Urban Nature

This introductory textbook with a global scope aims to train students of geography, sustainability, and urban and environmental studies to reimagine and transform cities to meet climate, biodiversity, and sustainability challenges. A dedicated team of authors critically examine the relationships between nature and urban areas, sharing an inspiring account of how nature helps us rethink our cities and their futures. Prior to this textbook, literature for courses covering urban nature was written by and for practitioners, whereas this textbook is written by experienced course instructors specifically to be accessible to diverse students. The textbook is illustrated with numerous photos and figures that bring key topics, challenges, and opportunities to life. It contains focus boxes and case studies from every continent, offering students an international scope and multiple entry points into the field. Chapters conclude with thought-provoking follow-up questions and recommended reading. The authors provide an array of supplementary online resources.

Kes McCormick is a Professor of Business Development and Sustainable Innovation in the Department of People and Society at the Swedish University of Agricultural Sciences. He also holds a position at the International Institute for Industrial Environmental Economics (IIIEE) at Lund University. With a background in political science and environmental science, he engages in a combination of research, education, and collaboration activities on sustainability, business, innovation, and governance, including *A Research Agenda for Sustainable Cities and Communities* (Edward Elgar, 2023). He is deeply engaged in online and in-person education, capacity building, and lifelong learning, including through Massive Open Online Courses.

Bernadett Kiss is a lecturer and researcher at the International Institute for Industrial Environmental Economics (IIIEE) at Lund University. For the past 20 years she has been working with sustainable cities and climate change, with special focus on urban governance, energy efficiency, policy learning and technology change, innovation systems, and nature-based solutions. Bernadett's interest lies in the integration of research and education, creating transformative learning environments and interdisciplinary capacity building programmes through knowledge co-creation with the engagement of urban stakeholders.

Yuliya Voytenko Palgan is an Associate Professor and Director of PhD Education at the International Institute for Industrial Environmental Economics (IIIEE) at Lund University. She has over 15 years of experience in multicultural, multidisciplinary, and interdisciplinary teams. She works in the areas of sustainability, urban governance, innovation, and sustainable consumption. Her research focuses on strategies for sustainability solutions in new economies (for example, the bioeconomy, the sharing economy, and the circular economy) and sustainable urban transformation (for example, nature-based solutions in cities and urban living labs). Yuliya works to promote education for sustainability at all levels: graduate, undergraduate, and professional.

Harriet Bulkeley holds joint appointments at Durham University and Utrecht University. Her research focuses on environmental governance and the politics of climate change, nature, and sustainable cities, including *An Urban Politics of Climate Change* (Routledge, 2015) and *Accomplishing Climate Governance* (Cambridge University Press, 2016). She was awarded the King Carl XVI Gustaf's Professorship in Environmental Science in 2014 and the Royal Geographical Society Back Award in 2018 in recognition of the policy impact of her work on climate change. She was elected a Fellow of the British Academy in 2019 and appointed to the Scientific Council of the European Research Council in 2023.

McKenna Davis is a Senior Fellow at the Ecologic Institute in Berlin, Germany, and Coordinator of Nature-based Solutions. Her work looks at the assessment of green infrastructure and nature-based solutions (NBS) and their governance frameworks, with a focus on linkages to human health and well-being, sustainable urban development, biodiversity conservation, climate change adaptation, and disaster risk reduction. She has published numerous papers and book chapters and led the development of the Urban Governance Atlas (https://interlace-hub.com/urban-governance-atlas), showcasing more than 250 global policy instruments supporting NBS. She is an expert in the Biodiversa BiodivClim Knowledge Hub on the 'Potential of NBS for mitigating and adapting to climate change'.

Rob Raven is an interdisciplinary scholar, professor of sustainability transitions, and deputy director (research) at Monash Sustainable Development Institute. His current research agenda is focused on the analysis of transformative change in urban contexts such as smart, sustainable, and net-zero cities. In 2022, Rob was included in Elsevier's top 2 per cent of the most influential researchers in the world across all scientific disciplines, and in 2023 in the Clarivate Highly Cited Researcher list. Rob is an editor for the journals *Environmental Innovation and Societal Transitions*, *Global Sustainability*, and *Nature Urban Sustainability*. A key focus of his work is how actors, sociotechnical experimentation, institutional change, and incumbency in urban regimes co-produce sustainable city futures.

Andrés Luque-Ayala is an Associate Professor in the Department of Geography at Durham University. He is an urban geographer and infrastructures scholar, focusing on the environmental governance of 'smart city' agendas and the digitisation of urban ecological flows. His work critically unpacks the role of digital technologies in how cities respond to climate change, through a research agenda that also examines how urban digital technologies rework notions of nature, particularly in response to the challenges posed by the urban Anthropocene. He is the co-author of *Urban OS: Reassembling the City through Computational Logics* (with S. Marvin, MIT University Press, 2020).

Kathrin Hörschelmann is Professor of Geography at the University of Bonn, where she leads the Cultural Geography Research Group. Her research focuses on the geographies of citizenship and participation, cultural geography, urban inclusion, youth identity, security, globalisation, and post-socialist change. In addition to numerous well-cited papers in international peer-reviewed journals such as *Transactions of the IBG*, *Progress in Human Geography*, *Political Geography*, and *Antipode*, she has published the textbook *Children, Youth and the City* (with van Blerk, Routledge, 2011) as well as several edited collections and special issues, including *Research Ethics for Human Geography* (with Henn and Miggelbrink, Routledge, 2022).

Urban Nature

New Directions for City Futures

Kes McCormick
Swedish University of Agricultural Sciences, Lund University

Bernadett Kiss
Lund University

Yuliya Voytenko Palgan
Lund University

Harriet Bulkeley
Durham University, University of Utrecht

McKenna Davis
Ecologic Institute

Rob Raven
Monash University

Andrés Luque-Ayala
Durham University

Kathrin Hörschelmann
Leibniz-Institut für Länderkunde

CAMBRIDGE
UNIVERSITY PRESS

CAMBRIDGE
UNIVERSITY PRESS

Shaftesbury Road, Cambridge CB2 8EA, United Kingdom

One Liberty Plaza, 20th Floor, New York, NY 10006, USA

477 Williamstown Road, Port Melbourne, VIC 3207, Australia

314–321, 3rd Floor, Plot 3, Splendor Forum, Jasola District Centre, New Delhi – 110025, India

103 Penang Road, #05–06/07, Visioncrest Commercial, Singapore 238467

Cambridge University Press is part of Cambridge University Press & Assessment, a department of the University of Cambridge.

We share the University's mission to contribute to society through the pursuit of education, learning and research at the highest international levels of excellence.

www.cambridge.org
Information on this title: www.cambridge.org/highereducation/isbn/9781108831734

DOI: 10.1017/9781108924122

When citing this work, please include a reference to the DOI 10.1017/9781108924122

First published 2025

A catalogue record for this publication is available from the British Library.

Library of Congress Cataloging-in-Publication Data
Names: McCormick, Kes, author.
Title: Urban nature : new directions for city futures / Kes McCormick, Lund University; Bernadett Kiss, Lund University; Yuliya Voytenko Palgan, Lund University; Harriet Bulkeley, Durham University, University of Utrecht; McKenna Davis, Ecologic Institute; Rob Raven, Monash University; Andreś Luque-Ayala, Durham University; Kathrin Hörschelmann.
Description: Cambridge, United Kingdom ; New York, NY : Cambridge University Press, 2024. | Includes bibliographical references and index.
Identifiers: LCCN 2024004961 | ISBN 9781108831734 (hardback) | ISBN 9781108927017 (paperback) | ISBN 9781108924122 (ebook)
Subjects: LCSH: City planning and redevelopment law. | City planning and redevelopment law – Political aspects. | City planning and redevelopment law – Environmental aspects. | Sustainable development – Law and legislation. | Climatic changes – Law and legislation. | Urban policy. | Biodiversity. | LCGFT: Textbooks.
Classification: LCC K3531 .M39 2024 | DDC 346.04/5–dc23/eng/20240206
LC record available at https://lccn.loc.gov/2024004961

ISBN 978-1-108-83173-4 Hardback
ISBN 978-1-108-92701-7 Paperback

Additional resources for this publication at www.cambridge.org/urban-nature

Contents

Detailed Contents

Figures

Tables

Boxes

Case Study Boxes

From Urban Nature to Nature-Based Solutions

External building greens

Urban green areas connected to grey infrastructure

Parks and semi-natural urban green areas

Allotments and community gardens

Green indoor areas

Blue areas

Green areas for water management

Wilderness or derelict areas

The term ***urban nature*** can be understood from a general perspective to refer to the blue and green areas present in cities. The emerging concept of ***nature-based solutions*** is more specific than urban nature, and focuses on what we have come to know as green and blue infrastructure – an urban nature that has purposefully been created, maintained or managed to provide multiple benefits for humans and the environment alike.

Preface

Urban nature holds great potential to address the complex web of challenges that cities are facing and to support sustainability transitions. Cities are working with nature in a diversity of ways. Blue infrastructure, such as lakes, ponds, drains, and wetlands, can regulate storm water, reduce pressure on the urban drainage system, and create sponge cities, which also lowers heat and offers recreational opportunities. Green infrastructure, on the other hand, such as urban forests and green roofs and walls, can improve air quality, reduce heat island effects, enhance biodiversity, and contribute to human health and well-being. Furthermore, urban gardens can increase access to local food and employment, while enhancing physical and mental health along with social integration.

Cities and nature are at the heart of the biodiversity and climate intersection and at the core of reshaping approaches to urban and global sustainability. Yet despite growing recognition of these challenges and the potential for synergistic nature-based solutions, policy-makers, business leaders, and practitioners continue to rely largely on traditional approaches of governance, finance, and engineering, which often take silo approaches to address these profoundly interconnected sustainability challenges. Considering cities as dense networks of interwoven sociospatial processes that are simultaneously local and global, human and physical, cultural and organic opens the door for more integrated measures. This is the perspective on cities, nature, and sustainability we adopt in this textbook.

As an author team, we offer students the benefit of a breadth of knowledge, experience, and perspectives from diverse fields and contexts. The complexity of cities and nature necessitates an interdisciplinary approach. As a team of eight, we offer what a single author could not provide: expert coverage of urban nature and nature-based solutions from many angles, including natural and social sciences, urban governance and policy, engineering, economics, geography, politics, and environmental science. We capture the conceptual emergence of thinking on cities, nature, and sustainability from across these areas.

TARGET AUDIENCE

Despite the recognised multi-functionality of urban nature and the multiple benefits that nature-based solutions can provide, there is a lack of textbooks that critically and thoroughly examine the relationships between nature and cities. As the research in this area dates back less than a decade, book-length treatments are scarce. In particular, we noted that what little there is available is inaccessible to undergraduate- and masters-level students in social science disciplines undertaking courses in geography, sustainability, urban, and environmental studies. This textbook is our response to these issues. It is an introductory and inspiring account of urban nature and its role in addressing climate change, biodiversity, and sustainable transformation of urban areas.

TEXTBOOK ORGANISATION

Urban Nature is a concise overview. It initiates students into the intersection of cities and nature, demonstrating why and how nature helps us to rethink and reimagine urban sustainability. In this perspective, cities and nature are not separate, but instead merge to become a combined concept or approach. Ten chapters in three parts investigate and illuminate the key topics, challenges, and opportunities for urban nature. The chapters in the textbook are illustrated with figures, images, and text boxes, and they also contain a list of thought-provoking follow-up questions and resource materials. All the chapters draw on knowledge and examples from a collection of global case studies on cities and nature, covering North America, Europe, Asia, Africa, and South America.

PEDAGOGICAL FEATURES

This textbook has been designed to engage students in a journey of discovery and learning. Each chapter includes sections that both break down and connect key topics, as well as two main case studies from cities around the world, providing students with insights into urban nature through a focus on sustainability challenges and opportunities. Throughout the textbook, there is a range of text boxes that introduce supplementary insights and ideas with a particular focus on revealing the design and impact of nature-based solutions. The textbook also uses photographs and visuals to provide key examples of cities and nature. This approach offers students an improved understanding of sustainable transformations and ways of reimagining new directions for urban futures.

ONLINE RESOURCES

We encourage students to engage more deeply with the concepts in our textbook by providing a curated selection of complementary online resources created by our author team:

- **Urban Nature Online Course:** A free Massive Open Online Course on nature-based solutions and innovation in cities.
- **Urban Nature Atlas:** A collection of more than 1000 inspiring nature-based solutions from cities in Europe and beyond.
- **Urban Nature Navigator:** A tool that helps to assess the contributions that different nature-based solutions can make to meeting urban sustainability challenges.

- **Urban Nature Podcast:** A podcast series that takes its listeners on a journey into the world of nature-based solutions.
- **Urban Nature Business Models Catalogue:** A catalogue for urban nature-based solutions that presents eight different business models.

Whether you are using this textbook as an instructor, a student, or a practitioner, we trust you will find ideas and inspiration. We encourage your feedback and questions.

Acknowledgement

This book has been funded by the European Union's Horizon 2020 research and innovation programme under grant agreement No. 730243, with additional contribution from the Swedish Institute Public Sector Innovation Programme 2023. Beyond the co-authors, this book project was supported by the expertise and resources of a number of institutions and committed individuals, to whom we are greatly thankful.

1 Introduction and Overview

Cities around the world are facing increasing environmental, economic, and social challenges. Population growth, climate change, and associated natural disasters, food shortages, waste and water management, biodiversity and ecosystem loss, resource inefficiency, social segregation, and urban vulnerability are some of these challenges. More than 50 per cent of the world's population lives in urban areas, which is projected to increase to 70 per cent by 2050 (UN, 2018). Rapid urbanisation in many parts of the world is having a direct impact on social inequalities and human well-being, as many cities struggle to provide sufficient shelter and services for their populations. In established cities, patterns of economic, social, gender, and racial inequality are persisting. The rapidly growing urban population is exacerbating demands on natural resources, both in terms of material consumption and increasing land needs. This has stark implications for our already vulnerable ecosystems and declining biodiversity. At the same time, urban centres concentrate activities that produce greenhouse gas emissions contributing to climate change and they are also vulnerable to the impacts of a changing climate.

The twin crises of biodiversity loss and climate change have created a critical need to rethink the relationship between cities and nature. At a global level, the key policy processes trying to address these crises are seeking the active commitment of cities to contribute to biodiversity goals (UN Convention on Biological Diversity) and shifting towards the use of urban nature for reaching climate adaptation and mitigation objectives (UN Framework Convention on Climate Change). Cities and nature are therefore at the heart of the intersection between the biodiversity and climate regimes and at the core of reshaping approaches to urban sustainability. Yet despite growing recognition of these interconnected challenges and the potential for synergistic solutions, policy-makers and practitioners continue to largely rely on traditional approaches of governance, finance, and engineering, which often take siloed approaches to address these profoundly interconnected sustainability challenges. Considering cities as 'dense networks of interwoven socio-spatial processes that are simultaneously local and global, human and physical, cultural and organic' (Swyngedouw & Heynen, 2003, p. 899) opens the door for more integrated measures, which are coordinated through a systemic approach (Brink et al., 2016).

Urban nature holds great potential to address the web of challenges that cities are facing and support transitions to a more sustainable future (see Box 1.1). Cities are working with nature in a diversity of ways, such as by using blue and green infrastructure. Blue infrastructure includes, for example, lakes, ponds, drains, and wetlands. These features can regulate storm water flows, reduce pressure on the urban drainage system, and create sponge cities that lower flooding risks while reducing heat island effects, enhancing biodiversity, and providing recreational opportunities. Green infrastructure can include, for example, urban forests, green roofs and walls, multifunctional parks, and river embankments. These areas can improve air quality and energy efficiency, reduce heat island effects, and contribute to human health and well-being, among other benefits. Furthermore, urban gardens can increase access to food and employment, while enhancing physical and mental health and social integration.

The term 'urban nature' can be understood from a general perspective to refer to the blue and green areas present in cities. The emerging concept of nature-based solutions is more specific than urban nature, and focuses on what we have come to know as green and blue infrastructure – an urban nature that has purposefully been created, maintained, or managed to provide multiple benefits for humans and the environment alike. These benefits include addressing key urban challenges like biodiversity loss, health and well-being of urban populations, and a changing climate. In this textbook, both the terms urban nature and nature-based solutions are utilised and explored in the broader context of cities and nature and are

Box 1.1 Recognising the benefits of nature in cities

Grey infrastructure – from roads and pipes to car parks and electricity substations, among many others – plays a dominant role in urban development. Nevertheless, blue and green infrastructure, capturing the natural properties of ecosystems, are also present in cities as established urban nature. Increasingly, these natural areas are being reconceptualised as nature-based solutions to limit the impacts of climate change, enhance biodiversity, and improve resilience, while also generating positive wider economic and social benefits.

- **Climate action for adaptation:** contributions to flood protection, shadow effects and reducing high temperatures (urban heat island) in summer.
- **Coastal resilience:** contributions to reducing flooding for cities located in coastal areas.
- **Cultural heritage and diversity:** contributions to the beauty and the cultural meanings of industrial, military, and other forms of heritage.
- **Economic development:** contributions to employment, nature-related sectors of the economy, and public finances through overall service provision.
- **Green space and biodiversity:** contributions to the availability and accessibility of green space, and animal and plant species.
- **Environmental quality:** contributions to the air quality and beauty of the living environment for urbanites.
- **Health and well-being:** contributions to mental and physical well-being through access to outdoor activities and enjoying the experience of nature.
- **Inclusive governance:** contributions to the accessibility of nature and feelings of safety among urbanites.
- **Regeneration and land use:** contributions to the greening of urban areas that have been or are to be regenerated.
- **Social justice and cohesion:** contributions to the equitable distribution of nature's benefits across urban areas and to social encounters.
- **Sustainable consumption:** contributions to providing local produce and to the pollination of food plants.
- **Water management:** contributions to storing water and reducing the pressure on sewerage systems.

demonstrated through a multitude of cases. The textbook provides an introductory account of how innovation with nature in cities can help to address climate change and biodiversity loss, while supporting the sustainable transformation of urban areas.

Through an interdisciplinary approach and drawing on knowledge from case studies from North America, Europe, Asia, Africa, and South America, this textbook provides insights into key challenges and opportunities for urban nature and nature-based solutions (see Box 1.2). Additionally, a number of thought-provoking

Box 1.2 Presenting the structure of the textbook

This textbook is divided into three sections and 10 chapters, the first of which is this overview chapter. It has been designed to engage you in a journey of discovery and learning. The chapters in the textbook are illustrated with figures, images, and text boxes, and also contain follow-up questions and resource materials. Each chapter includes two boxes with key case studies from cities around the world, providing you with insights into urban nature through a focus on sustainability opportunities and challenges.

Throughout the chapters and parts of the textbook, there are a range of boxes that introduce supplementary insights about urban nature and nature-based solutions. The 10 boxes that appear throughout the textbook on 'Cultivating Urban Nature – Key Lessons' provide you with specific suggestions on how to understand, expand, and develop urban nature in your city. These boxes appear throughout the textbook and connect to the themes of different chapters, namely:

1. **Develop Connections:** the converging challenges of urban sustainability demand solutions, like urban nature, that connect multiple issues (Chapter 1).
2. **Tend Creativity:** urban nature can feed our imaginations and our soul (Chapter 2).
3. **Recognise Trade-Offs:** urban nature involves trade-offs that need to be explicitly recognised (Chapter 3).
4. **Make Space:** urban nature needs space to grow (Chapter 4).
5. **Grow Collaboration:** collaboration comes in all shapes and sizes, and greater diversity and flexibility is needed for activities on urban nature (Chapter 5).
6. **Value Experimentation:** seeing is believing – experiments allow actors to try things out without losing too much (Chapter 6).
7. **Foster Investment:** urban nature requires investment of all kinds – financial, political, and cultural (Chapter 7).
8. **Embrace Diversity:** there is no one-size-fits-all for urban nature – beauty is in the eye of the beholder (Chapter 8).
9. **Ensure Equity:** too often, the benefits that urban nature provides are unevenly distributed across communities in cities (Chapter 9).
10. **Nurture Intermediaries:** new relationships and trust are needed to expand urban nature (Chapter 10).

questions and resource materials are provided to support independent and deeper learning (see Table 1.1). This approach provides learners with an overview of the conceptualisation of nature in cities and innovation, and with scientific and empirical evidence as well as an improved understanding of sustainable transformations and ways of reimagining new directions for urban futures (see Box 1.3).

Table 1.1 Overview of learning exercises in the textbook

Activity	Description
Individual reflection	This is a task carried out individually and focuses on understanding and reflecting. For example: Think of what constitutes nature in a city for you. How would you define it in your words? In your opinion, are we (humans) part of this nature or are we outside of it?
Peer discussion	This is a task carried out in groups with peers and focuses on discussion and critical thinking. For example: Discuss with your peers how the concept of 'urban nature' relates to other key concepts and fields of study discussed in this chapter: 'urban ecology', 'urban metabolism', and 'urban political ecology', for example. Relate this discussion to how the perspectives on nature in the city have evolved over time and across various disciplines.
Explore examples	This is a task carried out individually or in groups and involves exploring examples and contexts. For example: Explain what 'nature-based solutions' are and provide three examples of nature-based solutions. Which nature-based solutions can you identify from the case studies of Melbourne and Tianjin? Why do you consider these to be nature-based solutions? Explain why and how these nature-based solutions can be considered multi-functional.

Box 1.3 Cultivating urban nature – key lessons

Develop Connections: the challenges associated with achieving urban sustainability demand solutions – such as urban nature – that can connect multiple issues and provide diverse benefits.

Nature-based solutions are often heralded as being synergistic, able to simultaneously meet a range of environmental, economic, and social challenges. Yet the delivery of these benefits does not necessarily happen automatically and instead needs to be prioritised from the design stage of nature-based solutions projects through to their implementation and maintenance. Many nature-based solutions are currently being implemented without tapping their potential to provide wider benefits beyond their primary objectives, or to support action across multiple municipal policy agendas as well as address the key concerns of private and community-based actors. Recognising this potential and aligning with sectoral agendas can provide additional momentum and resources to fund and choose nature-based solutions alongside or instead of traditional grey infrastructure solutions. Finding these synergies requires bringing diverse actors around the table at an early stage of project design and using decision-support tools that allow the multiple benefits of nature-based solutions to be recognised and considered simultaneously. Looking for the root causes of unsustainability in the city – from water availability to health and inequality – can also provide a means for establishing nature-based solutions that can tackle multiple challenges simultaneously.

Part I

Understanding Perspectives

Urban nature and nature-based solutions, such as urban forests, have the potential to provide multiple benefits to a range of sustainability challenges facing cities (see Box P1.1). They can help to limit the impacts of climate change, enhance biodiversity and improve environmental quality while contributing to economic prosperity and social well-being. But how should we understand urban nature and nature-based solutions?

Box P1.1 Spotlight on implementation – urban forests

Urban forests are an emerging concept which not only incorporate trees, but also include other vegetation in streets, parks, plazas, river embankments, wetlands, railway corridors, community gardens, and on buildings, as well as the soil and water that supports them. Urban forests have been around for generations but have only recently been valued for more than their aesthetics and recreational value. This shift comes as a result of population growth, densification, and climate extremes and recognition of the potential environmental, economic, cultural, and political benefits they can offer. Urban forests are increasingly recognised as a tool to persuade and engage local actors to work with and expand urban vegetation. They can create resilient and sustainable urban landscapes that provide healthy and enjoyable places for people to live and work but this requires rethinking the role of green spaces in cities. Like other nature-based solutions, they must draw on strong visions and strategic target-oriented planning, coupled with new governing modes and partnerships, often reallocating and sharing responsibilities with private actors.

Urban forests represent a key approach to expanding nature-based solutions in cities.

Box P1.2 Understanding the value of nature in cities

Assessing the value and potential of urban nature and nature-based solutions requires an approach that takes account of the multiple benefits they can provide and the different criteria against which they can be evaluated. This necessitates utilising different kinds of knowledge and assessing the value of nature in the city in relation to urban sustainability goals.

Biophysical and ecological: nature-based solutions and urban nature can provide ecosystem services for cities, such as providing resources, regulating environments, creating habitats, and generating social and cultural activities. The extent and scope of these services varies with the conditions in which nature-based solutions are introduced, how they are designed, and the ways in which they are maintained over time.

Economic and financial: nature-based solutions and urban nature can bring a variety of benefits to cities. Understanding the economic and financial value of these benefits is important if they are to be taken into account in decision-making processes as an alternative or complement to traditional forms of infrastructure and urban development.

Social and cultural: the benefits of nature-based solutions and urban nature can also be social and cultural, from providing spaces for social interaction to recreational opportunities. At the same time, nature is seen to have values that are difficult to account for in economic terms but which are nonetheless important to society, such as contributing to human well-being as well as being inherently valued in their own right.

Part I explores how urban nature and nature-based solutions are conceptualised through different approaches and different ways of valuing nature, and the ways in which nature is being created for cities (see Box P1.2).

Conceptualising: This chapter outlines different conceptual frameworks that can be used to better understand the evolving role nature has played in cities. It distinguishes between socioecological systems and urban political ecology, each of which influence how nature has been regarded and treated in different time periods and urban settings. It seeks to provide an overview of these concepts and explain their implications for how urban nature and nature-based solutions are constructed and viewed today as an urban policy issue.

Key contents:

- Presenting different approaches to understanding urban nature, nature-based solutions, and the relationship between nature and cities.
- Discussing the emergence of nature-based solutions as a response to urban sustainability challenges.
- Case studies: Urban Forest Strategy (Melbourne, Australia) and the Eco-Valley of Tianjin Eco-City (Tianjin, China).

Valuing: This chapter provides an insight into the different kinds of values that nature has, how this plays out in the urban arena, and what this means about how it can and should be assessed. Through a detailed account of values and benefits as well as potential assessment techniques and their limitations, this chapter also presents how techniques capture the values of diverse stakeholders and discusses the implications when stakeholders attribute different and sometimes conflicting values and benefits.

Key contents:
- Exploring our understanding of the value of nature and highlighting the challenge of conflicting values and benefits with urban nature and nature-based solutions.
- Reviewing assessment techniques, including their limitations and potential approaches for further improvement.
- Case studies: Cape Town Environmental Education Trust (Cape Town, South Africa) and Beekeeping at Audi Hungaria (Győr, Hungary).

Developing:
This chapter investigates the technical and biophysical properties of nature-based solutions by presenting eight types of urban ecological domains that are illustrated with practical examples. In addition, the ecosystem services associated with different types of nature-based solutions, like urban forests, are outlined, including provisioning services, regulating services, habitat and supporting services, and cultural services.

Key contents:
- Presenting how urban nature is being developed in our cities in different ways and combinations – in particular through the concept of nature-based solutions.
- Outlining eight types of urban ecological domains and the ecosystem services associated with different types of nature-based solutions.
- Case studies: BiodiverCity (Malmö, Sweden) and the Tolka Valley Park (Dublin, Ireland).

2 Conceptualising

INTRODUCTION

There is no singular or universal way of thinking about nature. When it comes to cities, however, it is clear that nature is a plural concept (see Box 2.1). How we conceptualise urban nature matters, as it establishes what and who benefits from it. For some, urban nature refers to the many natural beings, ecosystems, and habitats that are present within cities. From this perspective, the city is seen as the opposite of nature: a concrete jungle, man-made and often grim, yet blessed by the sporadic presence of patches of non-human life. For others, urban nature encompasses humans and their actions in the city, as long as these actions work towards the promotion of both human and non-human life. This is the urban nature of activists

Box 2.1 Making sense of nature

Nature is a manifold concept with many different definitions. In its broadest sense, nature refers to the physical and material aspects of the earth, specifically in opposition to those aspects of the earth created by humans. Nature can also refer to all things alive. The etymology of the word, from the Latin *natura* (meaning birth, or constitutional quality), refers to an innate quality. Hence, people often talk about 'the nature of things' to refer to their 'essence'. In philosophy and social theory, debates around nature are usually marked by a reflection around the extent to which humankind is or is not to be considered part of nature. As you will see in this textbook, this debate will come in handy; is nature external to the city? Is there nature inside the city? Or would it be better to find ways to eliminate the city–nature dichotomy altogether? In making sense of nature, the work of geographer Noel Castree is very useful. Instead of asking questions around *what nature is*, he believes we should be asking *what nature is considered to be*: 'what we consider to be "natural" always bears the (usually) hidden or forgotten trace of particular assumptions, agendas and desires specific to a social group or a wider community, culture or society' (Castree, 2014, p. xvii). In focusing on how nature is represented by different groups of people, this approach highlights the extent to which nature is always political.

and reformers; one that exists through the affirmative actions of humans in defence of nature, striving towards more 'sustainable' or 'environmentally friendly' modes of living. Yet, this view of urban nature still views factories and highways as 'alien'. In both cases, the city is seen as a man-made landscape in which we, as humans, are decidedly unnatural.

Disconnecting from nature can be useful on multiple levels, not least regarding decision-making. It seems to be easy to cut a tree down when we do not feel that we are one of its branches. However, there is another reading of urban nature, where the city and the natural world (the countryside, the forest, the natural park, the oceans, or even an urban meadow) are not considered as separate places. Debunking the city–nature dichotomy highlights that what is at stake is not the quality of 'natural habitats' in cities, but rather the weight given to different representations of nature in urban politics.

In this chapter, the different ways of thinking about urban nature, what falls under this label, and where these perspectives stem from are examined to better understand the conceptualisation of the city–nature relationship (see Box 2.2). Starting from a biological and ecological perspective where humans are external to nature, a socioecological perspective on urban nature in which humans interact with and shape nature will be explored. The fields of *urban ecology* and *human ecology* focus on these interactions in cities. In this context, the idea of urban metabolism explores this further, and describes several flows and trends in which humans, nature, and cities are seen as shaping each other.

Box 2.2 Key terms and concepts used in this chapter

Anthropocene: A proposed geological epoch dating from the commencement of significant human impact on the Earth and its geology and ecosystems, including, but not limited to, anthropogenic climate change. Anthropocentrism refers to a human-centred point of view.

Ecology: A branch of biology that deals with the relations of organisms to one another and to their physical surroundings. One of the ways in which ecological models have been applied to cities is within the field of *urban ecology.* While urban ecology is open to the consideration of both social and biological processes, *human ecology* focuses more directly on the relationship between humans and their natural, social, and built environments. Both urban ecology and human ecology aim to study its subject matter from a socioecological system perspective. However, in Europe, the field of urban ecology focuses primarily on an analysis of the biota of urban areas. In contrast, the North American tradition of urban ecology draws inspiration from both ecology and the social sciences, looking at both natural and human processes through the same analytical approach and methodology. In this book, when we talk about urban ecology, we refer to the North American tradition. *Political ecology* studies critique the interplay of the environment and political, economic, and social factors, placing a focus on how spatial–ecological processes influence politics and power.

Ecosystem: Consists of all the organisms and the physical environment in an ecological system. These biotic and abiotic components are linked together through nutrient cycles and energy flows.

Garden city: A model of planned urban development designed by Ebenezer Howard in 1898 in England as a response to the poor housing and living conditions in large cities. It consists of independent parts of the city, which would be separated from each other by wide agricultural belts.

Socioecological systems: Based on a concept that humans are a part of nature and not separate from it. These systems include biophysical, geophysical, and social elements, which are in continuous and dynamic interaction with each other across time and space.

Sustainable development: A concept articulated in the 1987 report 'Our Common Future' (also known as the Brundtland Report) by the United Nations World Commission on Environment and Development. It refers to development that meets the needs of the present without compromising the ability of future generations to meet their own needs.

Urban metabolism: A concept that describes a range of material and energy flows which play an active role in creating the urban environment. It can provide a unified viewpoint to encompass all of the activities of a city in a single model.

Box 2.3 Cultivating urban nature – key lessons

Tend Creativity: Nature can feed our imaginations and our soul.

The language used around nature-based solutions is often highly technical and instrumental, in that there is a focus on the services and benefits that nature can provide and these are conveyed in scientific and economic terms. Such approaches may be necessary and useful for making the case for the importance of bringing nature into the city, but, at the same time, they carry the risk that some of the things we love most about nature can get lost, such as how it fills our senses, brings memories to life, offers a connection to others, and reminds us of the wonders of the world. To enable urban communities and places to thrive, nature-based solutions need to allow for creativity, generating spaces for play, imagination, awe, and reflection. Recognising the creative potential of urban nature also means working in partnership with cultural and spiritual leaders, from organised religions, the creative arts, museums, and heritage organisations to indigenous and local communities, to design and implement nature-based solutions. The potential for urban nature to play a key role in shaping the way we engage with key global and local environmental challenges – from climate change to biodiversity, plastic pollution to food waste – has yet to be fully realised. Tending creativity within nature-based solutions can provide a means through which urban communities can engage with nature and can enable them to use these experiences to make individual and collective changes in our world.

According to *urban political ecology*, another scholarly field examining the relationship between urban dwellers and nature, nature is made and sustained over time and humans and their social relations are inherently part of nature. Thus, power dynamics and the making of inequalities and injustice are related to human and non-human urbanites. At the end of this chapter, a conceptualization is suggested that informs the following chapters on valuing (Chapter 3) and developing urban nature (Chapter 4), in this way providing a foundation to the rest of the textbook (see Box 2.3).

Encountering Nature in the City

With the rise of industrialisation in the nineteenth century, a new way of life was introduced to city dwellers through immense developments in science and industry. Urban spaces were increasingly used as production and transportation sites, which pushed populations to either live in crowded accommodation or move to suburban areas. As a result, socioeconomic and environmental challenges were drastically aggravated, leading to a depletion of natural resources. For example, the use of chemicals and fuel in factories resulted in increased air and water pollution and an increased use of fossil fuels. In general, while broadening service provision, contributing to economic growth, and advancing meaningful improvements in many

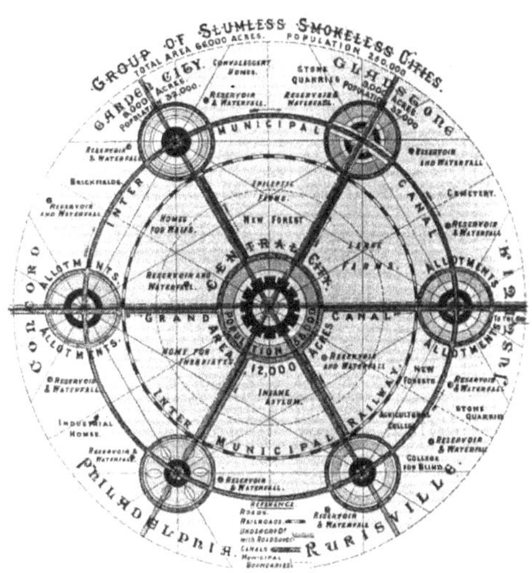

Figure 2.1 Ebenezer Howard's suggestive model of the garden city

spheres of life, industrialisation also led to severe societal problems, such as stressful lifestyles, ill health, and environmental degradation.

In the late nineteenth and early twentieth centuries, with the increasing recognition of the need to address challenges associated with the exploitation of resources and pollution – generated as a result of industrialisation – urban planners began to work with nature as a tool to create healthier living conditions (Angelo, 2021). One model that emerged and grew in popularity was the *garden city concept* proposed by Ebenezer Howard (see Figure 2.1). The model suggested that society should be reorganised into a network of independent garden towns, limited in size and managed by the citizens. While a number of physical plans for the garden city concept were proposed, it was also noted that cities should be organised as per the needs of people and the surrounding environment.

In the 1980s, the Brundtland Report *Our Common Future* put cities at the heart of the sustainability debate and recognised the critical role they play in *sustainable development* (Brundtland Commission, 1987). Since then, a more intentional incorporation of sustainability goals and urban planning approaches can be observed, with recognition given to the vital role of urban nature in the face of climate change and increasing environmental, economic, and social pressures. Areas such as parks, wetlands, forests, gardens, lakes, rivers, ponds, and, more recently, engineered urban nature such as green roofs and green walls have become essential elements of today's urban fabric.

As both climate change and the extensive scope of human impacts on the earth force the scientific community to name a new geological epoch – the Anthropocene – the city–nature relationship has once again taken centre stage. The Anthropocene is not just a discussion in the field of geology, but also one of nature, in which increasing levels of atmospheric carbon dioxide are leading to negative tipping points in ecological balances, increased levels of ocean acidification, habitat destruction, and the potential extinction resulting from wide-scale natural resource extraction. The city is seen as both a culprit and a saviour to this, being both a large source of anthropogenic change yet also being a site of potential for navigating the ongoing crisis and uncertainties of this era. Whether it is through 'smart city' and 'eco-city' narratives that imagine the city as a complex adaptive system that is both anticipatory and responsive in real time, or through the promotion of *urban resilience* as the means by which the city can absorb future shocks, the logic of 'Anthropocene thinking' is shaping how we now imagine the city (Derickson, 2018). The city of the Anthropocene is becoming a site of experimentation where new concepts and ideas are tested and come to be realised in practice. There is no one way but rather multiple ways to understand, conceptualise, and work with and around cities.

Multiple Ways of Thinking about Nature and the City

The Ecological Gaze Reaches the City

Rethinking the city through the lens of nature is not a new phenomenon. The garden city movement was an urban planning trend in Europe from the 1910s onwards. It propagated a life based on settlements with gardens for self-sufficiency, parks, and small businesses within the boundaries of cities. Historian Jennifer Light documents how North American urban planning, between 1920 and 1960, drew significantly from the natural sciences, advancing a 'tradition of urban research and policy in the image of the [United States'] approach to the analysis and administration of nature' (Light, 2009, p. 2). Throughout this period, the way ecology understood plant and animal life, and the ecological knowledge used to manage forests, farms, and other natural assets, provided a template for how cities were designed and improved.

Urban landscapes were seen as ecological communities that needed conservation, while urban planners were directed to ecological models in search of ideas for how to think about the city. The work of urban sociologist Robert Park, a pioneering figure within *human ecology* and a leading scholar within the Chicago School of sociology, illustrates this trend; Park would not only ask his students to read texts on plant and animal ecology, but would also advocate for urban planners to study 'human relations like "the zoologist dissects the potato bug"' (Light, 2009, p. 29). Theories about plant succession, ecological change, and 'zonation' (the classification of zones according to predominant species) were critical in the development of popular twentieth-century urban planning approaches, as exemplified by Ernest Burgess's Zonal Model of 'The City' (see Figure 2.2).

The work of the Chicago School of Sociology and their contributions to human ecology were also instrumental in the establishment of *urban ecology* in the second half of the twentieth century. Urban ecology aims to study cities as ecological systems. Its focus is not simply on analysing natural ecosystems within cities, but also understanding urban areas as socioecological systems, including both ecological and social processes. This is explicitly an interdisciplinary field, seeking to integrate the social

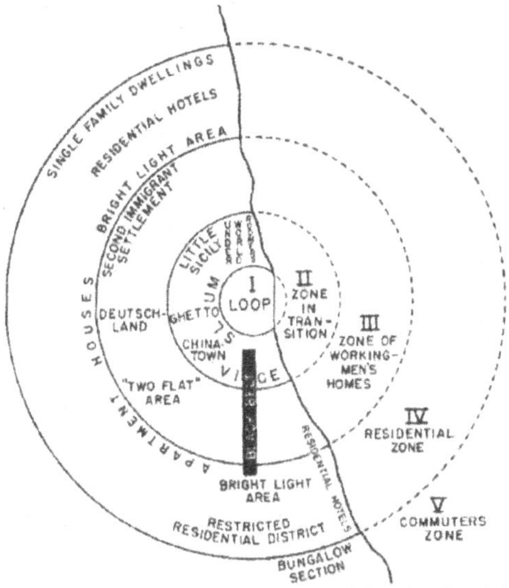

Figure 2.2 Ernest Burgess's zonal model of the city

and natural sciences (see, for instance, the work of the Baltimore School of Urban Ecology). Urban ecology strongly draws on ecology by applying notions of complexity, interdependence, and a range of ecological models to analyse the role of humans in transforming nature in cities. An example of such a model is *patch dynamics*, which is an analysis of how areas of a landscape interact with each other over time.

In acknowledging the importance of including social dimensions, Pickett et al. (1997) discuss how although it is useful to build on the ecosystem concept, an integrated model on urban ecosystems should also consider social as well as natural dimensions; this includes human behaviour, institutions, and the interactions among these, together with learning and feedback loops. Pickett et al. (2016) also identified three knowledge paradigms within urban ecology: (a) an ecology *in* cities, where emphasis is on land and water coverage within cities; (b) an ecology *of* cities, where emphasis is on socioecological systems, incorporating biological, social, and built components; and (c) an ecology *for* cities, where, drawing on the knowledge generated by (a) and (b), knowledge producers (for example, researchers or community members following this approach) are conceptualised as part of the city/system evaluated, and any knowledge resulting from this perspective is an explicit attempt to advance social and ecological goals of sustainability.

Urban Metabolisms

An analysis of metabolisms sits at the core of urban ecology, just as it does within ecosystem ecology. The notion of *urban metabolisms* exemplifies the extent to which intellectual connections between ecology and urbanism shape how we think about the city. This idea dates back to the 1960s and arose in response to deteriorating air and water qualities in American cities, thus emphasising the need to focus on the different processes which create an urban environment (Castán Broto et al., 2012). Here, a range of natural flows are recognised beyond simply existing within the city; these flows play an active role in making the city itself. Tracing the idea of urban metabolisms across a range of disciplines – including industrial ecology, urban ecology, ecological economics, political economy, and political ecology – Castán Broto et al. (2012) identified different trends of urban analysis that emerge from this perspective. These include: (a) viewing the city as an ecosystem; (b) drawing attention to the material and energy flows within the city; (c) exploring the interplay between economic and material relations; and (d) identifying the economic drivers of rural–urban relationships. In this way, through mobilizing the idea of urban metabolism, it is possible to (e) unpack the reproduction of urban inequality; and (f) advance a set of alternative, and arguably more sustainable, relationships between society and the natural world.

A range of scholars, however, have pointed to the limits of this approach, not least due to its artificial system boundaries and relation to certain material flows. Admittedly, the idea of urban metabolism draws heavy inspiration from the ecological and biological sciences, and as such relies on artificial and arbitrary system boundaries between the city and the countryside. This in turn creates a false sense of inputs and outputs. Equally, the focus on material resources such as water, energy, or wastes also tends to ignore economic flows, in particular the role of capital in shaping the dynamics of urbanism (Gandy, 2003). Ecological and biological readings of urban metabolisms stand in sharp contrast to *political* readings, which often use a Marxist political economy framework that sees the metabolism not only as a matter of flow or circulation, but also as a matter of exchanging and making. In the nineteenth century, Karl Marx borrowed the term 'metabolism' from the natural sciences to describe the (socionatural) production and transformation of landscapes effected by the workings of labour and capital (Kaika & Swyngedouw, 2011). In emphasising the extent to which urban metabolisms are connected to capitalist processes of accumulation, power relations are revealed, suggesting that the circulation of urban nature is tied up with who wins and who loses from processes of economic development operating at local and global scales (Swyngedouw, 2006).

Urban Political Ecology

Both mobilising and reconceptualising the idea of urban metabolisms, *urban political ecology* seeks to draw on political economy approaches to further deepen an engagement with the ways in which urban nature is produced, exploited, and marginalised (Angelo & Wachsmuth, 2015, p. 16). In this way, the focus is not on an abstracted or idealised version of nature, but rather on how nature has come to be urbanised both in and outside the city (Kaika, 2005). The urbanisation of nature is a historical and political process; for example, this work shows how in modern infrastructure networks, such as water infrastructures, electricity grids, or information and communication technology (ICT) networks, infrastructure has served not only to make society more independent from nature but instead woven nature and cities more closely together (Gandy, 2004; Kaika, 2005).

As a result, urban political ecology approaches typically critique any sense that there is a binary – an opposition – between the city and nature, and highlight how conflict, domination, and struggle are central to how city–nature relationships play out in the modern world. Urban nature is not just simply present but is created and sustained over time through metabolic and social relations, and these processes are infused with power relations (Swyngedouw, 2006, p. 106). This emphasis on conflict, domination, and struggle is also aligned with an underlying critique of capitalism in the urban political ecology approach, which suggests that urban nature and nature-based solutions often arise as a result of exploitative and capital-driven socioenvironmental processes *in* and *for* cities.

Urban Nature is More Than Just for Humans

Often, scholarly approaches and practical strategies to urban nature have centred around the needs of human populations and how to improve urban habitats for people, ignoring the existence, impacts, or needs of non-human species and local ecosystems. Recognizing the agencies and dependencies of a range of living and non-living actors, more-than-human approaches have arisen in several disciplines over the years. These, characterized by relational perspectives (e.g. Whatmore, 2002), attempt to understand what urban nature might mean beyond human rationality, dissolve binary categories, think in different time frames, and focus on processes while also resituating humans in relation to the multitude of non-human living beings and ecosystems. For example, by recognising all non-humans on which human life depends, the Law of the Rights of Mother Earth (Pachamama) illustrates how more-than-human thinking has got into the legislative domain in Bolivia.

Adapting relational approaches are increasingly becoming relevant as evidence shows that some animals and plants actually benefit from cities and others adapt better to urbanisation than it was previously assumed, contributing to improved habitats and urban biodiversity (Ives et al., 2016). As awareness and understanding of the interconnectivity and interdependency of different life forms has grown, the human focus of cities has increasingly been questioned; and not just in urban policy and planning. In this context, the potential of nature-based solutions has been discussed and prompted a human-centric approach towards a more eco-centric approach, remaking cities as places where multiple species and ecosystems can co-exist (Maller, 2020).

Conceptualising Urban Nature as Nature-Based Solutions

While this review of evolving concepts for understanding urban nature demonstrates that the idea of working with nature is not new, the term nature-based solutions has only recently been popularised to capture some of those approaches – particularly those that see in urban nature the possibility of replacing or complementing forms of man-made infrastructural provision towards human and ecological well-being. Discussions have increasingly recognised the current challenges facing urban areas and their populations, such as a reduced availability of physical space, threats to human health arising from climate change, increased densification, and decreasing connectivity with nature.

Consequently, urban planning processes have increasingly considered implementing multi-purpose measures that utilise natural systems to foster the delivery of ecosystem services and wider societal benefits. The emergence of nature-based solutions was the result of increasing interest in generating win–win, no-regret solutions and optimising environmental and economic agendas, not least in the face of increasing environmental degradation and a changing climate (Davis et al., 2018). Since then, the term has been broadened to cover and address multiple societal challenges while also delivering economic and environmental benefits, highlighting the interdependencies between people and nature.

Box 2.4 Concepts relating to nature-based solutions

Nature-based solutions: These can be considered as '... actions to protect, sustainably manage, and restore natural or modified ecosystems, that address societal challenges effectively and adaptively, simultaneously providing human well-being and biodiversity benefits' (Cohen-Shacham et al., 2016) and at the same time '... inspired and supported by nature, which are cost-effective, simultaneously provide environmental, social and economic benefits and help build resilience. Such solutions bring more, and more diverse, nature and natural features and processes into cities, landscapes and seascapes, through locally adapted, resource-efficient and systemic interventions' (European Commission, 2015).

Ecosystem-based adaptation: This refers to 'the use of biodiversity and ecosystem services as part of an overall strategy to help people adapt to the adverse effects of climate change' (Convention of Biological Diversity, 2009).

Ecosystem-based disaster risk reduction: This is 'the sustainable management, conservation and restoration of ecosystems to provide services that reduce disaster risk by mitigating hazards and by increasing livelihood resilience' (Cohen-Shacham et al., 2016).

Natural capital: Natural resources, including the world's geology, soils, air, water, and all living organisms. From a human perspective, these assets can provide people with free goods and services, also called ecosystem services (Guerry et al., 2015).

Natural water retention measures: Through natural processes, they 'aim to safeguard and enhance the water storage potential of landscape, soil, and aquifers, by restoring ecosystems, natural features and characteristics of water courses [...] [they also] regulate the flow and transport of water so as to smooth peaks and moderate extreme events (floods, droughts, desertification, salination)' (European Commission, 2015).

Nature-based solutions can be seen as an umbrella term for this family of related ideas (see Box 2.4) that have each emerged from distinct historical, sectoral, and geographical contexts. Nature-based solutions refer to deliberate, innovative interventions that seek to use the properties of nature to address a set of urban challenges as an alternative to purely grey methods of urban planning and development (Davis et al., 2018). Such challenges can include climate change, food insecurity, disaster risk reduction, and water resources (Pauleit et al., 2017). Nature-based solutions are seen as being capable of creating multiple ecological, economic, social, and urban planning benefits in parallel.

These solutions bring more diverse nature and natural processes into cities through locally adapted, resource-efficient, and systemic interventions. Nature-based solutions include interventions that span a host of actions, from managing floods to securing improved health outcomes for different groups of society to building green roofs and city parks that limit heat stress to creating city lagoons that store water and installing permeable surfaces, vegetation, and rain gardens to avoid storm water runoff (see Case Study Box 2.1). Yet despite their potential to generate multiple benefits, the application of nature-based solutions remains largely marginal, fragmented, and highly uneven within and between cities (see Case Study Box 2.2). In the following chapters, we use the approaches outlined above to consider how, why, and by and for whom nature-based solutions are being implemented.

Case Study Box 2.1 Urban Forest Strategy (Melbourne, Australia)

The Urban Forest Strategy is a central part of a comprehensive policy framework driven by an innovative and collaborative governance approach and is a first of its kind for the city of Melbourne. It is also a demonstrative example of a deliberate intervention seeking to use the properties of nature, while engaging with multiple stakeholders and a multi-disciplinary knowledge base to address a range of challenges.

Melbourne is the second-most populous city in Australia and Oceania with a growing, young, and international population. Densification is seen as a key measure to reduce urban expansion, which places increasing pressure not only on the built environment and urban services but also on the unevenly distributed green spaces and the well-being of citizens. Increasing climate extremes, such as heavy rains, floods, heatwaves, droughts, and bushfires, pose further challenges for the city's resilience.

The Urban Forest Strategy (2012–2032) is a timely and effective response to Melbourne's sustainability challenges. Its main aims are to adapt the city to current and future climate change impacts, mitigate the urban heat island effect, create healthier ecosystems, create a more water-sensitive city, and engage the community in these endeavours to support long-term sustainability. Recognising the hybridity of the city, the strategy creates a continuum across natural, social, technical, and cultural spaces, actively drawing on technical expertise and local (citizen) knowledge of urban ecosystems, the community's sense of place, and capacity for change.

The systematic provision and maintenance of green spaces in combination with soft and grey measures is a core part of the strategy and relies on concrete goals and implementation actions. Goals include to: (1) increase canopy cover; (2) increase

Case Study Box 2.1 (cont.)

urban forest diversity; (3) improve vegetation health; (4) improve soil moisture and water quality; (5) improve urban ecology; and (6) inform and consult the community. Implementation actions include the development of neighbourhood-scale strategies (Precinct Plans), Tree Capital Program (planting 3000 trees per year), Urban Forest Visual (mapped tree data), and training Citizen Foresters to participate in urban tree care. Importantly, the strategy's aim is to re-nature the city for and with citizens.

Figure 2.3 Melbourne, Australia

Case Study Box 2.2 The Eco-Valley of Tianjin EcoCity (Tianjin, China)

Tianjin Eco-City, and the green corridor (Eco-Valley) that cuts across it, demonstrate how natural systems and green spaces can be used as top-down planning tools to shape the existing urban materiality into promising sites that address relevant issues and future uncertainties. Tianjin hosts hundreds of international companies contributing to fast industrial development and population growth in the past decades. This resulted in major environmental challenges, such as air pollution, traffic congestion, lack of green space, and loss of agricultural land and soil organic matter content. Additionally, the city needs to improve its water retention capacity to combat droughts and intense rainfalls.

Recognising the impacts of rapid and large-scale urbanisation and the consequent sustainability challenges, 'ecological civilisation' has become an emerging pathway on the national political agenda, along with eco-urbanism as a new model for sustainable development. Tianjin Eco-City is one of the flagship projects of eco-urbanism in China, where green space development is generally a by-product of the rapid, large-scale, government-led urbanisation and industrialisation process.

Case Study Box 2.2 (cont.)

Starting in 2008, the Eco-City project has envisioned the transformation of a 34 km^2 barren, non-arable land and polluted wastewater ponds into a socially harmonious, environmentally friendly, and resource-efficient city. The 11-km Eco-Valley is the unifying element of this development, providing connectivity, sustainable transit, and recreational space in a scenic trail for the 70,000 current and 350,000 future residents. In the S-shaped green corridor that connects four residential districts, three subcentres, community spaces, commercial zones, and waterside areas, at least 70 per cent of plants used are native to the region.

The Eco-Valley is designed to meet Key Performance Indicator targets of the Eco-City such as a minimum 45 per cent green space and 12 m^2 green space per capita. It is also a national 'sponge city' pilot area, aiming to capture and use at least 75 per cent of rainfall. As the largest continuous open space in the Eco-City, the Eco-Valley also serves as a major fire barrier zone, earthquake safe zone, and an emergency evacuation route, creating multiple ecological, economic, social, and urban planning benefits in parallel.

Figure 2.4 Tianjin, China

OVERALL REFLECTIONS

In this chapter, we have introduced urban nature as a concept, highlighting how it is not new but rather established since times of increased industrialisation. Here, the garden–urban nexus became a centrepiece of architectural planning throughout Europe and North America as far back as the end of the 1800s. Yet it was not until the 1980s that cities were put at the heart of the sustainability debate and recognised for the critical role they have to play.

We have introduced several disciplinary perspectives that conceptualise the city–nature relationship. In the first instance, this multiplicity reflects different disciplinary emphases. It also reflects whether we think about urban nature primarily from: (a) a biological and ecological perspective, where humans are external to nature; (b) a socioecological perspective, where humans interact with nature in an urban space (urban ecology); or (c) a sociopolitical perspective, where humans and their social relations are considered inherently part of nature (urban political ecology). The latter also raises questions about other inherent parts of nature, such as non-human urbanites, and their role and representation in urban ecosystems.

Since the first half of the twentieth century, urban planning has been strongly influenced by the discipline of ecology. Even today, fields such as urban ecology see cities as complex systems that can be analysed through the same analytical tools developed within ecology and the natural sciences. However, contemporary urban ecology combines an ecological perspective with sociological insights that allow it to include human and institutional attributes (such as learning) within their analytical models. At the opposite end of the spectrum, the field of urban political ecology criticises a reliance on biological models to understand the city. This field, drawing on a Marxist-inspired reading of sociometabolic relations, prioritises a political reading of urban nature. Accordingly, urban nature here is something to be made and sustained and as such it is part of metabolic and social processes which are inherently infused by power relations.

We have also further elaborated on the concept of nature-based solutions as well as a series of related approaches. 'Nature-based solutions' is an umbrella term that refers to deliberate, innovative interventions that seek to use the properties of nature to address a set of urban challenges as an alternative to purely grey methods of urban planning and development. Nature-based solutions, from a socioecological perspective, can create multiple ecological, economic, social, and urban planning benefits in parallel. It does this, for instance, by providing ecosystem services that cater to needs highly valued by humans. However, in the sociopolitical reading of nature-based solutions, these are considered a part of a dynamic system in the constant, where ecological, social, and political processes alike shape the processes and their outcomes. With the perspective of more-than-human added to this, any sentient being is part of this shaping, and as such, part of the solution.

KEY LEARNING EXERCISES

1. **Individual Reflection:** Think of what constitutes nature in a city for you. How would you define it in your words? In your opinion, are we (humans) part of this nature or are we outside of it?
2. **Peer Discussion:** Discuss with your peers how the concept of 'urban nature' relates to other key concepts and fields of study discussed in this chapter, including 'urban ecology', 'urban metabolism', and 'urban political ecology'. Relate this discussion to how the perspectives on nature in the city have evolved over time and across various disciplines.
3. **Explore Examples:** Explain what 'nature-based solutions' are and provide three examples of nature-based solutions. Which nature-based solutions can you identify from the case studies of Melbourne and Tianjin? Why do you consider these to be nature-based solutions? Explain why and how these nature-based solutions can be considered multi-functional.

FURTHER RESOURCES

Bulkeley, H. (2021) Climate changed urban futures: environmental politics in the anthropocene city. *Environmental Politics*, 30(1–2), 266–284.

Dorst, H., van der jag, A., Raven, R. and Runhaar, H. (2019) Urban greening through nature-based solutions – key characteristics of an emerging concept. *Sustainable Cities and Society*, 49, 101620.

Wickenberg, B., McCormick, K. and Alkan Olsson, J. (2021). Advancing the implementation of nature-based solutions in cities: a review of frameworks. *Environmental Science and Policy*, 125, 44–53.

3 Valuing

INTRODUCTION

The value of nature tends to be taken for granted in our everyday lives. We might not notice, for example, how urban trees provide shelter from the hot sun, or how being surrounded by nature within an otherwise busy and hectic city makes us feel relaxed and at ease. Efforts are increasingly being made to make these multiple values of nature visible to citizens, decision-makers, and the private sector, both to conserve and restore the nature that already exists, but also to drive the uptake of nature-based solutions. This is a complex task, mixing both ecological and ethical lines of thinking in an attempt to provide diverse assessments of what nature might be worth to individuals and to society as a whole. Capturing the value of anything is challenging, even in markets where the exchange of goods and services for money exists. When it comes to nature, it is even more complicated. There are no markets per se, and economic values are not the only values which are being supplied. Valuation therefore becomes a contested cultural and political practice.

In this chapter, we start by exploring how the value of nature is conceptualised. We then identify the difference between approaches that consider nature to have primarily an *instrumental value* – where it is of use to society – and those that focus on the *intrinsic value* of nature, that is, where the value of nature is an end in and of itself. This provides the basis for thinking about alternative approaches, recognising that the way we relate to nature is what generates value, and that, in turn, such values are likely to be multiple and divergent. We then examine how economic techniques can be used to assess the value of nature. While controversial, such approaches are seen by some to be useful because they allow for the value of nature to be placed on a level playing field with the economic or monetary value of other urban features. The perceived strengths of economic evaluation – that is, that these approaches generate a common metric through which different forms of value can be aggregated and compared to one another – can also lead to some of the greatest weaknesses. Such evaluation approaches struggle to provide the space needed to recognise the multiple and diverse values of nature held by different communities across space and time (see Box 3.1).

Box 3.1 The critique of the economic valuation of nature

Admittedly, the economic valuation of nature has come a long way towards accounting for the contribution of nature to human well-being. Nevertheless, it has some serious shortcomings, which originate from the fact that the model is based on financial investment models, that is, the economic decision-making of an individual at a given time (Gowdy, 2004). Here we discuss a few, including but not limited to: (1) the social aspects of human decisions; (2) temporal and scalar issues; and (3) justice considerations.

First, economic valuations seem to overlook that individual preferences depend on a variety of cultural conditioning and psychological characteristics and, thus, significantly vary from individual to individual and from culture to culture.

Second, they seem to have limitations in encountering temporal and scalar changes, such as changes in the distant future or in large-scale ecosystems. Notably, they seem to work better on a local scale. There have been multiple local studies made successfully documenting values of specific threatened ecosystems with great policy relevance (Parks & Gowdy, 2013).

Third, while the economic valuation of nature has been critical to bring conservation efforts into the limelight, it has also contributed to bringing it into the world of financial markets, speculative investments, and landgrabs. Some regard this with concern and scepticism, as valuing nature economically might mean the application of the same logics that have resulted in the uneven accumulation and distribution of wealth and control over natural resources, social inequity, and power imbalances.

Box 3.2 Key terms and concepts used in this chapter

Hedonic pricing: An economic method to estimate the demand for a good or service which is based on the revealed preference of users or consumers. Hedonic pricing methods assume that the price of a product or service reflects its embodied characteristics. As certain environmental services influence market prices, hedonic pricing is often applied to assess the economic value of such services.

Instrumental value: In moral philosophy, things with instrumental value can help you achieve a particular end, that is, they are good as a means to achieve something else.

Intrinsic value: In contrast to instrumental values, intrinsic values are good and as such desirable in and of themselves. Intrinsic values can also be contrasted by extrinsic values, which can also be defined as a means, or for something else's sake.

Natural Capital Accounting (NCA): This is a process to calculate the total stocks and flows of natural resources and services in a given ecosystem or geographical area. Using one or more valuation techniques, physical indicators are often expressed in stocks and monetary indicators in flows.

Nature's Contribution to People (NCP): This refers to 'all the contributions, both positive and negative, of living nature (e.g. diversity of organisms, ecosystems, and their associated ecological and evolutionary processes) to the quality of life for people'. Beneficial contributions include food provision, water purification, and flood control, whereas unfavourable contributions include disease transmission and predation that damages people or their assets. Whether a contribution is perceived as positive or negative may be context-sensitive and depend on cultural, temporal. or spatial circumstances (Intergovernmental Science-Policy Platform on Biodiversity and Ecosystem Services (IPBES), 2018).

Return on Investment (RoI): This is a ratio between net income (over a period) and investment (that is, costs resulting from an investment of some resources at a point in time). If the RoI of a project is high, it means the investment's gains compare favourably to its cost.

In the context of environmental and social projects, gains are often understood as other types than financial gains. For example, social return on investment is a principle-based method for measuring extra-financial value relative to resources invested. This extra-financial value can be environmental and social value which is often not reflected in conventional financial accounts.

Willingness to Pay (WTP): In behavioural economics, this is the maximum price a user or consumer claims to be willing to pay for a product or service. Consumers' willingness to pay is context-sensitive and, as such, largely depends on the context in which the concrete decision takes place.

Box 3.3 Cultivating urban nature – key lessons

Recognise Trade-Offs: Urban nature and nature-based solutions involve trade-offs in comparison to other potential solutions. These need to be explicitly recognised and considered in decision-making processes.

While nature-based solutions can be designed to address multiple issues simultaneously, they will always involve trade-offs in terms of what and who is prioritised in comparison to alternative solutions. Priorities and related values have important implications when considering investment. Making trade-offs explicit is critical if these interventions are not going to always benefit the same places, communities, and agendas. By recognising the trade-offs and compromises involved, gaps that need to be addressed can be identified and new measures to foster greater inclusion can be established. At the same time, it is important to remain flexible when developing nature-based solutions so that as trade-offs emerge, these can be accommodated and addressed. Where such trade-offs emerge that may involve undermining fundamental principles – such as reducing inequality or ensuring that environmental risks are not displaced to other people or places – investment decisions can be reassessed and reworked. It is critical that divergent values and demands of different actors do not mean that such trade-offs are ignored, and that their consequences are neglected. Involved actors can support decisions surrounding nature-based solutions in being transparent about potential trade-offs and how these are managed by requiring the use of multi-criteria assessment approaches during all nature-based solution stages – from project design to implementation and evaluation.

We then consider the ways in which the value of nature is contested. We find that the value of urban nature is produced over time by particular ideas and practices that tend to favour some communities over others, leading to tensions about who should determine urban nature futures. At the same time, it is important to recognise that not all urban nature is valued, with some kinds of nature being regarded as unwanted, out of place, or even detrimental to urban life (see Box 3.2). Looking at which kinds of nature remain marginalised by and for whom also shows us that how nature comes to hold value is a cultural and political practice (see Box 3.3).

Thinking about the Value of Nature

How, why, and for whom nature has value has been the subject of long-standing ethical consideration and political–economic debates. The question of the value of nature concerns both its meaning – that nature has in our lives and societies – and its benefits. Further, it is about making the value of nature visible and recognised within society at large. Valuing nature is therefore not simply a matter for philosophers or economists, but rather a political and societal debate. It is also something that we do every day in multiple ways, often without even recognising it.

One approach to valuing nature focuses on its instrumental properties: what is it that nature delivers to society in terms of services and benefits? Urban nature provides a variety of services, including capturing rainwater, providing cooling, storing carbon, and creating soft surfaces for playing sports, as outlined throughout this book. These services, in turn, generate a range of benefits for society, such as reducing the costs of flood defences or the need for air conditioning or to create space for leisure activities. An instrumental perspective suggests that nature is valuable as long as it is delivering these services and benefits, and that the value of nature itself depends on whether it can deliver these 'better' than other approaches. For example, sustainable urban drainage systems (SUDS) are a nature-based solution that uses natural systems to help manage water in the city. These solutions are valued because they are more resilient and cost-effective in the long term than traditional purely concrete systems if considering the delivery of additional benefits like biodiversity conservation and aesthetic appeal alongside the main function of managing water.

In contrast to the instrumental approach to valuing nature, other perspectives focus on the intrinsic qualities of nature. In this view, nature is valued in and of itself rather than being viewed as a means to achieve other outcomes. The intrinsic value of anything – nature included – is a challenging concept to grasp and has been subject to intense philosophical debate. For some, this form of value exists whether or not society recognises it; it is entirely internal to nature. For others, what is recognised as the intrinsic value of nature is instead a mark of how societies come to value nature for its own sake, for example in terms of the awe it can inspire, the spiritual connections that it forms, the relations of care that looking after nature for the future generates, and so on. In this perspective, the value of nature is not to be found in how it performs, but in the sheer fact of its existence. Seen from this perspective, natural drainage systems in cities would be valued for the nature they contain, regardless of their efficiency or effectiveness as compared to grey infrastructure alternatives. In short, looking at the value of nature as intrinsic means that any loss of nature is a loss of value.

The debate about whether we should see nature as having instrumental or intrinsic value has been fierce and often challenging to apply in policy contexts. As a result, efforts have been made to find alternative positions that occupy a more middle-ground position, recognising both the services and benefits that nature produces as well as its inherent qualities. Chan et al. (2016) thus argue that 'few people make personal choices based only on how things possess inherent worth or satisfy their preferences (intrinsic and instrumental values, respectively)', but rather 'also consider the appropriateness of how they relate with nature and with others, including the actions and habits conducive to a good life, both meaningful and satisfying'.

At the global scale, focus within the science-policy domain of IPBES (the Intergovernmental Science-Policy Platform on Biodiversity and Ecosystem Services) has shifted towards thinking about the relational value of nature. This approach recognises that the value of nature is generated through the different relations society establishes with it. The relational value of nature can be focused on its direct benefits but also account for the meaning, connection, and affect it generates such as beauty, solace, and inspiration. This wide range of ways in which nature generates benefits and meaning for individuals and society as a whole has been recognised by the term 'nature's contribution to people', which forms a cornerstone of the IPBES Global Assessment on the current state of nature and the need to ensure its future. For its proponents, nature's contributions to society encompass 'all the positive contributions, or benefits, and occasionally negative contributions, losses or detriments that people obtain from nature' (Pascual et al., 2017, p. 9). Further, these multiple contributions are understood as being situated within diverse cultural perspectives and forms of knowledge, such that the value of nature is recognised as multiple, diverse, and contextually embedded.

In reality, each of these perspectives on the value of nature – instrumental, intrinsic, and relational – are present in society and therefore also in decision-making processes about nature. They inform not only how we think about nature in the present, but also in the future and the ways in which decisions are made (see Figure 3.1). Despite the importance of these values in shaping what kinds of nature and which urban futures are being imagined, planned, and delivered, they often remain hidden from view or challenging to make explicit. As a consequence, other kinds of value such as the economic returns on

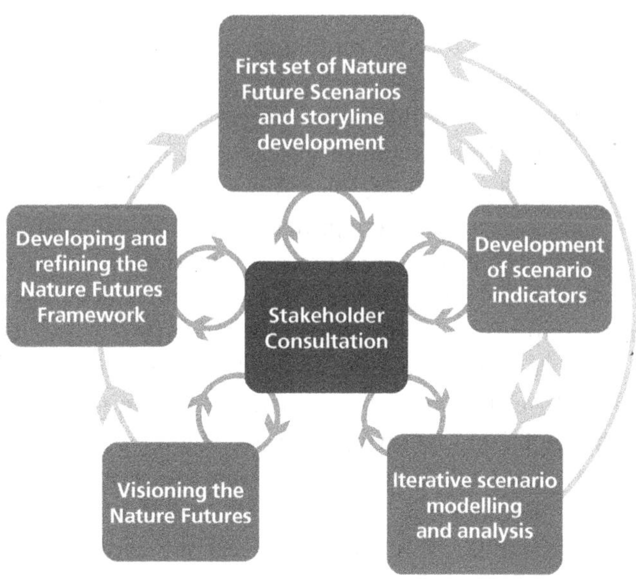

Figure 3.1 Iterative process for nature futures scenarios development

investment in new urban developments are often much more visible in decision-making processes. Significant effort has thus been made to make the value of nature more explicit in decision-making.

Making the Value of Nature Explicit

Recognising that nature has value is one thing, but actually valuing it is another. Historically, the value of nature has rarely been numerically calculated or explicitly taken into account in decision-making. Since sustainable development emerged as a global policy goal, a wide range of approaches have been developed through which to capture the value of nature in order to be considered alongside the value of, for example, economic development. These valuation techniques seek to identify the benefits that nature generates using different indicators and metrics that allow the value of nature to be compared to the value of other goods and services. The service of carbon storage, for instance, can be valued through indicators that measure the amount of carbon that can be captured and stored by diverse ecosystems. This valuation can be undertaken in ecological terms – in this case in terms of tonnes of CO_2 stored per m^2 – or it can also be monetised, with a monetary value in this case related to the price per tonne of CO_2 within carbon markets. While the valuation of nature does not have to take place in monetary terms, it is often the case that decision-makers and policy-makers are interested in calculating the monetary value of nature as this is a key criterion shaping the planning and implementation of urban projects.

When it comes to calculating the economic value of nature, valuation techniques are commonly used to capture three kinds of benefits. First, *direct-use values* arise from the use of ecosystem services directly, such as the use of nature-based solutions to cool buildings, provide clean water, or create space for recreation. Second, *indirect-use values* provide *positive externalities*, which are additional benefits to their core purpose, such as a green roof retaining water and reducing flood damage across the city. Third, *option values* occur when people are unsure about their future demand for a service that nature provides – for example, coastal protection – and are willing to pay to keep open the option of using a resource in the future, or to avoid irreversible negative impacts on the resource. It is more challenging to use economic valuation to capture *non-use values*. Within this approach, three distinct forms of non-use value are often considered: (a) existence value (based on utility derived from knowing that something exists); (b) altruistic value (based on utility derived from knowing that somebody else benefits); and (c) and bequest value (based on utility gained from future improvements in the well-being of one's descendants). These are forms of relational value, generated through specific kinds of relation between the individual and the form of nature they are valuing.

Economic valuations of this kind predominantly rely on the use of techniques that seek to reflect either the presence or the value of nature in existing markets or to use surveys or other methods to capture if and how individuals would assign monetary value to nature (see Box 3.4). For example, the *hedonic pricing* method is based on observing how house prices vary with proximity to nature and using this variation to infer how much that form of nature is worth in that particular urban context. Other techniques work by identifying the precise services that nature provides – for example, air cooling or flood protection – and comparing this to the cost of delivering the same level of service through traditional grey infrastructure approaches or technologies. Where markets or analogues that reflect the value of nature are not available, such as for non-use value, economists rely on stated preference methods where individuals are asked their willingness to pay for specific benefits or to accept certain forms of harm to nature.

These valuation techniques have a number of advantages: they allow different forms of urban nature and diverse nature-based solutions to be assessed on the same terms and in relation to traditional urban development approaches through the use of comparable indicators (for example, carbon stored, degrees of cooling provided) and their monetary value. They bring a heightened awareness of the services that nature provides in cities and a clear means of making this visible to decision-makers and policy-makers for whom nature may not be a first priority.

Box 3.4 The economic value of nature-based solutions

Urban nature in cities can deliver high value

Attempts are continuously being made to monetise our natural assets; primarily to raise awareness among decision-makers and practitioners about the value of nature, in economic terms. Bockarjova et al. (2020), for instance, analysed the economic value of a set of nature-based solutions in Europe based on data from the Urban Nature Atlas. They used the willingness-to-pay method to estimate values of nature-based solutions, measuring perceived direct and indirect value to urban residents, as well as value that exists even when individuals are unlikely to use the site. They found that the total economic value of 168 nature-based solutions in various cities in Europe is US$1.52 billion per year and the average value per year by hectare is US$83,203 per year. Notably, this is approximately twice the average GDP per capita in the European Union.

Nature-based solutions can deliver excellent return on investment

In their study, Bockarjova et al. (2020) calculated the return on investment for some 60 cases and compared the estimated total economic benefit to the respective capital investment cost. As the economic benefits are delivered to the urban population, but are not related to monetary flows, they could estimate the social return on investment per project. They found that more than half of the interventions recouped investment costs within 5 years, including 25 nature-based solutions which recouped investment costs within 1 year, and benefits continued in subsequent years.

Box 3.4 (cont.)

Examples of how nature-based solutions can provide economic and social value

Name	Types of nature-based solutions	Investment (US$ million)	Economic value (US$ million/year)	Social return (US$/year/dollar invested)
Krupp in Essen, Germany	Restoration of urban parks	6.771	44.503	6.63
Lambro river, Milan, Italy	Regeneration of urban rivers and canals	4.2	11	2.66
Haukaas Marshlands, Bergen, Norway	Peri-urban forests and wetlands	1.65	4.1	2.48

At the same time, there are also significant challenges in using these techniques. In practical terms, they are limited in the kinds of nature that are considered; for example, most hedonic pricing looks at the value of large urban parks and may not be relevant to other kinds of urban nature-based solutions such as green roofs and walls. They can also be resource-intensive to conduct due to the use of extensive surveying techniques and, therefore, not feasible for all cities. This challenge could be overcome through benefit transfer techniques, which seek to identify the findings from previous research and enable this to be used across multiple urban contexts. Nonetheless, this relies on which kinds of urban nature have been included in the initial studies that were conducted.

Beyond the practical challenges of using economic valuation methods, there are also wider concerns. While attempts have been made to capture the non-use value of nature, this remains challenging in practice. For example, individuals are not always able to articulate in monetary terms what they would be willing to pay for nature or what they would accept in terms of harm towards it. This is not only because we are not used to thinking about nature in this way or answering such questions, but also because it raises moral challenges: what is nature worth to us on a day-to-day basis, and can we put a price on it? Indeed, for some people, putting a price on nature is an act of devaluing it as it serves to change nature's meaning from something that is seen as priceless to a thing that has a (limited) monetary value. In this sense, it can be seen as a similar dilemma to putting a price on the value of a human life.

One outcome of the use of such techniques has been the implementation of payments for ecosystem services. However, such schemes have attracted widespread criticism for only being able to recognise a narrow range of nature's values and for neglecting the diverse values that indigenous people and local communities hold towards and within nature. Using common indicators or monetisation to make the value of nature commensurate with other values also entails the risk that if nature does not provide sufficient value, it may become seen as something that can be removed or substituted by other forms of infrastructure or development, especially when the latter appear to have equal or more financial value.

Contested Values

The articulation of values does not only take place through instruments of economic valuation, despite their prevalence in urban planning and policy. Indeed, every explicit act of identifying parts of urban nature as worthy of protection or destruction, restoration, or use is a form of valuation. As Aalto and Ernstson (2017, p. 310) suggest, these are forms of value articulation that are 'active, creative, selective, and ultimately political' processes which in turn are underpinned by practices 'influenced by class, race, gender and historical and ideological factors'. It is therefore no surprise that the value of urban nature is usually diverse and highly contested (see Case Study Box 3.1).

Case Study Box 3.1 Cape Town Environmental Education Trust (Cape Town, South Africa)

The case of the Cape Town Environmental Education Trust illustrates how social, economic, and environmental goals and inherent and instrumental values come into alignment. This initiative also demonstrates how pairing urban nature conservation with employment opportunities can offer great opportunities to improve inclusion for disadvantaged communities in urban green spaces. Cape Town is located in a global biodiversity hotspot and has both stark inequity and high levels of unemployment, all of which make equity, job creation, and nature conservation key challenges for the city. Cape Town forms part of a UNESCO World Heritage Site called the Cape Floral Region Protected Area, which includes nearly 20 per cent of Africa's flora in 0.5 per cent of Africa's area.

There are 16 nature reserves within Cape Town that protect many endangered species and ecosystems, but threats to the staggering biodiversity of the area and the pressing needs of Cape Town's citizens are difficult to reconcile. In addition, structural inequality due to the history of apartheid has prevented many disadvantaged and racialised communities from accessing recreation, economic, cultural, and other opportunities within protected nature reserves. Youth unemployment is over 50 per cent in Cape Town. New approaches are seeking to address the interconnections between these challenges to try to conserve biodiversity while strengthening economic opportunity and social inclusion in urban nature reserves.

Case Study Box 3.1 (cont.)

The non-profit organization Cape Town Environmental Education Trust has partnered with the City of Cape Town to create what they term a 'crèche to career' model of environmental education that supports on-the-ground nature conservation. The initiative strives to raise awareness about valuing nature differently, for instance by showing children from low-income communities the inherent, spiritual, and economic value of nature conservation, while improving job skills through skill training and formal apprenticeships.

This way, nature conservation takes a more inclusive approach that offers opportunities to low-income and racialised communities. These efforts have connected nearly 6000 children to nature, employed 151 people as conservation monitors, and conserved 728 hectares of land. The goal is that, step-by-step, nearby communities take ownership of the surrounding nature and start regarding it as something beneficial offering spiritual, social, and economic values.

Figure 3.2 Cape Town, South Africa

Economic valuation approaches are seen by some as advantageous because they seek to make diverse values *commensurate*, that is, able to be measured against one another and aggregated to provide an overall valuation of urban nature. However, where values are diverse and contested, such approaches can also serve to hide different values. Because these techniques are better equipped at capturing some forms of value over others, important values for urban nature may be persistently overlooked or integrated with other approaches, where in practice they may not be commensurate. For example, some local residents may value urban green spaces for the peace and tranquillity they provide. Others may value them positively or negatively for the possibilities for sociability that they afford, generating noisy play or large social gatherings. These contrasting value positions are continually negotiated, with some value positions becoming established and institutionalised – for example in 'keep off the grass' signs that populate urban parks in the UK – while other value positions are hidden, such as the use of urban green spaces as spaces for shelter among homeless people in cities.

The case of the Broadway estate in Tilbury, London, UK, provides an example of how the value of urban nature can be multiple and contested (Aalto & Ernstson, 2017). Here a vacant green space in a housing estate initially built for temporary purposes was subject to vandalism and the local authority was considering fencing the space to prevent members of the local communities accessing the site. Realising this would not solve the issue, a multi-agency partnership was formed to deliberate on the way forward. The art and architecture practice *muf* was recruited to develop alternative solutions. Working with story-telling techniques to elicit local values related to the site, *muf* enabled the articulation of values relating the importance that the area held for the Traveller community and the importance of horses in their everyday practices.

Although the local authority was initially opposed to formalising use of this space by this community and their horses, they were convinced to provide space for such a use by the articulation of the cultural and social values that this area of urban nature held for members of this community. As the park has become developed, more and more diverse communities have sought to have their needs recognised, for example in terms of providing space for horticulture or activities for elderly people (Aalton & Ernstson, 2017). As this and the above example show, urban nature remains continually contested and changes with time. Therefore, approaches that allow for a deeper engagement with diverse and conflicting values are needed to support decision-making alongside techniques of economic valuation.

In some cases, valuing nature can provide the basis for a more overt politics of exclusion that seeks to protect nature and the services it provides to the city, as a whole, from specific groups of people. In Sao Paulo, Parque Várzeas do Tietê (PVT; Tietê Lowlands Park) was first announced in 2009 and envisaged as the world's longest linear park. It has been designed as a nature-based solution that will provide flood protection as well as economic development to the region. However, in order to create the park, some 7500 families who currently inhabit the banks of the river were intended to be removed (Henrique & Tschakert, 2019). Central to the design and implementation of the project was the classification of current uses of the plot as either compatible, uncomfortable, or predatory and undesirable when it came to the future development of the area (Henrique & Tschakert, 2019).

While existing parks were used for leisure, the university campus and football grounds were seen as desirable, the land uses associated with the informal residents of the area were designated as undesirable and their removal legitimised (Henrique & Tschakert, 2019). The residents sought to resist the forced removal process. Areas targeted for this intervention were consolidated with more people moving in and building more robust structures. While nature-based solutions may be innovative, as Henrique and Tschakert (2019, p. 190) conclude from their analysis of this case, they 'can still exacerbate old vulnerabilities and engender new ones in communities already marginalised'. Nature-based solutions may reinforce particular hierarchies about what forms of nature come to be valued, by and for whom. Addressing the potential inequalities that nature-based solutions can generate requires inclusive approaches to decision-making where different groups and the divergent values they hold for nature are recognised and trade-offs are negotiated.

Unwanted Nature

Most of the discussion of the value of nature focuses on its benefits, that is, the services and meanings that nature holds for society as a whole and for individuals in their everyday lives. At the same time, some forms of nature have come to be seen as unwanted in particular urban settings, either because they are seen as having no or only limited value, or because nature's presence may be detrimental to other (proposed) forms of urban nature or urban and/or economic development. Urban bird populations often fall into this category.

In the cities of Newcastle and Gateshead, located on either side of the River Tyne in the north-east of England, an urban colony of an endangered sea gull – the Kittiwake – has been established since the late 1940s. The presence of a rare species along the city skyline is both celebrated and resisted. The BALTIC Centre for Contemporary Art, one of a number of important nesting sites for the birds along the river, celebrates the annual return of the migratory bird to the city and even organises a tour, while a live feed of the colony is broadcast by a local wildlife trust. At the same time, building owners across the two cities have put up spikes, netting, and other deterrents to prevent the birds from nesting on their properties. Here, a species regarded as having significant value in conservation terms is seen to generate economic costs rather than benefits.

Elsewhere, the value of more ordinary forms of urban nature is seen as marginal. Walthamstow Wetlands, located on the River Lee in East London, UK, was developed in 2016 as a project to create Europe's largest urban wetland from existing river landscapes and reservoirs by the local authority, water utility, and wildlife trust in order to create better access to nature for local communities and also support biodiversity in the area. Multiple measures were introduced to support wildlife and, in keeping with the designation of the area as a Site of Special Scientific Interest, the focus was mainly placed on species designated as important or rare and on those which were regarded as charismatic in order to support greater public engagement (Clancy & Ward, 2020). Within this project, the presence of Canada geese has proved controversial. Introduced to the UK for their ornamental value among the aristocracy in the seventeenth century, their population remained relatively low until both the growth of new water bodies and specific programmes for their relocation in the 1950s. Canada geese now occupy many sites across the UK and are classed as residential as their breeding conditions have compromised their migratory instincts (Clancy & Ward, 2020). These semi-wild species are not considered significant in conservation terms or for any services that they provide to society, but are rather considered a nuisance in urban parks.

In the case of the Walthamstow Wetlands, Clancy and Ward (2020) found that this caused something of an ethical dilemma, as the long history of residence of the geese in this area has come into conflict with the restoration and renaturing work being undertaken as a nature-based solution to enhance biodiversity and urban liveability. This work has included measures to deter the geese from continuing to occupy areas of the site. As Clancy and Ward (2020, p. 3) go on to argue, the 'construction of a nature reserve in the city involves carefully selecting the bodies and voices that fall under the banner of "biodiversity", to then be made worthy of concern'. In other words, the very design and implementation of nature-based solutions involves the valuing of some forms of nature over others (see Case Study Box 3.2).

Case Study Box 3.2 Beekeeping at Audi Hungaria (Győr, Hungary)

Győr is a fast-growing regional hub of north-western Hungary in one of the most important traffic and logistics corridors of Central Europe in the Budapest–Vienna–Bratislava triangle. The city is strategically located at the confluence of three rivers and a stone's throw from the main channel of the Danube, branding itself as 'the city of rivers'. There has been vibrant city life in the area for many centuries, resulting from a sequence of many cultures, thriving agriculture, and a long tradition of industry. With about 129,500 residents and 357,000 in its metropolitan area, the city is also an administrative and economic centre, with commerce and industry being dominant.

With industrial development come emissions, risks to biodiversity, and impacts on human health and well-being. While green space is relatively abundant at 63 m^2/person, most of it is due to single-block peri-urban forests such as Püspökerdő, which is considered the 'green lung' of the city. Nature-based solutions in Győr originate both from the distant past and from more recent times. The former have had to survive many developments but now thrive under modern urban development agendas, while the latter have emerged from new projects, such as green roofs and multi-functional urban parks.

This nature-based solution is a unique and innovative fusion of ecological landscape management with native species, pollution biomonitoring research, awareness raising, marketing, and environmental education intertwined with beekeeping at the Audi

Case Study Box 3.2 (cont.)

Hungaria factory. The Audi plant in Győr is the world's largest car engine factory. It is also Hungary's largest factory, directly employing over 11,000 people. The company has shown commitment to social development and the environment since the start of its operations in Győr; 1.76 per cent of the 5,167,366 m^2 factory area is green space, which borders brownfields and Natura 2000 territories.

Audi Hungaria identified biodiversity as a priority in 2008, which led to the development and implementation of its flora and fauna protection plan, including the restoration of native ecosystems, a bird protection programme, the protection of rainwater reservoirs, the installation of green roofs and walls, and the planting of over 1000 trees and 5000 bushes based on local ecological conditions. As an external expert assessed, the premises feel like another city, with native plants bringing the artificial factory surfaces to a more human and liveable dimension. Beekeeping was initiated by Audi AG in Ingolstadt, Germany, as a Corporate Social Responsibility programme, and established at the site of Audi Hungaria in 2015 on native Pannonian sandy grasslands and wildflower meadows. Awareness-raising focuses on employees and schoolchildren, while the project also contributes to pollution biomonitoring research using bees as bioindicators.

Figure 3.3 Győr, Hungary

As these examples show, the value of nature is not always straightforward or able to be assumed. It cannot simply be written off from the ecological status as a result of the benefits it generates or from its economic value. Rather, it is socially and materially produced through active practices that serve to identify both some forms of nature as holding more value than others and the values of some communities and individuals as more significant than others. Valuation is above all a cultural and political process.

OVERALL REFLECTIONS

In this chapter, the complexity surrounding the value of nature has been discussed. The efforts and techniques mixing both ecological and ethical lines of thinking to assess the multiple values of nature and to make it visible to people have been presented. How cultural and political practices challenge capturing these values has also been discussed.

First, the differences between valuation approaches that consider nature to primarily have a value that is of use to society (instrumental value) and those which value nature itself for what it is (intrinsic value) were explained. This provided a basis for understanding why it is necessary to develop middle-way or alternative approaches, because how we relate to nature becomes focal (relational value). From this perspective, nature generates both benefits and meaning for individuals and society in various ways, but nature's negative contributions have also been recognised (nature's contribution to people). We have also shown that each of these perspectives is present in reality when valuing nature, even if often remaining hidden.

Valuation techniques – and especially economic valuations – are thus important, because the often hidden or non-explicit value of nature can be revealed and placed on a level playing field with the economic or monetary value of other urban features. Methods of hedonistic pricing, stated preferences or willingness to pay, make the economic value of environmental services visible to citizens and decision-makers alike. While these methods generate a common denominator through which values can be aggregated and compared, we have also shown that they are controversial. Mostly because they struggle to recognise the multiple and diverse values held by different communities across space and time.

Capturing the multiple and diverse values of urban nature is particularly challenging, as these are changing over time and space. Some forms of nature and certain practices are favoured by some communities over others, which in turn can create tensions about who should determine the future of urban nature. Understanding different forms of nature and related social practices, including those regarded as unwanted, can inform us about how nature comes to hold value, by whom and for whom, in the present. It can also inform us what kinds of nature and which urban futures are being imagined, planned, and delivered in the future.

KEY LEARNING EXERCISES

1. **Individual Reflection:** Reflect on the different ways of economic valuation of urban nature: hedonic pricing, comparing costs, and stated preference methods. Why may knowing these techniques be important for urban planning? What are

the challenges associated with the economic valuation of urban nature? Propose the ways to overcome these challenges.

2. **Peer Discussion:** Imagine a situation where the local government plans to remove an urban park in your neighbourhood and construct new housing with green roofs, green courtyards, and access to urban farming plots instead of the park. In a group of three, choose one role position of valuing nature per person: intrinsic, instrumental, and relational. Starting from your role value position, choose whether you support the new housing development or oppose it. Make a list of arguments for your position starting from your role values. Discuss in which ways your position and your peers' positions are contested and when your arguments align. As a group, propose an alternative development which is plausible for all three peers.
3. **Explore Examples:** Use examples of nature-based solutions to explain what direct use values, indirect use values, and non-use values are. Provide examples of 'unwanted nature' close to the place where you live. Why is it 'unwanted' and what are the ways to avoid conflicts with this nature?

FURTHER RESOURCES

Bockarjova, M., Botzena, W. and Koetse, M. (2020) Economic valuation of green and blue nature in cities: a meta-analysis. *Ecological Economics*, 169, 106480.

Intergovernmental Science-Policy Platform on Biodiversity and Ecosystem Services (IPBES). (2022) *The Assessment Report on the Diverse Values and Valuation of Nature*. Bonn, Germany: IPBES.

Seddon, N., Chausson, A., Berry, P., et al. (2020) Understanding the value and limits of nature-based solutions to climate change and other global challenges. *Philosophical Transactions*, 375(1794), 20190120.

4 Developing

INTRODUCTION

Transforming cities into more sustainable, green, climate-resilient, and biodiversity-rich systems is increasingly being integrated into urban development agendas. The multitude of societal and ecological urban challenges has accelerated the discussion on the prominent role nature can play in this transformation process, for instance by providing multiple sustainability benefits for a diversity of actors. There is, however, a growing gap between the rhetoric of the potential and actual implementation, not least due to the different ways in which urban nature is conceptualised and valued, which, in turn, determines how it is developed into its physical appearance.

Nature can take different forms in a city, and we can categorise these forms in different ways. It is therefore is important to appreciate how urban nature is being viewed, for instance, through the lens of nature-based solutions. Furthermore, nature is often considered something untouched by humans that exists far away from cities and that must be brought back into urban areas. It is often overlooked that there is already nature all around the city, even inside our homes, and not all of it desirable or beneficial for all actors involved. When flooding forces rats out of the sewerage system into our living rooms, or our food leftovers trigger an ant invasion into our kitchens, we may not view these appearances of nature as beneficial.

Albeit from an ecological perspective, we contribute to habitat and subsistence creation for non-human urbanites. Similarly, pigeons swarming around our cities are often viewed as unwanted nature by many. But this is still urban nature. While placing out bird feeders in city parks with regular maintenance, bird-watching places, and educational information boards can quickly turn these urban areas into a nature-based solution through which we intentionally create an urban nature space with benefits for different human and non-human actors of the urban ecosystem. For some, in derelict urban areas, long-term construction sites might not be desirable places to pass by, while for others, they may provide a social sphere, shelter, and habitat.

In this chapter, the focus is on understanding how urban nature is being developed in our cities in different ways and combinations – in particular through the concept of nature-based solutions (see Box 4.1). Some existing green and blue areas in cities may provide ecosystem services and become instrumental once they are

Box 4.1 Key terms and concepts used in this chapter

Ecological categories: Nature-based solutions can be divided into eight ecological categories and a range of subcategories. These categories include (external) building greens; urban green areas connected to grey infrastructure; parks, semi-natural, and natural urban green areas; allotments and community gardens; green indoor areas; blue areas; green areas for water management; and derelict areas.

Innovation types: In this chapter, to aid understanding of nature-based solutions, we use a typology of ecological, social, technological, and system. Ecological innovations with urban nature, for example, are grouped along three key areas of action, including creation and transformation of green, blue, and grey areas, maintenance and management of existing urban nature sites, and ecosystem restoration. Similarly, social, technological, and system innovations have a variety of focus areas that are key to the development, implementation, and mainstreaming of projects featuring urban nature and nature-based solutions.

Urban landscapes: These include: coastalscape, riverscape, underscape, gardenscape, parkscape, woodscape, farmscape, roofscape, builtscape, streetscape, railscape, and barescape. Urban nature and nature-based solutions may also be located in and across multiple urban landscapes.

Box 4.2 Cultivating urban nature – key lessons

Make Space: Urban nature needs space to grow.

The allocation of urban space to nature will mean that it cannot be used for grey development purposes, many of which may be perceived to offer more economically rewarding returns on investment. Making space for urban nature involves engaging landowners and asset-holders and promoting the multiple benefits that such interventions can bring, designing nature into new urban developments from the outset, and developing legal requirements or voluntary mandates for their inclusion. It is also critical to find ways of integrating nature into existing urban landscapes. One approach could involve removing sealed artificial surfaces, such as taking up paving and road space, reusing roof or wall space, or uncovering rivers. Another strategy is to engage with landholders in cities who might not realise that through repurposing their assets, they could contribute to a wide range of sustainability goals; for example, hospitals, schools, religious organisations, retail parks, and office complexes. At the same time, we know that making more space for nature can come at a cost with increasing land prices and rents, which can price nature out of the reach of existing inhabitants and marginal communities in the city. These issues need to be addressed from the outset to avoid urban nature having unintended consequences, like contributing to urban inequalities and social injustice.

recognised as having the potential to solve particular issues. At the same time, however, rather than being a solution, parts of urban nature may be regarded as a problem or seen to interfere with other benefits being fully realised. It is important to remain mindful of the tensions in this regard as well as the significant possibilities of nature-based solutions (see Box 4.2).

This suggests that the value of urban nature-based solutions addressing specific challenges could change over time, vary amongst different constituents, and be contested. Such conceptions and visions are important when it comes to developing interventions that create, manage, or restore urban nature and its features. Such nature-based solutions may be physical/ecological and involve, for example, the creation of new natural areas, adapting a maintenance regime for an existing natural area, or restoring degraded green spaces. They may also be social/political in character and involve changes to governance arrangements, business models, and forms of financing and the engagement of citizens around urban nature. These are not necessarily neatly separated; single interventions can take many forms simultaneously.

Exploring the Forms of Nature-Based Solutions

The diversity of physical forms that urban nature can take depends on a variety of factors, including how urban nature is conceptualised and valued in a given cultural, environmental, economic, and social context. Therefore, when trying to make sense of the diversity of nature-based solutions, it is helpful to utilise some basic typologies that assist us, for instance, in better understanding the relation between a certain type of urban nature (for example, a pond) and its intended role in addressing a specific urban sustainability challenge (for example, heavy rainfalls and consequent flooding).

In this context, we can think about nature-based solutions as ecological sites in the city (see Table 4.1) and the related actions and processes through which these sites have been created and developed in different urban landscapes (see Table 4.1). We have discussed in Chapter 3 that these processes can be social and political in their

Table 4.1 Processes and actions to develop nature-based solutions

Process/action (type of innovation)	Focus area	Explanation and examples
Ecological	Creation and transformation	Creating new natural spaces: green roofs, green urban areas (e.g. parks), sustainable use areas, and habitats (e.g. national forest areas), and transforming grey infrastructure into green spaces (e.g. renaturing brownfield sites or former industrial areas).
	Maintenance and management	Maintaining and managing existing green and blue spaces (e.g. protected areas and corridors), improving maintenance and delivery of ecosystem services (e.g. management measures under Natura2000 areas, river basin management plans).
	Restoration	Restoring ecosystems and their functionality to deliver a wider range of ecosystem services and benefits (e.g. wetland and floodplain restoration, dike relocation, remediation of polluted areas, removal of concrete along the rivers).
Social	Policy	Policy action refers to new or significant changes in public policy frameworks (e.g. new forms of regulations and public incentives). Interventions include legal designations, regulation, strategic prioritisation; development of policy instruments (e.g. voluntary agreements, certifications, benchmarks).
	Governance	Governance process refers to new or significant changes in governance frameworks or arrangements. Interventions include new forms of collaboration between public and private actors or new methods of citizen engagement.
	Knowledge	Knowledge generation includes new or substantially improved arrangements or methods for generating knowledge about nature in the city that changes how it is viewed, understood, and used, as well as how urban nature projects are designed and implemented. Interventions include forms of digital monitoring, new techniques for evaluation, mapping, and data collection from the citizens.

Table 4.1 (cont.)

Process/action (type of innovation)	Focus area	Explanation and examples
	Economic	Economic process refers to new or significant changes in economic frameworks or modes of operation. Interventions include new business models, financing arrangements, and ways in which value is assessed and marketed.
	Cultural	Cultural process refers to new or significant changes in cultural frameworks (e.g. new concepts or cultural categories). Interventions include artistic or creative endeavours, reconnecting nature to particular cultural histories, or forms of heritage.
Technological	Product	Product generation is the introduction of a good or service that is new or has significantly improved characteristics or intended uses. Interventions include new plant species used in urban planting, the use of different materials for drainage channels, and new products for green roofs.
	Process	Process generation refers to the implementation of a new or significantly improved production or delivery method. Interventions include processes supporting the production of urban agriculture or the maintenance of river systems.
	Infrastructural	Infrastructural process refers to a new type of or significant changes to existing infrastructure that enable the flow of goods, people, and resources. Interventions include redesign or re-engineering of river channels, road verges, railway sidings, streets with space for nature, and development of new forms of blue and green infrastructure.
System	System	System process leads to systemic changes in both social (e.g. values, regulations, attitudes) and technical (e.g. infrastructure, technology, tools, production processes) dimensions and, most importantly, in the relations between them. Examples include multi-functional interventions as part of a large-scale transformation of an urban district, neighbourhood, or catchment area. Interventions include new master plans, integrated catchment plans, and urban redevelopment.

Table 4.2 Urban landscapes

Landscape	Explanation and examples
Coastalscape	Coastal areas (built and wild)
Riverscape	River areas (natural and managed), riverbanks
Waterscape	Lakes, ponds, fountains, wetlands (natural/managed/artificial)
Soilscape	Surface and subsurface soil
Underscape	Underground water bodies, bedrock
Gardenscape	Private gardens (domestic and commercial)
Parkscape	Public parks (may contain wooded areas) and allotment gardens
Woodscape	Public and private forested and wooded land
Farmscape	Farmland areas within or on the boundaries of urban
Roofscape	Roof space – public, private, commercial (a subset of the builtscape, but critical for urban nature competing with other sustainability interventions, e.g. solar panels, white coatings)
Builtscape	Built fabric – walls/facades, pavements, car parks, indoor greens
Streetscape	Road infrastructure (e.g. hedges, marginal land, roundabouts)
Railscape	Rail infrastructure (e.g. marginal lands, embankments)
Barescape	Abandoned and derelict land, buildings, infrastructure

nature; in Chapter 7, this will be further explored in detail with another type of process, namely innovations, innovation processes, and their driving factors.

First, nature-based solutions can be divided into eight ecological categories and a range of subcategories. These categories include (external) building greens; urban green areas connected to grey infrastructure; parks, semi-natural, and natural urban green areas; allotments and community gardens; green indoor areas; blue areas; green areas for water management; and derelict areas. An explanation and specific examples of each subcategory are provided in this chapter and in the subsequent sections, which feature one case study per ecological category.

Second, we can think about the processes through which urban nature and nature-based solutions can be developed. According to innovation system thinking, these can be grouped into four main types of innovations – ecological, social, technological, and system, each of which accommodates several focus areas (see Table 4.3). Ecological innovations with urban nature, for example, are grouped along three key areas of action, including creation and transformation of green, blue, and grey areas, maintenance and management of existing urban nature sites, and ecosystem restoration. Similarly, social, technological, and system innovations have a variety of focus areas that are key to the development, implementation, and mainstreaming of projects featuring urban nature and nature-based solutions (see Case Study Box 4.1). These are summarised and explained in Table 4.1, and further elaborated on in Chapter 7.

Table 4.3 Ecological categories of nature-based solutions

Category	Subcategory	Explanation and examples
(External) building greens	Green roofs	Roof vegetation on thin substrate with varying degrees of irrigation and management; vegetation established either artificially by seeding or naturally; this includes perennials, grasses, small trees, rooftop farming, mosses, succulents, herbs, and grasses.
	Green walls or facades	Ground-based climbing plants intended for ornamental purposes or plants growing in facade-bound substrate (e.g. containers or textile-systems).
	Balcony greens	Plants on balconies and terraces planted mostly in pots.
Urban green areas connected to grey infrastructure	Alley and street trees/ hedges/greens	Trees planted in alleys or along roads and paths, either solitary or in rows. Hedges along roads or paths. Non-tree, mostly shrubby or grassy verges along roads.
	Railway banks and tracks	Green space along railways.
	House gardens	Areas in the immediate vicinity of private houses cultivated mainly for ornamental purposes or non-commercial food production.
	Green playgrounds/ school grounds	Green areas intended for playing or outdoor learning.
	Institutional green spaces	Green spaces surrounding public and private institutions and corporate buildings.
	Green parking lots	Parking lots surrounded by or interspersed with trees, grass patches, flower beds, bushes, or other vegetation.
	Riverbank greens	Green space alongside rivers, streams, and canals, usually with foot or bike paths.
Parks and (semi-) natural urban green areas	Large urban parks or forests	Larger green (forested) area within a city intended for recreational use by urban population; can include different features such as trees, grassy areas, playgrounds, water bodies, and ornamental beds.
	Pocket parks/ neighbourhood green spaces	Small green areas around and between buildings vegetated by ornamental trees, shrubs, grass; often in residential areas, but also between other building types.
	Botanical gardens	Educational and ornamental areas planted with large diversity of plant species.
	Green corridors	Networks of linked landscape elements that provide ecological, recreational, and cultural benefits to the community.
Allotments and community gardens	Allotments	Small garden parcels cultivated by different people, intended for non-commercial food production.
	Community gardens	Areas collectively gardened by a community for food and recreation.
	Horticulture	Land devoted to growing vegetables, fruits, and flowers.

Table 4.3 (cont.)

Category	Subcategory	Explanation and examples
Green indoor areas	Indoor vertical greeneries (walls and ceilings)	Ground-based climbing plants intended for ornamental purposes or plants growing in facade-bound substrate (e.g. containers or textile-systems) inside of a building.
	Atriums	Green areas surrounding/enclosed in a building, planted mostly with ornamental plants.
Blue areas	Lakes/ponds	Natural and artificial standing water bodies containing freshwater with (semi)natural aquatic communities; banks can be human-made or natural.
	Rivers/streams/canals/estuaries	Natural and artificial running water bodies containing freshwater (mixed fresh and saltwater in estuaries) with (semi)natural aquatic communities; banks are human-made or natural.
	Deltas	Landform at the mouth of a river formed by sediment deposits.
	Sea coasts	Contact areas between the sea and the land of different characteristics (e.g. sand beaches, cliffs, coastal dunes).
	Wetlands/bogs/fens/marshes	Areas with soil permanently or periodically saturated with water and characteristic flora and fauna.
Green areas for water management	Rain gardens	Shallow, vegetated basins that collect and temporarily store rainwater runoff from rooftops, pavements, and streets or allow for its infiltration.
	Swales/filter strips	Vegetated and gently sloped pit or shallow drainage channels for filtering surface runoff.
	Sustainable urban drainage systems	A systemic approach to manage drainage in and around properties, often combining green and grey components; can include, for example, green roofs, permeable surfaces, infiltration trenches, swales, or detention basins.
Derelict areas	Abandoned and derelict spaces with growth of wilderness or green features	Recently abandoned areas, construction sites, and former industrial areas with spontaneously occurring pioneer or ruderal vegetation.

Third, we can consider how urban nature and nature-based solutions can be integrated into different urban landscapes. These include: coastalscape, riverscape, underscape, gardenscape, parkscape, woodscape, farmscape, roofscape, builtscape, streetscape, railscape, and barescape (see Table 4.2). Urban nature and nature-based solutions may also be located in and across multiple urban landscapes. For example, sustainable urban drainage systems that utilise both natural and grey infrastructure features to manage water in cities extend across the urban soil and waterscapes (see Case Study Box 4.2). In the following sections, we introduce each of the eight categories of ecological sites of nature-based solutions, and elaborate with illustrative real-world examples.

Case Study Box 4.1 BiodiverCity (Malmö, Sweden)

The BiodiverCity project, initiated and led by the Environmental Department of Malmö City, is a great example of the diversity of forms urban nature and nature-based solutions can take. Between 2011 and 2017, the project delivered more than 30 multi-functional green and blue nature-based solutions across the city of Malmö, across different urban landscapes, leading to ecological, social, and technical changes and the relations between them.

After its industrial past, Malmö has and continues to transform to a service-oriented city. While becoming an important economic, educational, and cultural centre of southern Sweden, the growing population and increasing densification poses a threat to urban greenery and biodiversity. Recognising these challenges, as part of Malmö's transition, the green and blue nature-based solutions of the BiodiverCity project carry invaluable social, ecological, and economic benefits and lessons to learn from for further projects. The project aims for a denser, greener, and more diverse city with a mixed use of spaces, where the residents will be close to nature and rich biological diversity.

Supported by the discourse of densification calling for innovative solutions for urban greenery, BiodiverCity has delivered a variety of green roofs, green walls, mobile plant systems, three-dimensional greenery, and a range of urban biotopes to the city. While each individual intervention of the project has its own characteristics and often differs in the type of innovation (ecological, technological, social, or cultural, or a combination of all of these) in their emergence, they also carry many common traits of transformative and incremental innovations. Some of these include: (a) using already existing networks where innovations originate and travel through; (b) making technical, financial, and human resources available, knowing that, for example, the lack of substrates, species, skilled and committed developers, and ecological knowledge have previously been impeding factors for learning, innovation, and mainstreaming nature-based solutions; (c) coherent project design, for example the inclusion of maintenance and well-defined goals and responsibilities; (d) creating continuity in leadership, commitment, and ecological knowledge; and (e) engaging the private sector, such as property owners and developers, through the entire project, not least to establish showcases for further learning.

Indeed, the active participation of committed and experienced people throughout the project, and the combination of engaged building developers and competent multi-disciplinary working groups (not least across municipal departments), have been important to achieving project goals such as developing new products, services, and processes to create a basis for evaluation, learning, and later dissemination of nature-based interventions. The continuous involvement of housing companies from planning through implementation and commercialisation assured a project continuum by providing conditions for continuous learning, while the multi-disciplinary working groups set the ground for horizontal and vertical knowledge development and dissemination.

Case Study Box 4.1 (cont.)

Figure 4.1 Malmö, Sweden

Case Study Box 4.2 Tolka Valley Park Wetlands and Greenway (Dublin, Ireland)

Tolka Valley is an example of how environmental degradation and the scarcity of resources can drive institutional and technical innovation across a range of urban landscapes, resulting in more sustainable solutions. Tolka Valley Park suffers from chronic soil and water pollution. Sustainability policy prioritises its environmental remediation, altering the function of this green space for surrounding communities. The Tolka River runs through a park on the northern edge of Dublin City, bordering an industrial estate, low-income residential areas, and a newly developed block of luxury apartments. The north-east of the park was a landfill decommissioned in the 1970s.

The rest of the park was used for illegal dumping and other criminal activities and was stigmatised as an unsafe place for years prior to its regeneration. The park had several

Case Study Box 4.2 (cont.)

environmental challenges, including a polluted storm-water stream that discharged into a fishing river via an ornamental pond, and increasing numbers of flooding events in the south-east of the park due to upstream over-urbanisation. While building an integrated wetland to de-pollute the pond during the first phase of regeneration (1999–2001) was relatively inexpensive (costing €40,000), the second phase (2009–2013) of the project including a Greenway and additional wetlands was more costly (costing more than €3 million) and challenged by the economic crisis of 2008.

The regeneration of Tolka Valley Park was led by the Dublin City Council. It resulted in improved ecological quality and enhanced biodiversity while opening the park to a diverse public. Tolka Valley Park feeds into a Special Protection Area, the South Dublin Bay and River Tolka estuary, whose catchment area spans three local authorities. The regeneration project involved two Integrated Constructed Wetlands (ICWs) and other soft engineering methods and landscaping improvements. The first ICW has attenuated pollutants from an underground tributary of the Tolka River, reducing unpleasant odours, enhancing the pond's amenity value, and creating new wetland habitat for biodiversity.

Having distinct patches of different plant species results in greater biodiversity and also improves its pollutant-retention capacity. The second ICW absorbs pollution from run-off and slows storm-water drainage into the River Tolka. In addition, a cycling and walking path was installed through the park. The transformation of a previously polluted open space into a much-frequented public park has benefitted the surrounding neighbourhoods. However, socioeconomic inequalities and cultural divisions are still reflected in how and by whom the park is used.

Figure 4.2 Dublin, Ireland

External Building Greens

External building greens include green roofs, green walls, green facades, and balcony greens. This vegetation can be established either artificially by seeding or naturally. It includes perennials, grasses, small trees, rooftop farming, mosses, succulents, herbs, and grasses. External building greens offer a range of benefits, including the improved insulation of buildings, climate and flood control, and biodiversity enhancement. They can also increase the aesthetic value of the urban landscape.

One example can be identified as the green roof of the Ministry of Economics and Finance in Athens, Greece. This project was implemented on the rooftop of a 10-floor building with a floor space of 1.4 hectares, installing a green roof of 650 m^2. The motivation behind the roof installation was to study the thermodynamic impact of green roofs in Athens, which has a very hot climate. Targets included: (1) to achieve energy savings of up to 50 per cent for air conditioning on the floor directly below the installation; (2) to reduce the energy bill for air conditioning and heating; (3) to improve the biodiversity of the rooftop area; (4) to keep the wet weight of the built-up area under 50 kg; and (5) to maintain high water storage capacity.

The project was implemented in 2008 with a shallow substrate depth of less than 10 cm used as the base for the rooftop garden. As the weather conditions are typically harsh in the summer, native plant species were planted at the base. Primarily, the plant selection was composed of indigenous Hellenic aromatic herbs. A number of wild perennial flowers such as *Hypericum* and *Phlomis*, and annuals such as poppies, grasses, and chamomile, were also added, all within a proprietary substrate from Oikosteges. The second stage of the study was performed after 12 months. Between these two studies, more biomass was added to the base to increase the biodiversity of the garden. The shallow substrate depth and the use of light weight materials with high water storability contributed to the project's success.

Results from the study concluded that the green roof significantly affected the thermal performance of the building; energy savings of 50 per cent were observed for air conditioning on the floor directly below the installation. In addition to the energy-saving benefits, the biodiversity in the area increased; a plethora of birds and beneficial insects were observed on the roof, ranging from European robins, yellowhammers, yellow tits, coal tits, and sparrows to kestrels hovering above the roof. Other species were also witnessed, such as honeybees, tiger swallowtail, monarch butterflies, dragonflies, and ladybirds. The lightweight was achieved by incorporating several strategies including shallow substrate depth (less than 10 cm) and lightweight substrates.

Urban Green Areas Connected to Grey Infrastructure

Urban green areas connected to grey infrastructure include alleys, street trees, hedges and greens, railway banks and tracks, house gardens, green playgrounds and green school grounds, institutional green spaces, green parking lots, and

Figure 4.3 External building greens

riverbank greens. These offer a range of benefits including air pollution and climate control, flood retention, food production in the case of house gardens, recreational and aesthetic amenity.

One illustrative example is the green area inner-city tree planting agreement in Bologna, Italy. The project aimed to tackle climate change – both the mitigation and adaptation effects of urban forestation – and air quality through an integrated policy. It sought to apply private partnership tools, developed within the framework of corporate social responsibility experiences, and distribute guidelines. Specifically, the project developed a public–private partnership model for urban forestation through the adoption of a Green Areas Inner-City Agreement (GAIA). This was expected to include three specific protocols for green urban areas and result in 3000 trees planted across Bologna. These three protocols aimed to:

- Develop a model of environmental governance that merges the mitigation and adaptation effects of climate change and show how they impact on air quality.
- Demonstrate the feasibility of local policies tackling climate change through the development of partnerships between private and public bodies for the management of green urban areas.

Figure 4.4 Urban green areas connected to grey infrastructure

- Initiate a process for assisting public administrations in promoting co-responsibility by introducing an innovative management tool that fosters tree planting in urban areas to compensate for the construction of infrastructure.
- Define a common and replicable methodology for calculating the greenhouse gases and air pollutants sequestration.
- Offer an instrument that local businesses can apply to offset their carbon footprint.

The GAIA project ultimately developed an instrument by which local enterprises and firms can decrease their carbon footprint and, at the same time, generate environmental and social benefits for the community. Even though it was initially difficult to engage the private sector in these kinds of initiatives, the project succeeded in persuading 18 private companies to participate and plant 1000 new trees. It has also developed the three protocols: a technical protocol for evaluating trees in terms of CO_2 sequestration and air pollutant removal; an analytical protocol of eco-physiological threats of 20 tree species; and a management protocol for identifying juridical characteristics of the private–public agreement. Moreover, the project designed a carbon toolkit for calculating environmental targets in terms of CO_2. Finally, it carried out a survey of the best national and international practices in the field of public–private partnerships.

Parks and Semi-Natural Urban Green Areas

This category of urban nature and nature-based solutions includes large urban parks or forests, pocket parks and neighbourhood green spaces, botanical gardens, and green corridors. These provide a range of ecological benefits including improved air quality, flood retention, climate control, increased biodiversity, and noise reduction. They also offer social and health benefits by offering places for recreation, exercise, and aesthetic amenity.

An illustrative example of parks and (semi-) natural urban green areas can be seen in Petuelpark, a 7.4-hectare park located to the north of Munich, Germany. The goals of the project included: (1) to decrease the above-ground traffic; (2) to unite Schwabing-Nord and Milbertshofen, parts of the city which had been separated by the Petuelring road for decades; (3) to continue the green network of Olympapark, Luitpoldpark, and the English Garden to the north; (4) to create a meeting point for people of different ages and social and cultural backgrounds, including uniting the people of two neighbourhoods (Germans and migrants, both old and young); and (5) to create a meeting point for humans and nature, and art and landscape.

The park was created as part of a complex transportation development project that aimed to reduce above-ground traffic with the help of the Petueltunnel (partially situated in the park) and improve the quality of life in the area with the help of green developments. The park also aimed to create a space for recreation and leisure,

Figure 4.5 Parks and semi-natural urban green areas

not least by including several (water) playgrounds and a fountain, café, and artwork. A 'Generation garden' was also included as part of the park, designed to serve as a meeting place and a space for gardening. As such, garden beds were provided in the garden for free use by residents. The elevated parts of the park above the tunnel were also covered extensively with grass, while other parts had thematic gardens added and the Nymphenburg-Biedersteiner canal.

In terms of the impacts, citizens utilising the park appreciated the quietness of the area, the reduced noise exposure being a result of cars being underground instead of above it. Several different types of trees were planted, increasing urban biodiversity; the landscape architects Stefanie Jühling and Otto Bertram equipped the park with ornamental cherries, birch trees, various pines, plane trees, hedges, and climbing plants. Cattails and swamp lilies were also introduced to the watercourses and so-called 'disruptive stones' in the canal to ensure a greater oxygen content in the water, thus improving the living conditions for fauna and flora.

Allotments and Community Gardens

This category includes allotments, community gardens, and horticulture land devoted to growing fruits, vegetables, and flowers. The major benefits of these are socioeconomic in nature, as they offer alternative food production opportunities and thereby strengthen food security in cities, as well as offer spaces for recreation and social interaction, and opportunities to teach urban citizens gardening skills. They may also offer climate and air quality co-benefits.

An illustrative example of allotments and community gardens exists in the urban orchards of Mallorca, Spain. Five orchards were constructed, reclaiming abandoned urban spaces by the Mallorca city government in 2010. The project has three pillars which include: (a) strengthening social cohesion and inclusion; (b) creating opportunities for education; and (c) offering space for recreation. The orchards were also constructed with retired citizens in mind, with the desire to design the gardens as a community space where retired citizens could gather and meet. The area was created by converting a vacant spot and turning it into a green space where locals could grow food and enjoy organic farming. The locals grow food in the garden for their own consumption, as well as for the community café, which distributes food to the locals as a neighbourhood food service. The service is also an approach taken by the community in response to the COVID-19 pandemic crisis.

Since opening, the garden has become a hub for many community activities including arts, cultural, and musical events and it is in the focus of many projects with local partners. These range from local school children learning about plastic pollution to adults protecting urban wildlife. The garden community also offers practical advice and support, and delivers regular training workshops on topics relating to gardening, biodiversity, and the environment. The garden is an emotionally therapeutic space that helps people recover from the stresses and strains of everyday life. The community gardens also offer opportunities for people to spend time outdoors in nature and contribute to creating local green spaces in the city. Additionally, the community garden also included planted trees that helped improve the local climate and air quality, and reduce local air temperatures. In 2020, new orchard developments were planned to include new focus groups but due to the COVID-19 pandemic these plans were affected negatively.

Green Indoor Areas

Green indoor areas include indoor vertical greeneries such as green walls, green ceilings, and atriums, that is, green areas that surround or are enclosed in a building. While mainly used for ornamental and aesthetic purposes, green indoor areas can also improve the micro-climate and air quality inside buildings. In addition, the proximity of green inside tends to have positive effects on people's general well-being.

An illustrative example of green indoor areas can be seen in the green wall at the Eiffel Palace Office Building in Budapest, Hungary. The 53 m^2 hydroponic living wall is located inside the office building. The goal of implementing the green wall was to balance humidity inside the building and to produce oxygen, thus creating a comfortable working environment. As part of the development of the office building, two 12 m wide and 3.5 m high green walls were created equalling a total size of 53 m^2. The investors planted tropical plant species that are common in Hungary in the indoor areas and species with a high degree of air purification effect.

Figure 4.6 Allotments and community gardens

The green walls were installed with an automatic irrigation system that uses grey-water, collected to irrigate the green walls and to manage storm-water runoff.

The building was the first in Central-Eastern Europe to gain the double environmental certification of BREEAM Very Good and LEED Gold, featuring vegetation on multiple terraces and sun collectors. The Eiffel Palace green wall has also been recognised as a multi-award-winning monumental green building, being the largest regional plant wall at the time of the installation. It has been rated as one of the best indoor green walls for its benefits in increasing humidity and supplying oxygen to the interior. The project also addresses water management by only using rainwater for irrigation. This is an example of a growing number of buildings integrating larger and more sophisticated green indoor areas into their design and physical structures.

Blue Areas

Blue areas include various water reservoirs such as lakes, ponds, rivers, streams, canals, estuaries, deltas, sea coastlines, wetlands, bogs, fens, and marshes. The major benefits of blue areas are in providing habitats to many species and enhancing biodiversity in cities as well as in contributing to local climate regulation, while also providing space for recreational activities.

An illustrative example of a blue area as urban nature is demonstrated in the Larkhill Gardens Lake and further improvement of the area in Liverpool, England. The project was a collaborative project between the City Council, the Environment Agency, and the local community and was funded by the local City Council and the Environment Agency. The project was included as part of the long-term project Liverpool Park Lakes, which aimed to tackle the many problems faced by shallow park lakes such as structural decline, a lack of water, poor water quality, poor habitat quality, loss of management of the user, and the lack of proactive management by the City Council.

Lark hill Gardens Lake was expected to be the flagship project for the whole restoration process, with the lake chosen due to it being the smallest of the main park lakes and one which faces common challenges. The improvement of the lake included changing its structure to create a deep-water fishing area, a shallow-water area, and wetland. Water supply was addressed through the installation of a borehole; an outflow was fitted with a top water level and a summer water level within the wetland, a previously adjacent area of land prone to flooding. The bank profiles were reduced and marginal planting undertaken by the use of locally sourced native species. Access and reduction of user conflict was facilitated by the incorporation of a boardwalk and fishing platform. The extensive physical improvement works have resulted in the fishery now supporting balanced fish stocks and a wide variety of aquatic and marsh plants.

Figure 4.7 Green indoor areas

Green Areas for Water Management

Green areas for water management include rain gardens, swales, filter strips, and sustainable urban drainage systems. The benefits provided include storm-water management, flood control, and increased biodiversity. Green areas for water management also often provide spaces for recreational activities, while enhancing general well-being.

An illustrative example of a green area used for water management exists in a rain garden placed on a city island near Amsterdam, the Netherlands. Blok 54 is a new building on the city island IJburg in Amsterdam, on which a green roof and a rain garden were created to manage the storm-water flow from the green roof, through a groove with diverse vegetation, replicating a natural creek. The vegetation used in the project included fruit bushes, which serve as a sensory garden for handicapped children. The creek also flows into bioswales (which are storm-water runoff conveyance systems using plants that provide an alternative to typical storm sewers). Blok 54 can thereby be considered an ecocity garden. The goals of the project were outlined as:

- To maximise storm-water retention to make sure that most of the rainwater does not flow into the sewage system.
- To increase the flood protection of the building and relieve the central sewerage system through the creation of a green roof, in combination with the rain garden, which operates as a sustainable drainage system.
- To promote biodiversity through the creation of habitat for birds and species by means of tree stumps, diverse vegetation, and water surface.
- To improve social cohesion through events around implemented green and blue structures.

Figure 4.8 Blue areas

Figure 4.9 Green areas for water management

According to publicly available records, some achieved impacts of the intervention have already been recorded; however, as the project was only recently completed, most of the benefits are to be expected. Currently, the roof garden on Blok 54 already stores 60 per cent of the storm water and has increased the size of the green area in the district through the roof garden. It is expected that it will be possible to store most of the storm water through these natural elements. Only in cases of extreme rainfall is it expected that the excess storm water will flow into the sewerage system. The intervention thus contributes to the city's resilience to climate change impacts. Fruit trees and bushes are expected to provide fruits such as apples, strawberries, and other berries once they mature.

Wilderness or Derelict Areas

Derelict areas include abandoned and derelict spaces with growth of wilderness or green features. Their major benefits are that they can provide recreational spaces, support biological treatment and regeneration of the soil, as well as increase biodiversity locally. They may also constitute sites of industrial heritage in cities and may therefore be of interest from a cultural perspective.

An illustrative example of a derelict area as a nature-based solution can be seen at a former fishing harbour in Tallinn, Estonia. The abandoned fishing harbour in Tallinn is a derelict, privately owned but publicly used open space of approximately 5 hectares and known as the former fishing harbour (*Kalasadam*). It is part of the old industrial waterfront belt waiting to be regenerated. The site was formerly closed and controlled but was reopened for public use in the early 1990s after the re-establishment of Estonia's independence. The proposed redevelopment plans have not succeeded in satisfying all the various interest groups, leading to the proposals being rejected. This has led to the site remaining derelict and becoming an example of urban wilderness.

The site is a green open space with high recreational value. Inserting a few pieces of equipment and taming the urban wilderness very slightly has significantly increased the number of users. This derelict site of a fishing harbour demonstrates how the place holds an important position as a representation of the country's specific heritage; a complement for the city's open spaces as a piece of urban wilderness and diverse public space supplement for the neighbourhood and for diverse activities in the city. At the former harbour, the concrete piers are used daily by anglers, the slipway is used for water-scooters and boats, and the sandy side of the shore is used for swimming. People come to the site to sit on the stones and chunks of old concrete and enjoy the view over the Gulf of Tallinn. Children enjoy playing with the pebbles while their parents use the opportunity to sunbathe in privacy, although they are in the centre of the city, or to sit in the shade of the spontaneous vegetation.

As all of the above examples show, the response to urban challenges is not always straightforward and the form that nature can take varies considerably as a result. We also see that nature-based solutions are often a simultaneous integration of multiple categories. Thus, the categories above should only be regarded as examples of how urban nature and nature-based solutions can be understood, developed, and designed based on the ongoing ecological, cultural, and political frames, socioecological and sociopolitical concepts, and the socially and materially produced values they hold for different social groups or individuals. As processes of governance and finance enable (or hinder) the development of urban nature and nature-based solutions, what shapes and forms they take in different cities is likely to change over time.

OVERALL REFLECTIONS

In this chapter, departing from a blend of socioecological and sociopolitical perspectives guiding the development of urban nature, examples of how nature can be framed and utilised in relation to specific urban sustainability challenges have been presented. While urban nature can be recognised as both natural and human-made, this chapter has discussed nature-based solutions as purposefully developed from scratch or designed from existing green, blue, and grey areas in different cities and cityscapes.

In order to show the diversity of nature-based solutions, eight categories based on their ecological properties have been suggested. These range from simple indoor vegetation and balcony greens (single ecological interventions) to more complex outdoor systems interlinked with grey infrastructure in the built environment. Such systems

Figure 4.10 Wilderness or derelict areas

include sustainable storm-water management systems, where multiple forms of urban nature, including open green water channels and ponds, are simultaneously applied.

Besides the diversity of forms urban nature and nature-based solutions can be materialised in, through embedded case studies, how nature-based solutions can be guided by different frames and values – such as sustainability goals and aspirations and how they were pursued by various urban actors – has been shown. Among these, city planners, businesses, and civil society groups play a key role in ensuring that urban nature projects deliver multiple ecological, socioeconomic, and health co-benefits to urban ecosystems, human, and non-human city dwellers alike. The design of many of these projects also rested on and combined innovations of not only ecological but also social, technological, and systemic nature.

It can also be seen, however, that during the development of nature-based solutions, views and values might vary and clash among different constituents, leading to conflicts, contestations, and further challenges; this being perceived as nature-based solutions creating more problems than solutions. As will be explored, although from an efficiency point of view these processes seem to slow down the development, implementation, and efficient mainstreaming of nature-based solutions, they are critical in ensuring a just transition to urban sustainability.

KEY LEARNING EXERCISES

1. **Individual Reflection:** Next time you commute to your place of study or work, or when you walk in a city, take a pencil and a piece of paper with you and write down all the examples of urban nature you encounter on your way from Table 4.3. Which are the most common ones? Reflect why this may be the case just for your city. Are there any examples that you have not thought of as 'urban nature forms' before? Why?
2. **Peer Discussion:** Select two types of innovation from Table 4.1 to discuss with your peers. Argue why and how these types of innovation may be important for designing, developing, maintaining, and mainstreaming urban nature in a city. Collectively think of examples (either real-life or hypothetical) to support your line of argument.
3. **Explore Examples:** Are there any ecological forms of urban nature listed in Table 4.3 and discussed in this chapter that you have never encountered in real life? Why do you think this is the case?

FURTHER RESOURCES

Frantzeskaki, N. (2019) Seven lessons for planning nature-based solutions in cities. *Environmental Science & Policy*, 93, 101–111.

International Union for Conservation of Nature (IUCN) (2020) *Global Standard for Nature-Based Solutions*. Gland, Switzerland: IUCN.

Nesshöver, C., Assmuth, T., Irvine, K., et al. (2017) The science, policy and practice of nature-based solutions: An interdisciplinary perspective. *Science of the Total Environment*, 579, 1215–1227.

Part II

Enabling Processes

Urban nature and nature-based solutions are an increasingly popular means for tackling economic, environmental, and social sustainability challenges, and the idea that we can use nature – including both green and blue infrastructure (see Box P2.1) – to work with us in order to improve our cities is now seen as vital. But how do we enable urban nature and nature-based solutions to thrive in our cities?

Part II provides insights into emerging governance structures and financial and business models for investing in urban nature and nature-based solutions, and innovation pathways to enable nature-based solutions to develop in cities. It also accounts for and critically discusses the potential challenges arising in relation to these approaches (see Box P2.2).

Governing: This chapter sets the context for understanding how urban nature and nature-based solutions are governed by providing a typology of governance approaches through which the roles, constellations, and responsibilities of actors, financial sources, and institutional arrangements are outlined and discussed. Furthermore, this chapter highlights the importance of some core principles underpinning effective governance and explores the challenges and potential conflicts arising when many of these principles are applied at the same time.

Key contents:

- Governing urban nature and nature-based solutions, covering from government to governance, defining governance, and types and forms of governance.
- Emerging trends of governance for urban nature and nature-based solutions including the roles of different actors and constellations.
- Case studies: Isar River Restoration (Munich, Germany) and the Stavros Niarchos Foundation Cultural Centre (Athens, Greece)

Financing: This chapter provides an account of different sources of finance for urban nature, the actors involved in providing these sources of finance, and various financial mechanisms through which the sources and the actors are mobilised. It focuses on the four principal models of investing in urban nature, which include funding solicited through public funds, private capital, community/not-for-profit funding, and hybrid and collaborative approaches to funding. The chapter discusses the current situation, barriers and opportunities for investing in urban nature, along with relevant examples. It concludes with insights on how to facilitate more investments in nature-based solutions.

Key contents:

- Presenting sources, actors, and mechanisms for financing urban nature and nature-based solutions.
- Discussing public, private, community/non-profit, and hybrid funding of urban nature, related barriers and opportunities, and insights to facilitate more investment.
- Case studies: Parc Marianne Ecodistrict (Montpellier, France) and Mexico City Water Fund (Mexico City, Mexico)

Box P2.1 Spotlight on implementation – water management

Water infrastructure is critical for cities to maintain a clean sustainable water supply and build resilience to floods and droughts. Nature-based solutions for water challenges are innovative approaches to tackle social and environmental challenges. Growing urban populations around the world are causing a rising demand for water. Concurrently, changing climate is increasing extreme events in cities, from drought to floods, with severe social and economic consequences. Many cities around the world already face water stress, and demand for water is projected to increase significantly. This calls for extensive renewal and expansion of urban water infrastructure, changes that provide opportunities to redesign, retrofit, and better manage water resources to deliver multiple benefits for all. It is important that cities can work with nature and technological solutions while recognising the complexity of urban water systems, their relationship with the built environment and green infrastructure, and interconnections with communities and stakeholders. Rethinking water in cities, new partnerships and funding arrangements, new ways of working, enhanced public participation, increased collaboration, and long-term city planning are key factors to achieve environmental, social, and economic benefits and create healthier, more resilient, and more prosperous cities.

Water management presents a key challenge for utilising nature-based solutions in cities.

Box P2.2 Enabling the expansion of nature in cities

In the face of climate change and increasing environmental, economic, and social pressures, building resilience and sustainable development has become a strategic issue for cities. Nature-based solutions and urban nature are on the agenda as a vital approach to meeting urban challenges. Developing governance approaches, navigating innovation pathways, and creating business models are key ingredients to advancing nature-based solutions and expanding urban nature.

Governance approaches: Across multiple domains, from climate change to biodiversity, urban regeneration to health, nature-based solutions and urban nature offer new approaches for responding to the challenges facing cities. Their implementation requires a supportive policy environment from the international level through to the national domain and local realities of cities.

Innovation pathways: What are the enabling conditions and driving forces for nature-based solutions in the context of urban sustainability transitions? And how do innovation pathways play a role for nature-based solutions and urban nature? Innovation pathways are journeys that involve key drivers, decision-making junctures, agents, and opportunities, which can combine to facilitate nature-based solutions and urban nature.

Business models: Taking action on nature-based solutions and urban nature does not only depend on establishing the right policy conditions and financial resources, but also on establishing business models that can ensure their sustainability over time. Nature-based solutions and urban nature often create a complex array of public and private benefits, and developing business models that are able to capture and realise this value can be challenging.

Innovating:

This chapter presents innovation pathways for urban nature and nature-based solutions, which are journeys that involve key drivers, decision-making junctures, agents, and opportunities. Nature-based solutions emerge through a combination of innovative governance types and forms, financial arrangements and novel business models, and new institutional settings.

Key contents:

- Presenting examples of the interconnections between nature, innovation, and urban sustainability – the emergence of a global agenda.
- Exploring innovation pathways for urban nature and nature-based solutions that are appearing in cities.
- Case studies: River City (Winnipeg, Canada) and Little France Park (Edinburgh, United Kingdom)

5 Governing

INTRODUCTION

In previous chapters it was discussed how urban nature and nature-based solutions are conceptualised through different approaches and different ways of valuing nature, and the ways in which nature is being created for cities. Growing recognition of the socioeconomic and cultural benefits provided by urban nature and nature-based solutions has spurred a shift in policy and planning at international, national, and city levels. Internationally, nature-based solutions are promoted as means to support human resilience, development, and environmental, economic, and social sustainability. National governments around the globe have also started integrating urban nature and nature-based solutions into decision-making processes due to their potential to respond to climate change, enhance biodiversity, and improve environmental quality while contributing to economic regeneration and social well-being, among other objectives.

The focus of this chapter is on governing urban nature-based solutions (Box 5.1). With more than half of the world's population living in cities, the multi-functionality of nature-based solutions is increasingly important. Tapping into the potential to deliver wider benefits to enable an urban transition to sustainability requires an understanding of how they are organised and what the most effective ways to govern them are. In short, effective governance can help maximise the promising co-benefits and unlock the potential of urban nature and nature-based solutions in addressing sustainability challenges in cities.

But what is understood by 'governance'? What forms does it or can it take? What are the types of governance arrangements when it comes to the implementation and uptake of nature-based solutions in cities? What are the ways to achieve more effective governance of urban nature? These are some of the key questions that this chapter tackles and explores. It also presents how to distinguish between different forms and types of governance and approaches to governing and how to plan for more effective governance of urban nature-based solutions (see Box 5.2).

Box 5.1 Key terms and concepts used in this chapter

Bottom-up governance: Initiatives started and led by grassroots movements, citizen and community groups, non-governmental organisations, or businesses.

Co-benefits: The added socioeconomic and environmental benefits from the implementation of nature-based solutions.

Collaborative governance: Initiatives started and led by various stakeholders in collaboration with other actors who hold similar interests but represent different sectors.

Governance: The act of governing, rather than government in its narrow sense.

Horizontal coordination: A coordination process which describes the relations between different agencies and policy divisions within governments.

Multi-level governance: Multiple scales of government action including that across and between international, national, regional, and local levels.

Top-down governance: Initiatives started and led by government actors such as politicians, planning and regulation authorities, and decision-making experts.

Vertical coordination: A coordination process which encompasses the relations between municipalities, regional authorities, national, and supra-national governments.

Box 5.2 Cultivating urban nature – key lessons

Grow Collaboration: Collaboration comes in all shapes and sizes and greater diversity and flexibility is needed.

Across all stages of the process of cultivating nature-based solutions – from design to implementation and upkeep – collaboration between diverse stakeholders and communities is critical for nature-based solutions. Despite strong recognition of the importance of collaboration, it can be difficult to undertake in practice and tends to follow relatively well-trodden pathways. Community consultation can be relatively superficial, with limited opportunities for groups to challenge and reframe the purpose and content of nature-based solutions. A growing focus on co-design and co-production can provide more space for community voices, but it can also tend to include the usual suspects and require rather formalised, resource- and time-intensive processes that exclude those who cannot commit to this level of engagement. Developing shared knowledge banks or repositories of the possibilities of nature-based solutions that diverse stakeholders contribute to, generating understanding that is more than the sum of the parts, can be a valuable basis from which to build new collaborations and create new reasons for diverse actors to work together. Providing examples of what is possible generates a new willingness to engage across multiple stakeholders. Creating openings in the development of nature-based solutions to allow for improvised and spontaneous forms of collaboration alongside formal processes, as well as keeping design and implementation processes flexible, is one approach that could be further developed, especially where nature-based solutions are designed for neighbourhoods-in-the-making whose residents and communities are not yet present.

The chapter starts by distinguishing between 'government' and 'governance'. It proceeds by exploring and providing a typology of governance approaches to urban nature and nature-based solutions and discusses the roles that different actors play in these governance arrangements while putting the governance of urban nature into a multi-level perspective. The chapter then highlights challenges and opportunities for governing urban nature (see Box 5.2) and proposes a set of eight principles and values that are important for enabling successful governance arrangements for nature-based solutions.

From Government to Governance

First, let us discuss the core concept of this chapter – governance. While government refers to formal structures, systems, or institutions by which a state, a region, or a municipality is organised and governed, governance is often considered a broader term referring to the act of governing. It involves multiple public and private actors as well as citizens and communities who engage in debates and contestations, and compete to gain and maintain power over an issue that is being governed.

Governance can be defined as the system or processes by which entities are directed, influenced, and even controlled. At the same time, different forms of governance offer opportunities to strategically integrate various policy instruments, connect different sectors, and engage multiple stakeholders in a dialogue, thereby enhancing collaboration for sustainability transitions. In cities, governance processes are important when steering and defining the planning, use, and maintenance of common goods, such as public green and blue spaces, as they offer opportunities to find the smartest ways to benefit citizens and urban nature.

Traditionally, urban nature initiatives have predominantly been managed by local governments; however, over the years their governance has been complemented by experimentation with multi-level governance schemes, which refers to multiple scales of government action including that across and between international, national, regional, and local levels. The next section will explore and provide a typology of governance approaches to urban nature and nature-based solutions as well as discuss the roles that different actors play in these governance arrangements.

Governance Approaches to Nature-Based Solutions

Depending on the origins and degrees of power exercised by a particular group of actors, governance approaches to urban nature can be divided into three broad 'ideal' categories: top-down, bottom-up, and collaborative. Top-down governance refers to initiatives started and led by government actors such as politicians, planning and regulation authorities, and decision-making experts. Bottom-up governance relates to initiatives started and led by grassroots movements, citizen and community groups, non-governmental organisations, or businesses. Collaborative governance is about initiatives started and led by various stakeholders in collaboration with other actors who hold similar interests but represent different sectors.

Each of these governance approaches can be further broken down into subcategories, depending on how the governance is exercised, which governance modes prevail, and which actors dominate the governance relationships in terms of power (Bulkeley, 2019):

- Top-down governance: in-house (municipality), publicly provided, consortium (public–private provision), rule-driven, and incentive-driven.
- Bottom-up governance: enabling, business, philanthropic, community.
- Collaborative governance: society-led partnership, business-led partnership, government-led partnership.

We provide a detailed explanation of each of these governance subcategories in Table 5.1 and then link these with the three broad forms of governance of nature-based solutions, complemented with concrete examples from different cities. In practice, it should be noted that there are very few examples of

Table 5.1 Typology of governance approaches

Governance categories	Governance approach	Governance definition
Top-down governance		The nature-based solution is designed, implemented, and financed within the municipal organisation
		The nature-based solution is provided by a public authority or public agency: it is designed, implemented, and financed by (one or more) public authorities/agencies
		The nature-based solution is provided by a group of public and private authorities, agencies, and organisations that are linked through a formal institution or legal agreement (e.g. they form a consortium, a partnership with legal standing). The nature-based solution is designed, implemented, and financed through this consortium (i.e. there are no other organisations that work in partnership with this entity but remain external to it in formal/legal terms)
		The design and implementation of the nature-based solution is undertaken by a private-sector organisation or civil society group in response to a regulatory requirement provided by a public authority or agency (at any level of governance). Financing could either be provided by the initiating actors or come from another source (public/private/civil society)
		The design and implementation of the nature-based solution is undertaken by a private-sector organisation or civil society group in response to an incentive provided by a public authority or agency (at any level of governance). The financing of the nature-based solution could either be provided by the initiating actors or come from another source (public/private/civil society)

Table 5.1 (cont.)

Governance categories	Governance approach	Governance definition
Bottom-up governance		The design and implementation of the nature-based solution is undertaken by a private-sector organisation or civil society group in response to enabling and supporting measures – such as support with developing knowledge about nature-based solutions/their potential, signposting to relevant sources of financial or other support, the provision of access to resources or land, donation of some resources – provided by a public authority or agency (at any level of governance). The financing of the nature-based solution could either be provided by the initiating actors or come from another source (public/private/civil society)
	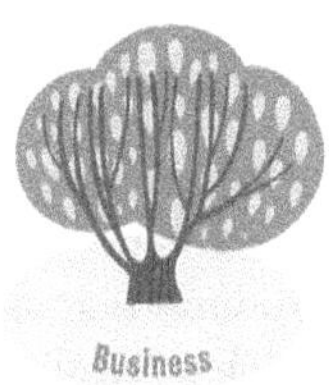	The design and implementation of the nature-based solution is undertaken by private-sector organisations or civil society groups, where the initiation of the nature-based solution is driven by a private-sector organisation and it provides the enabling conditions/support required for its implementation. The financing of the nature-based solution could either be provided by the initiating actors or come from another source (public/private/civil society)
		The design and implementation of the nature-based solution is undertaken by private-sector organisations or civil society groups, where the initiation of the nature-based solutions is driven by a philanthropic or not-for-profit organisation and it provides the enabling conditions/support required for its implementation. The financing of the nature-based solution could either be provided by the initiating actors or come from another source (public/private/civil society)
		The design and implementation of the nature-based solution is undertaken by civil society groups, where the initiation of the nature-based solutions is driven by a community group and it provides the enabling conditions/support required for its implementation. The financing of the nature-based solution could either be provided by the initiating actors or come from another source (public/private/civil society)

Table 5.1 (cont.)

Governance categories	Governance approach	Governance definition
Collaborative governance		The design, implementation and financing of the nature-based solution is undertaken in partnership, where different authorities, agencies, organisations, and groups contribute towards a joint undertaking but without becoming constituted as one entity in legal or institutional terms. In this instance, the partnership was initiated and led by a civil society organisation or group (i.e. composed of actors from civil society and operating on a not-for-profit basis)
		The design, implementation, and financing of the nature-based solution is undertaken in partnership, where different authorities, agencies, organisations, and groups contribute towards a joint undertaking but without becoming constituted as one entity in legal or institutional terms. In this instance, the partnership was initiated and led by a private-sector organisation or group
		The design, implementation, and financing of the nature-based solution is undertaken in partnership, where different authorities, agencies, organisations, and groups contribute towards a joint undertaking but without becoming constituted as one entity in legal or institutional terms. In this instance, the partnership was initiated and led by a public-sector authority, agency, or group (at different levels of government)

nature-based solutions governed by a single actor (Sekulova & Anguelovski, 2017) and there is also a high frequency of nature-based solutions that are governed by hybrid approaches. For example, a nature-based solution may be initiated by a government in a top-down manner, but then later funded and co-designed by a private entity, and monitored by public actors in a collaborative manner.

Top-down governance initiatives are started and led by government actors such as politicians, planning and regulation authorities, and decision-making experts. Traditionally, many urban green initiatives have been governed by state actors operating at the national scale (Sekulova & Anguelovski, 2019). However, over time, this has changed to local public administrations – and mayors in particular – taking on an increasingly prominent role in the overall vision, planning, and management of urban green infrastructure (Young & McPherson, 2013). Today we can still say that municipality-led nature-based solutions dominate in cities, with municipalities typically being in charge of strategic planning and implementation of urban trees, forests, and parks (Kiss et al., 2019).

Bottom-up governance initiatives are started and led by grassroots movements, citizen and community groups, non-governmental organisations, or businesses. Non-governmental actors are often in charge of urban community gardens and insect-oriented initiatives (Kiss et al., 2019) – the former being not simply gardening plots in a city, but arenas where conflicting public and private interests for the land use meet, and where the battles for a socially just and inclusive city take place (Follmann & Viehoff, 2015).

Collaborative governance initiatives are started and led through collaborations between a variety of actors who hold similar interests but represent different sectors (see also Case Study Box 5.1 and Case Study Box 5.2). Here, for example, policy officers at local or national levels might work together with citizens, businesses, knowledge institutes, and civil society. Coming from multiple disciplines, sectors, and policy arenas, these actors combine their expertise in order to design, develop, and implement nature-based solutions in cities (Kiss et al., 2019). As such, business practitioners offer practical experience and professionalism; academia and knowledge institutes provide scientific knowledge and expertise; and public administration actors contribute with decision-making power, experience, and data as well as help articulate urgent sustainability challenges which nature-based solutions have the potential to address (Sekulova & Anguelovski, 2019).

Putting Governance in a Multi-Level Perspective

Multi-level governance represents 'multiple scales of government action' (Hodson & Marvin, 2010). It includes two sets of coordination processes (see Figure 5.1). The first is vertical coordination, which encompasses the relations between municipalities, regional authorities, and national and supra-national governments. The second is horizontal coordination, which describes the relations between different agencies and policy divisions within municipal governments. Horizontal and vertical coordination among state actors forms the background of so-called 'Type I' multi-level governance (Bulkeley et al., 2009). 'Type II' multi-level governance involves new governance arrangements

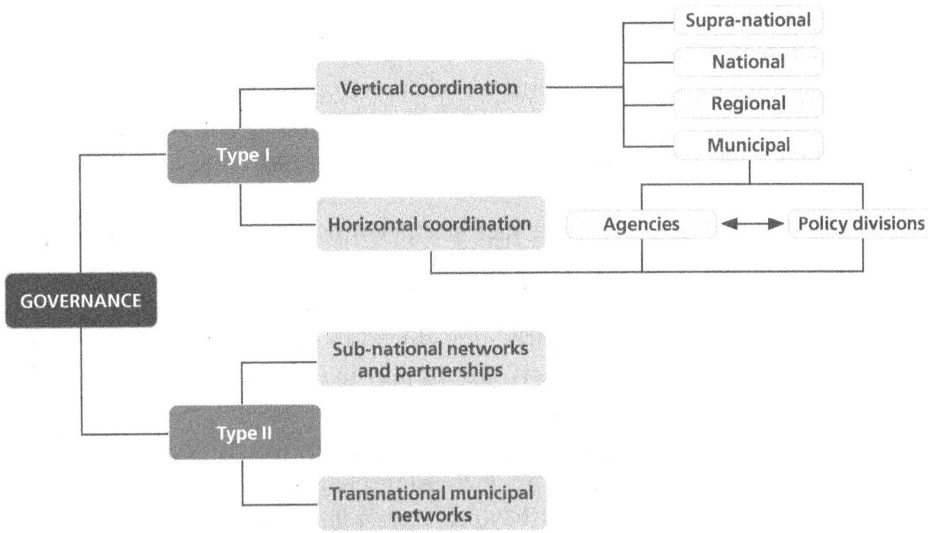

Figure 5.1 Types of multi-level governance

such as networks and partnerships that operate between and across political levels. It includes subnational networks and partnerships, and transnational municipal networks (Bulkeley et al., 2009).

Transnational municipal networks are organisations and platforms that aim to support cooperation between cities, such as Local Governments for Sustainability (ICLEI), the Climate Alliance, C40 Cities Climate Leadership Group, and Global Covenant of Mayors. These organisations have become an important driver for municipal action on advancing nature-based solutions. Transnational municipal networks can facilitate the exchange of information and experience between cities, catalyse learning, provide access to expertise and external funding, and they can offer political credibility to individuals and administrations seeking to promote actions internally.

Lessons for Governing Nature-Based Solutions

While governance can take various forms, there is no universal 'one-size-fits-all' approach. Instead, different types of governance can be used together in implementing nature-based solutions, depending on the local situation and context. What works in one city may not be the right governance approach in another city, and what functions well in one neighbourhood might not work in another area even within the same city.

When it comes to achieving the effective governance of urban nature and nature-based solutions, there is clearly a strong emphasis on enabling and facilitating more collaborative governance approaches (Bulkeley, 2019). Research looking at 1000 examples of urban nature-based solutions in Europe indicates an overall trend of transforming existing governance schemes from traditional top-down approaches to collaborative ones. It is clear that business and non-profit sectors are also undertaking a more encompassing role in designing, producing, and maintaining nature-based solutions in cities.

At the same time, while such partnerships are essential for the continuity and governance of nature-based solutions, the extent to which they are beneficial for the realisation of these solutions, without compromising public interest, is still being searched for. Similarly, it is crucial to recognise the vitally important roles that citizens and civil society groups play in implementing nature-based solutions and contributing to broader democratic processes in urban arenas. However, the potential of bottom-up, citizen-centred initiatives to scale and sustain nature-based solutions remains an increasing challenge. Therefore, governments and their agencies within and beyond cities remain central in establishing the right contexts for action and delivering nature-based solutions for local communities. In particular, aligning the policy goals of supranational (for example, European Union) and national governments with those of local authorities, community groups, and businesses developing nature-based solutions on the ground is important to enable the nature-based solutions to contribute towards multiple sustainable development goals.

Effective governance for urban nature-based solutions depends on strong roots, that is, core principles and values that underpin the development and implementation of these initiatives (Bulkeley, 2019). A set of eight principles and values that are important for enabling successful governance arrangements for nature-based solutions are presented and explained in Table 5.2. The principles cover the following key terms: ambitious, inclusive, just, abundant, relevant, practical, informed, and transparent.

Building Governance Principles for Nature-Based Solutions

While many successful projects on nature-based solutions follow several of the principles described in this chapter, very few adhere to multiple principles at the same time. One reason for this is that the principles may conflict. Recognising these conflicts and purposefully addressing them is vital for nature-based solutions to thrive. However, these underlying principles and values are often central to effective and good governance: they need to be recognised, articulated, and strengthened if nature-based solutions are to endure (see Figure 5.2). To enhance and develop good governance of nature-based solutions we provide some key advice for municipal governments, national governments, and business, and civil society organisations.

For municipal governments, we need to identify new opportunities for aligning their work with national and regional strategies; establish organisations that work

Table 5.2 Principles and values underpinning governance of nature-based solutions

Principle	Definition
Ambitious	Setting goals and implementing actions that explicitly contribute towards an ambitious vision of how nature-based solutions can contribute to urban sustainability; nature-based solutions are integrated into strategic goals/policy for sustainability.
Inclusive	Enabling the participation of stakeholders and communities in the design and implementation (and monitoring) of nature-based solutions; explicitly recognising marginal groups and supporting their inclusion.
Just	Developing nature-based solutions such that their benefits (and risks) are shared equitably between different actors and groups; explicitly seeking to address issues of existing inequity through the design and implementation of nature-based solutions; addressing ecological and environmental justice through ensuring that nature-based solutions do no harm to valued and intrinsically valued forms of nature.
Abundant	Nature-based solutions are designed and implemented to be comprehensive; addressing multiple sustainability goals and/or to enable multiple benefits/contributions of nature-based solutions for different communities and stakeholders.
Relevant	Nature-based solutions are socially and ecologically relevant when they: deliver local benefits and support local development priorities; enable the restoration/conservation of valued forms of nature at the local scale and across land/seascapes; contribute to ecological connectivity and ecosystem integrity.
Practical	Nature-based solutions are designed to be realistically implemented by the actors involved, given local mandates, finances, and capacities.
Informed	Scientific, civic, and traditional knowledge is used to inform the design and development of nature-based solutions either in a traditional 'evidence-based' model of policy/project design or through a learning-by-doing mode via the iterative development of knowledge and mechanisms for learning throughout the project.
Transparent	Determining what constitutes the success of nature-based solutions through appropriate forms of consultation and establishing a set of indicators that can be measured, reported, independently verified, and evaluated.

across sectors; work across the city to find those who can champion and benefit from nature-based solutions; talk to community groups and private-sector organisations to see how they can enable and empower their work or join together to form partnerships; evaluate their existing nature-based solutions and consider how to strengthen their roots.

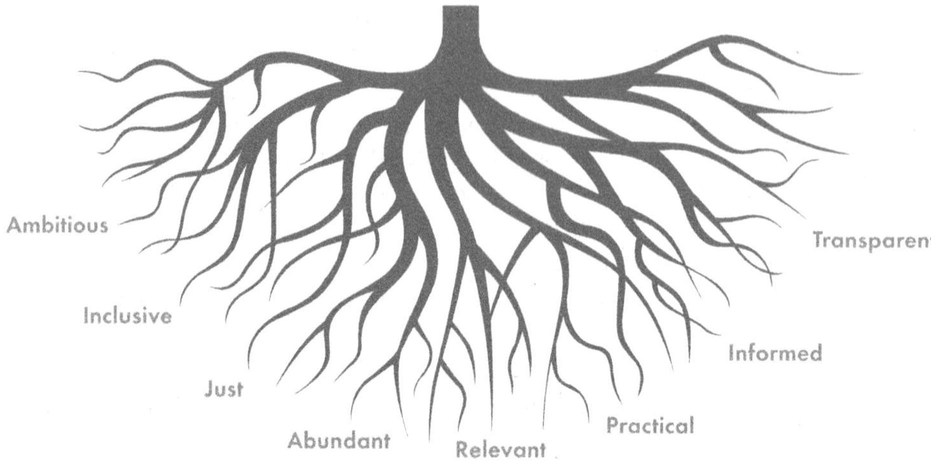

Figure 5.2 Planting governance seeds and ensuring strong roots

Case Study Box 5.1 Isar River Restoration (Munich, Germany)

Munich is the most densely populated and one of the fastest growing cities in Germany. With around 1.5 million residents in the city proper and 6 million in its metropolitan region, the twelfth largest city in the European Union is a top-ranked destination for immigrants and expatriates. However, progress towards its sustainability goals is challenged by loss of green space, increased flooding, and heatwaves. Munich grew on the banks of the River Isar, a natural feature that has always played an important role in the region's development and profile. The river has powered mills, transported timber, and provided electricity, recreation, and ecological qualities to residents and visitors alike.

More frequent floods beginning in the 1980s, however, have called for an integrated and innovative approach to restoring its original Alpine gravel dynamics, as much as possible, within the tight manmade corset of Munich. The 'Isar Plan' restoration project began in 1995 to improve flood protection, ecological function, and recreational areas. The Isar Plan grew from a close collaboration between several actors, including the City of Munich, the Bavaria Ministry, and a range of civil society organisations.

Through the 'Isar Alliance', a coalition of environmental non-governmental organisations (NGOs), a joint interdisciplinary planning group was formed, comprising water engineers, landscape architects, city planners, and biologists from the regional and city administrations, as well as community groups. While the Isar Alliance had long been concerned about river-water quality, the 1990s floods focused the community's attention and sparked action. Restoration of an 8-km river corridor through the city started in 2000. Development goals were defined based on an assessment by the project's interdisciplinary working group.

Case Study Box 5.1 (cont.)

Although the main goal was improving flood protection, it was very important it should not override any other goals, such as restored riverscape, enhanced water quality, improved biodiversity, and recreational opportunities. The restoration allowed the river more space to move and reshape itself while regaining its natural features. The monotonous riverbed was replaced by a diverse, rewilded landscape that not only provides ecologically valuable habitat, but also became a year-round attraction for residents, who could actively contribute to its design and quality. Through multi-level, inclusive, relevant, and practical modes of governance, the Isar Plan has harmonised the interests of flood protection, nature conservation, and urban lifestyles in a multiple-use river area.

Figure 5.3 Munich, Germany

For national governments, we need to identify how nature-based solutions can be integrated into policy areas which matter for local communities, businesses, and cities working with nature, such as health and economic development; consider how funding schemes can support the development of intermediaries and nurture change agents; support municipalities in scaling up their work; identify ways in which to enable and empower the work of businesses and civil society groups through providing knowledge and support; and consider the adoption of key principles to strengthen the roots of nature-based initiatives in cities.

Case Study Box 5.2 Stavros Niarchos Foundation Cultural Centre (Athens, Greece)

Air pollution and the heat island effect constitute persisting challenges for Athens, which has the lowest per capita green space in the European Union, and with the crisis worsening due to the availability of resources for urban greening. The dense urbanisation in Athens has been rather recent, rapid, and disorderly. The geomorphology of Athens causes a temperature inversion phenomenon, partly responsible for two types of air pollution problem: high concentrations of particles and photochemical smog. The intense use of automobiles, poor public transportation services, weak cycling network, and lack of green space throughout the city contribute to frequently unsafe air quality levels. This combined with a lack of ventilation in Athens enhances the urban heat island effect, noticed especially during the summer.

The Stavros Niarchos Foundation Cultural Centre (SNFCC) was previously a parking lot left over from the 2004 Olympic Games; now it is a 170,000 m^2 landscaped park, an artificial hill beneath which the Greek National Library and the Opera are located. As the first large-scale sustainable construction in Greece that is publicly available, the space hosts a range of educational and cultural activities that have so far been provided for free, including gardening courses, lectures and workshops on environmental and botanical topics, as well as environmental activities, such as tree identification. It also claims flood-regulating functions with embedded storm-water infrastructure, air quality improvement, and shade provision, among others. The project also addressed long-lived concerns of neighbouring municipalities for its regeneration and greening.

Some sustainability measures include a 17,000 m^2 green roof, thermal and noise insulation, drought-tolerant vegetation, drainage systems for rainwater capture, compost generation and use, and light pollution reduction techniques. The SNFCC complex (2009–2017) was funded entirely by the SNF foundation (a private international philanthropic organisation, founded by the Greek ship-owner Stavros Niarchos), constructed on previously derelict public land, and passed on to the Greek state after its completion. According to a special law signed as an agreement between the two parties, SNF and the Greek state, the government must comply with certain conditions, or else the SNF maintains the right to withdraw its donation.

SNFCC is a unique landmark project, albeit dependent on private investors. Not surprisingly, this legal setting and governance mode has been questioned and contested in terms of the economic burden incurred by the public sector and the actual benefits for the National Library, Opera, and the general public. This case exemplifies how public–private partnerships and nature-based initiatives that are predominantly motivated by private actors often focus on innovativeness and investment returns, rather than on social welfare and equity in access. This case also shows that the costs of construction and maintenance are often prohibitive for scaling-up such interventions for the broader public; for example, building public schools or other public spaces/buildings has proven to be cumbersome without the involvement of private actors.

Case Study Box 5.2 (cont.)

Figure 5.4 Athens, Greece

For business and civil society organisations, we need to make the co-benefits of their work with nature visible and valued by identifying the multiple beneficiaries who can gain from nature in cities; identify organisations that can act as intermediaries, building bridges between diverse opportunities, and work with them to establish partnerships; recognise and celebrate their role as change agents in urban sustainability; try out different governance approaches to enable urban nature projects in partnerships with diverse organisations; and adopt principles for working with nature-based solutions that will ensure that they can endure.

OVERALL REFLECTIONS

In this chapter, we have defined 'governance' and discussed different types and several subforms of governance for urban nature and nature-based solutions. Governance refers to the act of governing rather than government in its narrow sense. Multi-level governance encompasses multiple scales of government action, including that across and between international, national, regional, and local levels.

There are two principal types of multi-level governance: Type I and Type II. Type I includes vertical and horizontal coordination whereas Type II encompasses subnational networks and partnerships and transnational municipal networks. Three broad forms of governance include top-down, bottom-up, and collaborative governance, each of which can be further split into more nuanced approaches to governing.

We have provided several examples of nature-based solutions from different cities to exemplify the core concepts introduced in this chapter. We have also explained that achieving effective governance of nature-based solutions is challenging, although possible. We have therefore proposed a means to do this by adhering to eight key principles and values. These key principles and values emphasise the importance of developing urban nature and nature-based solutions that are ambitious, inclusive, just, abundant, relevant, practical, informed, and transparent.

Undoubtedly, many governance actions at various levels that promote the use and uptake of urban nature and nature-based solutions are on their way. However, the challenge remains of how to better integrate nature into cities. We also need to find new ways to secure long-term funding to ensure the implementation and maintenance of nature in cities. Lastly, we need to increase the knowledge base to foster wider support and awareness of nature-based solutions as a multi-functional approach to addressing societal challenges.

Multiple governance approaches can be used to effectively deliver nature-based solutions in cities, but there is no 'one-size-fits-all'. While partnership working dominates, municipal governments play important roles in directly providing nature-based solutions and creating the enabling conditions in which others can take action. Private sector, civil society, and community actors are also all playing their part. If we are to derive the full benefit of nature in cities, we will need to harness all of these approaches to generate and implement these interventions.

KEY LEARNING EXERCISES

1. **Individual Reflection:** What does 'multi-level governance' mean? Choose three transnational municipal organisations and search their websites. How do they engage with the urban nature agenda? In your opinion, what is their role in governing urban nature? Are any of the selected organisations more engaged in governing urban nature than the others? Why do you think this may be the case?
2. **Peer Discussion:** In groups of three, from Table 5.1 select one top-down, one bottom-up, and one collaborative approach to governing urban nature. Collectively think of urban nature examples representing the governance approaches you have selected. Identify the key actors involved in each example. Discuss which actors have more power and influence in each example. Why do you think this is the case? What could be done to strengthen the influence of other actors involved?
3. **Explore Examples:** Choose an urban nature example that you know well. It can be a park or a pond in your neighbourhood, or any of the case studies from this book. How does this example adhere to the eight principles and values in Table 5.2? If it does not adhere to some of these principles and values, what could be done to improve this and thus enable successful governance of your urban nature example?

FURTHER RESOURCES

Kabisch, N., Frantzeskaki, N. and Hansen, R. (2022) Principles for urban nature-based solutions. *Ambio*, 51, 1388–1404.

Tozer, L., Bulkeley, H., Kiss, B., et al. (2022) Nature for resilience? The politics of governing urban nature. *Annals of the American Association of Geographers*, 113, 599–615.

van der Jagt, A., Kiss, B., Hirose, S. and Takahashi, W. (2021) Nature-based solutions or debacles? The politics of reflexive governance for sustainable and just cities. *Frontiers in Sustainable Cities*, 2.

6 Financing

INTRODUCTION

In the previous chapter it was discussed how urban nature can be governed and that achieving effective governance of nature-based solutions is challenging, but certainly possible. It was also pointed out that while many governance actions at various levels promoting the use and uptake of nature-based solutions are on their way, this requires new approaches to secure long-term funding that will ensure the implementation and maintenance of nature in cities. The theme of governance flows into this chapter and it is the foundation of developing and expanding nature in cities.

Box 6.1 Key terms and concepts used in this chapter

Financial players for urban nature: Public, private, and community actors who are investing in urban nature projects. Examples include government agencies, municipalities, banks, funds, foundations, insurance companies, real estate investors, trusts, and community groups.

Funding sources for urban nature: General sources of finance such as loans, subsidies, and grants, and instruments that are specifically designed for climate resilience and urban nature-based development such as natural capital finance facility, environmental impact bonds, specialised subsidies, and natural hazard insurance.

Investing in urban nature: The provision of capital funding for urban nature projects by financial players and other relevant actors, such as real estate agglomerates.

Mainstreaming urban nature: Strategic intervention in the governance, financial, and urban development domains to enable the functioning of urban nature innovations over the long term and support their potential to deliver ecological, economic, and social benefits.

The focus of this chapter is on *investing* in nature-based solutions, which here refers to the provision of capital funding for urban nature projects by financial players and other relevant actors, such as real estate agglomerates (see Box 6.1). Considering the role of investing and investors in urban nature is important because of the sheer scale of the investment need. In fact, in 2020, the World Bank estimated the global annual investment need in urban infrastructure to be $4.5–5.4 trillion, which includes the development of climate-resilient and low-carbon infrastructures. While in this chapter we focus on investing in urban nature mainly through the provision of financial resources, it is important to acknowledge that investments may also include other resources such as human and material resources in terms of time, space, knowledge, skills, technologies, and infrastructure. While these are important to consider along with direct financial investments, we only include these types of resources here when they directly support access to financial resources.

Different types of urban nature require different types of investment (see Box 6.2). For example, investing in river development or urban forests will be different to investing in a green roof programme in terms of the types of funding and the actors involved. Available financial resources and funding structures are fundamental pillars of investing in urban nature. They comprise the sources of funds and specific instruments of different public, private, and community actors who engage in the development, implementation, and long-term maintenance of sustainable urban infrastructure, including urban nature.

The *sources of funds* for urban nature projects include both general funding sources such as loans, subsidies, and grants, and instruments that are specifically designed for climate-resilience and urban nature-based development. The former

Box 6.2 Cultivating urban nature – key lessons

Foster Investment: Urban nature and nature-based solutions require investment of all kinds – financial, political, and cultural.

The challenge of securing financial investment for nature-based solutions is increasingly recognised. A first step is to generate political investment from across a wide range of actors who share a vision and commitment to the use of nature-based solutions, building trust and a sense of collective endeavour across the multiple stakeholders who will need to bring finance to the table if nature-based solutions are to flourish. It will also be crucial to work with financial actors to create the knowledge and tools needed to support investment in nature-based solutions, while at the same time opening up the conversation on what constitutes a 'good' return on investment in sustainability terms. For example, nature-based solutions are likely to generate long-term benefits that cannot always be captured in monetary terms, or they reduce risks rather than generating profits. Equally, working with nature will always generate public goods alongside private benefits and new forms of co-finance are needed that can sustain the mixed economy of returns on investment that nature-based solutions generate. This can provide the basis for diversifying the forms of finance and financial actors who engage with nature-based solutions and open new collaborative approaches for sustaining nature-based solutions over time.

could come from national and international funding bodies, for example green roof subsidies or grants provided for urban nature projects. The latter include natural capital finance facilities, environmental impact bonds, specialised subsidies, and natural hazard insurance. Examples of *actors* involved in investing in urban nature are municipal departments, banks, foundations, insurance companies, real estate investors, community groups, and non-governmental organisations (NGOs).

In this chapter, we introduce different sources of finance (*what*), the actors involved in providing these sources of finance (*who*), and various financial mechanisms through which the sources and the actors are mobilised (*how*). We organise this material by the four principal models of investing in urban nature, which include funding solicited: (1) from *public* funds; (2) through *private* capital; (3) via *community/not-for profit* funding; and (4) through *hybrid* and *collaborative* approaches. Furthermore, we discuss the current situation, barriers, and opportunities for investing in urban nature, along with relevant examples. The chapter concludes with insights on how to facilitate more investment in urban nature and support its mainstreaming in cities.

Public, Private, and Community Investors

There are many actors, actor groups, and networks engaged in investing in nature in cities. These are presented in Table 6.1 according to the three principal investment models: public, private, and not-for-profit/community investment in urban nature.

Table 6.1 Different types of investors in nature-based solutions

Public investors	Private investors	Community investors
Supra-national public actors (e.g. European Commission)	Commercial banks	Citizens and communities (e.g. crowdfunding)
National governments	Insurance firms	Cooperatives
Regional and state governments	Real estate and utility companies and corporations	NGOs
Local governments and municipalities	Road companies	Philanthropic organisations (e.g. lotteries, foundations, trusts)
Public (development) banks	Commercial greening firms	
	Other institutional investors	
Hybrid investment, product development, and collaborative action		
Collaborative development funds		
Product development by insurance and other emerging financial actors		
Mobilising finance through sustainable business and global NGO networks		

In addition, different types of investors can fund together an urban nature intervention or financing for such intervention can come from a common fund that pools together public, private, and community funding. In this case, it is relevant to discuss co-financing or hybrid investment. Each of these models is explained in the following subsections and examples are provided.

Public Investment in Nature-Based Solutions

The traditional financial players investing in urban nature are public bodies. Urban nature interventions like parks, street trees, and water management infrastructure are traditionally seen as the responsibility of municipalities, who often act as the main funders for the implementation and maintenance of those interventions. Apart from municipalities, other public investors in urban nature include public organisations at supra-national levels such as the European Commission or international organisations in the World Bank Group as well as national, regional, and local governments, and public banks like the European Bank for Reconstruction and Development (EBRD).

One way of investing in urban nature is through the mobilisation of public funds at a supra-national level, such as funds available for countries in the European Union (EU). There are several EU programmes and funds that can be used to develop urban nature-based solutions and relevant expertise, along with other types of 'eco-innovation'. These include the Horizon Europe (in past, Horizon 2020) Programme, the LIFE Programme, the Programme for the Competitiveness of Enterprises and Small and Medium-sized Enterprises (COSME), the Cohesion Fund, and the European Structural and Investment Funds (ESIF). The LIFE Programme funds environmental and climate action by public, private, and/or third-sector organisations, including nature-based solution projects; for example, LIFE-myBUILDINGisGREEN in Spain. The ESIF consists of five streams and finances aspects of the Operational Programme developed by each EU Member State. Among the ESIF, particularly the European Regional Development Fund (ERDF), the European Social Fund (ESF), and the Cohesion Fund (CF) bear most direct relevance to urban nature-based solutions. The European Commission prepared a 'Guide to Multi-Benefit Cohesion Policy Investments in Nature and Green Infrastructure' to share knowledge on how green infrastructure could be funded under each of these funds in synergistic ways. For example, the ERDF could be used to fund green infrastructure for economic regeneration, whereas the ESF could fund new professional training opportunities associated with green infrastructure development. Many of these EU funds require co-funding by local partners, with the percentage varying depending on the fund, for example 60–70 per cent for LIFE projects.

The second way by which public actors invest in urban nature is by channelling taxation income to nature-based investment at national, regional, or local levels in the form of subsidies, grants, and earmarked funding. For instance, municipalities draw on taxation income to act as significant investors in urban nature projects and other amenities, both in terms of capital investment and ongoing maintenance. This is the situation in Sweden given the highly decentralised nature of the Swedish government, the high degree of freedom, and the significant funds that municipalities receive through incoming tax payments. Another example is the Scottish Green Infrastructure Fund in the UK, which makes governmental funds available to municipalities for developing urban nature to meet strategic needs, such as improved access to nature for deprived communities. For example, earmarked taxation programmes, generated from real estate development and uplift, can also be channelled to urban nature funding.

A third way in which public finance becomes available for urban nature is through public banks. The EBRD Green Cities programme provides access to funding for urban nature interventions mainly for cities in the countries outside of the EU. The European Investment Bank (EIB) is a joint EU institution qualifying as the world's largest provider of climate finance. Additionally, it has a loan programme dedicated to financing natural capital investments, the Natural Capital Finance Facility (NCFF), requiring a minimum of €5 million investment (for example towards green infrastructure or other urban nature) and a minimum rate of return. Athens in Greece is the first city to make use of the NCFF to help deliver urban climate change resilience measures on over 400 sites through green–blue infrastructure.

Similar to other EU funding, 25 per cent co-funding by local partners in NCFF projects is required. There are also examples of public banks operating at national or regional level. In Sweden, the public-sector bank Kommuninvest provides loans to municipal and regional governments to invest in sustainability projects requiring long-term funding. In Germany, regional public banks play an important role by supporting policy objectives with financial instruments, such as green roof subsidies. Existing regulations and subsidies for energy efficiency measures provide a suitable platform for adding similar regulation and incentives for green roofs, as the contacts and processes already exist.

Finally, the fourth way through which the public sector engages with investing in urban nature is via policy and regulation. Municipalities can set up mechanisms and incentives such as green procurement, which refers to the realisation of one's own assets or demands for products and services through nature-based solutions. For example, the MKB housing association owned by Malmö municipality, Sweden, invests in green roofs in Malmö. The Swedish national government is also influential through establishing the regulatory frameworks for institutional investors to operate in. As such, the Swedish National Pension Fund (AP Funds) can only invest in funds with high environmental and ethical standards, which creates an incentive for investing in urban nature. Earmarked taxation programmes are also supported by urban nature and biodiversity regulation at a city or state level. Versions of 'no net loss' or 'net gain' regulation that generates funds from developments to replace lost urban nature elsewhere in the city are developed in Germany and the UK.

Private Investment in Nature-Based Solutions

The need for private (co-)investment in urban nature has been increasingly emphasised. Private investors in nature include commercial banks, insurance firms, real estate (see Case Study Box 6.1) and utility companies and corporations, road companies, commercial greening firms, and institutional investors (for example, pension funds). An increasing number of banks, insurers, and other private investors are exploring the potential of investing in nature because of customer demand,

Case Study Box 6.1 Parc Marianne Ecodistrict (Montpellier, France)

The City of Montpellier faces strong population growth, being France's eighth largest and fastest-growing city. The city faces flood risk due to increasing climate extremes: longer periods of drought, more intense rainfalls, and sea level rise. These challenges affect the rich biodiversity in the city and the citizens' quality of life and well-being. Montpellier, due to its location next to the Mediterranean Sea, is one of 35 hotspots of biodiversity on the planet.

Densification and organised expansion are key measures to reduce urban sprawl, placing increasing pressure not only on the built environment and urban services, but also on green spaces. The green densification model integrates urban nature into (often large-scale) real estate development. The cost of creating and maintaining these urban nature projects has become an embedded part of a larger business case of 'sustainable urban living', captured through real estate value and economic growth. The Parc Marianne Ecodistrict in Montpellier is an example of 'organised sprawl', where new homes were built in combination with green and blue infrastructure to reduce flood risk, and improve the city's liveability and the health and well-being of its inhabitants.

The Parc Marianne Ecodistrict was built between 2010 and 2018 as part of a larger new-district development, Port Marianne, in direct response to the population growth of Montpellier. Controlled land prices made it possible for the City of Montpellier to

Case Study Box 6.1 (cont.)

buy the land (in the 1980s–1990s) and develop long-term plans for the area. The master architect and the city council developed detailed social and environmental requirements for the development of the new area. In 2003, as a result of an architectural competition led by a semi-public organisation, SERM (Société d'Equipement de la Région Montpelliéraine), three architectural firms were selected for the development of the three areas. The Architecture-Studio, in close collaboration with SERM and the City, became responsible for the design of Parc Marianne. Following the long-term vision of the former mayor George Frêche, the area was to be designed to better connect Montpellier with the sea. In order to do so, the municipality bought a lot of land with tax money, controlled prices, and planned projects like Parc Marianne.

Accordingly, this project was financed by developers who bought the land from the municipality. Their total investment was about €110 million. The municipality prescribed the rents that the developers could ask for each flat, and the price was not a factor in the tender allocation. In this case, the cultural history and a long-term vision were supported by a financing structure, which allowed the city to continue building on floodplains and channelling rivers to avoid becoming a swamp by elevating the neighbourhood so that the natural terrain could be used as a retention basin, which collects and directs storm water to the sea or lagoons. These measures not only reduce flood risk but also have recreational and biodiversity benefits. The district received ecolabel certification (2015) on thermal performance, quality of life, nature and biodiversity, and mobility.

Figure 6.1 Montpellier, France

government regulation, and a desire to minimise climate-related risks to their investments. For instance, in the Netherlands, ASN bank has adopted biodiversity conservation as the main criterion for building its investment portfolios and it leads work on developing methods to assess the biodiversity performance of its portfolio. As such tools become more widely available and used in the private sector, this will support private investment in nature, including that in cities.

There are also several large firms investing in urban nature to mitigate the environmental losses because of their activities. Such examples can be considered part of the Environmental, Social, and Governance (ESG) initiatives of firms. For instance, 'habitat banking' proposed in Spain was a method through which private firms could voluntarily buy credits to compensate for habitat loss as a result of their activities. These credits could then be invested in environmental restoration projects elsewhere. Tools such as habitat banking are promising, but often lack a legal mandate that would help mainstream investment in nature and ecosystems. These schemes have also been criticised on the grounds of their market-based character (Maestre-Andrés et al., 2021). Another example of private firms investing in urban nature is that of Audi, which invested in improving the nature value of habitats located on its factory site in Győr, Hungary. Bees were also introduced through beekeeping and used as bioindicators for monitoring emissions.

Community Investment in Nature-Based Solutions

Next to private and public actors, community and not-for-profit stakeholders can play an important role in funding urban nature projects, particularly smaller or local ones. Local urban nature projects are sometimes financed through crowdfunding initiatives, ranging from funding individual street trees to local green playgrounds or urban gardens, or by philanthropy organisations and NGOs. Such projects generally have high citizen acceptance as they reflect the local context, are often co-created by the residents, and provide hands-on evidence about the state of urban nature habitats, for example volunteer bee health monitoring.

Germany offers many examples of community-funded urban nature initiatives. For instance, in Leipzig, the Strassenbaume portal allows citizens to 'adopt' a specific street tree. The Princess Gardens (Prinzessinnengärten) in Berlin is an urban community garden with more than 500 different types of vegetables and herbs grown collectively by urban residents in the middle of the city. The Princess Gardens were created in 2009 on a previously neglected wasteland and they are now among the most well-known community gardens in Germany. They are open to anyone: adults and children, gardening enthusiasts and beekeepers who want to grow, learn, teach, or help in any other way. The Princess Gardens do not receive any direct funding. Land rental, personnel and material costs, infrastructure development, and operational costs are covered from the volunteers' own income in gastronomy and horticulture, through tours, lectures, and gardening workshops, and through the sale of plants, harvested crops, and meals in a garden café.

There are examples of citizen-led funding of urban parks through memberships and lotteries (for example, Bremen Bürgerpark in Germany). Lotteries, foundations, and trusts also invest in urban nature projects. For instance, the Heritage Lottery Fund is a national funder in the UK that provides grants for activities which preserve places with a heritage value. The Heritage Lottery Fund – in partnership with the Big Lottery Fund – invested more than £12 million to restore and upgrade Newcastle's historic parks. This funding helps protect the past investments and further test and develop proposals that emerged from an earlier project, Rethinking Parks, which was financed by the Heritage Lottery Fund and delivered by the National Trust in partnership with Sheffield City Council. The maintenance and upgrades in Central Park in New York City are performed by the Central Park Conservancy, which is mainly funded by individual donations and annually invests nearly $78 million into the Park's care, reducing the need for municipal investment significantly.

Apart from direct financial or in-kind (that is, labour) investments in urban nature projects, NGOs may play an important translational role between green urban investments and policy development. For example, Germany has a strong network of active environmental NGOs that are usually member-funded and driven by volunteers who care about local green developments. These NGOs play an important monitoring role when it comes to the execution of governmental policies. In the urban context, the push for additional houses is threatening existing urban green areas, which represent the cheapest locations for realising new housing development projects quickly, and NGOs can take the role of 'watchdogs' to strive for a balance between greening and housing objectives.

Different Investment Mechanisms for Nature-Based Solutions

Apart from public, private, and community actors who invest in urban nature, the investment sources can also be combined to share the investment burden. Furthermore, different actors can undertake collaborative action and, in this way, advance innovative business models that enable investments in nature-based solutions in cities. Here we describe several mechanisms that have been developed to organise such 'hybrid' investment in urban nature. These include collaborative development funds and public–private partnerships, product development by insurance and other emerging financial actors with a sustainability focus, and mobilising finance through sustainable business and global NGO networks and their member organisations.

One mechanism for hybrid investment in nature is through setting up collaborative development funds. In the city of Kecskemét, Hungary, a City Development Fund was established: 30 per cent of the money comes from private investors and 70 per cent is public funding. The fund targets city development projects that have a lower return but higher social benefits. Dividends are higher for private investors in contrast to public investors: losses of up to 10 per cent are carried by the public investor, considerably reducing the investment risk by private partners.

Furthermore, different municipal departments working with environment, public health, education, culture, and other matters benefit from urban nature projects in various ways and may therefore decide to combine their funds and attract external funds to invest in and maintain nature-based infrastructure in a city together, for example by creating urban forest funds. As such, in Melbourne, the municipality created the Urban Forest Fund, where voluntary offsetting funds from urban infrastructure projects and resources from different municipal departments are used for a 50 per cent subsidy for citizens and businesses who decide to green their property. An international NGO, The Nature Conservancy (TNC), co-develops Water Funds worldwide to coordinate co-investment into (urban) nature (see Case Study Box 6.2).

Case Study Box 6.2 Mexico City Water Fund (Mexico City, Mexico)

Water represents an existential challenge for Mexico City, which is threatened by both water scarcity and flooding. The solutions lie in its existing natural assets. Reminders of the lake come each year when heavy rains bring flooding. At other times, water scarcity is a problem and subsidence due to water extraction is ongoing, damaging infrastructure including pipes where 40 per cent of water is lost due to leakage. The metropolitan population of 20 million requires a lot of water and produces a lot of waste. Seventy per cent of the water comes from overexploited aquifers and 30 per cent is piped in from increasing distances.

All of this is done at great cost and there are fears that the current approach will soon reach its limits. Fortunately, the natural dynamics of its watershed has the potential to solve Mexico City's water problems. Attention is being increasingly focused on opportunities to conserve, restore, and manage existing ecosystems in ways that ensure their capacity to absorb and filter rainwater and to recharge aquifers, thus mitigating flooding and ensuring sufficient quantity and quality of water. NGOs, government, and business recognised the lack of financial mechanisms aimed at strengthening water security through the protection of ecosystem features and thus established a Water Fund.

The development of Mexico City's Water Fund was initiated in 2015 by The Nature Conservancy (TNC) Mexico on behalf of the Latin American Water Funds Partnership, together with the Inter-American Development Bank (IDB) and the city's municipal government (CDMX). Business partners are also an important part of the initiative. The Water Fund now operates through a purposefully created nonprofit called Por el Agua de la Ciudad de México (For the Water of Mexico City). The strategy has been integrated into the city's Resilience Strategy, which among its five pillars includes to 'promote water resilience as a new paradigm to manage water in the Mexico basin'.

Case Study Box 6.2 (cont.)

Efforts are currently focused within the city's designated 'Conservation Land' (an area of 80,000 hectares representing half the land area of Mexico City), beginning with a 13,000 hectare portion that has been identified as having particular capacity for water infiltration and aquifer recharge. The presence of large patches of Conservation Land within Mexico City provides an important opportunity; however, its potential is still threatened by irregular developments and economic incentives that undermine its preservation. In order to preserve natural resources, besides strong leadership and a commonly agreed vision, this financing mechanism requires a strategic economic commitment of the involved actors, guided by social and environmental sustainability principles.

Figure 6.2 Mexico City, Mexico

There is also an increasing understanding within the insurance sector that climate change and other sustainability challenges are putting at risk both their assets (that is, investments) and their liabilities (exposure to damage costs). A mechanism of collaborative action that supports investments into urban nature is through insurance product development. As such, some insurers are raising climate-risk awareness among households, firms, and municipalities regarding their assets. For example, German insurance firms collect worldwide data on climate risk to their investment portfolios, some of which is made available to the business sector (for example, the NATHAN portal by Munich Re).

The Dutch insurance company Achmea has developed the BlueLabel tool, which maps urban climate risk (heat and flooding) at a granular parcel scale. Other insurance companies were approached by The Nature Conservancy and other NGOs to develop insurance products for natural assets, such as coral reefs, to invest in their protection and reduce damage costs, an approach that could also be expanded to urban nature. Another way in which insurance companies are involved in enabling urban nature is through stimulating markets for urban nature projects. For example, the Dutch insurance firm Interpolis stimulates the uptake of green roofs by home owners through marketing campaigns and discounted prices based on expectations of lower damage costs because green roofs protect from water damage.

A third, more indirect but nonetheless important mechanism is the role played in some European countries by sustainable business networks and their member organisations. These networks act as knowledge brokers, translating EU regulation to financial institutions. For example, several sustainable finance networks are active in Germany, each playing a knowledge brokering, networking, and often lobbying role. These include CRIC (sustainable investor network), FNG (sustainable network for financial institutions in Germany, Austria, and Switzerland), and the Green and Sustainable Finance Cluster Germany. Alongside the government-run Sustainable Finance Hub, these networks play an important visioning and knowledge-brokering role in developing sustainable finance in the German financial sector. Such networks also contribute with new accreditation schemes and metrics. For example, FNG created a label for sustainable investment and a transparency index for investment funds, the 'Transparency Codex'.

Globally operating actors in the finance domain also take initiative themselves to support sustainable investment. For example, the Platform Carbon Accounting Financials (PCAF) acts on behalf of financial institutions worldwide to develop assessments of investment portfolios' carbon footprints. This could indirectly support development of urban nature projects as an offsetting activity. Likewise, the Global Alliance for Banking on Values (GABV) is an international network for sustainable banks and banking cooperatives, whereas the Network of Central Banks and Supervisors for Greening the Financial System (NGFS) is a global partnership of Central Banks interested in greening the financial system. Several globally operating insurance companies (for example, AEGON, Allianz, and Swiss RE) have signed up to the UN Environment Programme Finance Initiative (UNEP FI) Principles for Sustainable Insurance (PSI).

There is also increasing facilitating action by global NGOs including TNC, World Wildlife Fund for Nature (WWF), and the International Union for Conservation of Nature (IUCN) to develop their own expertise and funds in sustainable finance, also for urban nature. WWF and IUCN are also among the founding actors of the Natural Capital Coalition (NCC), a worldwide coalition of public-, private-, and third-sector organisations involved in understanding the dependency of their production processes and long-term viability on natural capital, as well as their impacts on it, through the Natural Capital Protocol.

Barriers and Opportunities for Investing in Nature-Based Solutions

Mainstreaming urban nature relates to strategic intervention in the governance, financial, and urban development domains to enable the functioning of urban nature innovations over the long term and support their potential to deliver ecological, economic, and social benefits. To identify the pathways to mainstream urban nature (Chapter 10) it is key to understand how urban nature can be governed (Chapter 5), how current investment and finance regimes are shaping decision-making practices in urban environments (this chapter), and what innovation pathways for urban nature exist (Chapter 7). Below we will focus on discussing key barriers and opportunities for investing in and ultimately contributing to the uptake and mainstreaming of urban nature.

Current Barriers to Investing in Nature-Based Solutions

The first important barrier to growing investments in urban nature is that it suffers from a general lack of priority and lack of clear standards. Investing in urban nature has a large unmet potential to contribute to the uptake of urban nature by providing finance, particularly from large mainstream commercial financial institutions. While a growing number of financial actors are increasing their share of sustainable finance and investment, financial return remains non-negotiable. Some global sustainable banks are leading the way by only investing in activities that generate a positive social and environmental impact, often requiring a lower financial return. Public-sector banks also tend to invest more sustainably, supporting the implementation of government policy.

However, in many cases sustainable investments still do not prioritise urban nature as an investment target, due to the lack of standardisation and scale of these investments. Other sustainability targets such as those for climate mitigation are often prioritised, for example, by the development of renewable energy or energy efficiency projects, because metrics and calculation methods used in this domain have been developed over a longer period of time and are being standardised. The lack of evidence and indicators to quantify the benefits of urban nature is a typical barrier to investment, particularly for private actors. This is because private investors tend to operate following a high-gain, low-risk paradigm, preferring to invest in projects that generate high returns in short time frames. This is not always supportive of urban nature projects because their benefits often cannot be expressed clearly in financial values, which makes them less attractive when calculating returns on investment. In addition, benefits such as climate resilience play out in longer time frames and require acknowledgement of long-term climate risks or costs, which makes them less attractive for investors seeking short-term returns.

Furthermore, the benefits of urban nature projects – even when measured – are captured in a 'scattered' manner between different stakeholders, meaning that for an individual actor, investments usually do not cover costs, and coordination of investment between stakeholders is complex. These are key reasons why many private banks and other private institutional investors still do not invest in nature.

Another important barrier when investing in urban nature relates to the importance of maintenance to create durable investment objects. Different types of urban nature and their properties (for example, the ability to grow, absorb water and CO_2, cool, isolate) affect their ability to create value for urban sustainability and also represent potential risks that can make investments challenging. Without clear models of maintenance that keep nature alive, invested assets may quickly run dry. Similarly, to be sustainable in the long run, community-based not-for-profit investments in urban nature require a high level of commitment from investing parties and their continuous involvement in the urban nature project maintenance. In the following subsection we will discuss opportunities and ways to overcome barriers and advance investment in urban nature projects.

Future Opportunities for Stepping Up Investment in Nature-Based Solutions

There are several promising opportunities that could drastically increase the amount of finance available for urban nature. These include recognising and articulating the potential of urban nature projects for climate-risk mitigation and cost reduction associated with climate-induced damage, as well as the role of urban nature in increasing urban biodiversity. In addition, ensuring the viability and long-term sustainability of urban nature interventions requires the support of current business models that are advancing nature in cities and establishing new business models that leverage innovative ways of collaborating and investing in urban nature (Box 6.3).

First, mitigation of climate-related risks by financial institutions can be an important rationale for investments in climate-proof or climate-mitigating assets. Climate risk is increasingly viewed as affecting financial portfolios in a negative way at a global scale. Central Banks and regulators increasingly require financial institutions to report on these risks. For instance, the Taskforce on Climate-related Financial Disclosures (TCFD) advocates reporting at a global scale and the EU is mandating financial institutions in Europe to make the climate exposures in their portfolios transparent.

Because higher risk carries a price for financial actors (higher cost of capital, lower ratings, lower expected financial returns), such reporting requirements benefit urban nature investments as the costs of investing in urban nature decrease in relation to investments with higher associated climate risks. This is particularly true for the insurance sector, which is directly affected by climate risks and costs through its liabilities. Hence, engaging insurers more actively poses a specific opportunity because they are well positioned to raise awareness on risk mitigation with their customers, and they collect granular data on actual damage costs that can establish the value of (and stimulate investment into) mitigating measures such as urban nature projects.

Second, biodiversity is starting to show up on the radar of some financial institutions, from both an impact and a risk perspective. The European Investment Bank is pioneering Natural Capital investments through its Natural Capital Finance Facility Pioneers like the Dutch ASN bank, which has chosen biodiversity as a central objective of its investment policy. This creates an opportunity for urban nature because urban nature can increase the conditions for raising urban biodiversity.

Third, advancing business models for urban nature is vital to ensure implementation, maintenance, and long-term viability of urban nature projects. Tools to advance such business models were developed in the NATURVATION project and include the Business Model Catalogue and Business Model Puzzle (see Box 6.3).

OVERALL REFLECTIONS

The challenge of securing financial investment for urban nature is increasingly recognised. As shown in this chapter, developing and maintaining different types of urban nature and their ownership structures requires activating different financial instruments and sources of funds. There is no universal solution that would fit all types of urban nature and the financial models range from a single green roof investment by a business as a part of green procurement process to long-term public–private investment models that incorporate and value multiple urban nature benefits for various stakeholders.

Box 6.3 Advancing business models for nature-based solutions

Mainstreaming urban nature does not only depend on establishing the right policy conditions and financial resources, but also on establishing business models that can ensure their sustainability over time. Urban nature projects often create a complex array of public and private benefits, and developing business models that capture and realise this value can be challenging. There is both a need to support the current business models that are advancing nature in cities and to harness business model innovation to enable future action on urban sustainability.

The NATURVATION project developed two resources for these purposes. First, the Business Model Catalogue for urban nature presents eight business models that were identified based on 54 in-depth case studies of urban nature-based solutions, in Europe and beyond. These models explain which value propositions can drive urban nature funding. Importantly, by combining different models, the funding capacity for urban nature can be increased.

Second, the Business Model Puzzle for urban nature is a dialogue tool for understanding which values can drive the realisation of an urban nature project and which stakeholders may be willing to pay for this value. It builds on the Business Model Catalogue and allows stakeholders like municipalities, real estate developers, NGOs, and insurance firms to identify values they can adopt to realise urban nature projects.

Investing in urban nature requires the availability of capital funding and both the willingness in the financial sector to invest in urban nature as well as the capacity of the insurance industry to include urban nature interventions in its calculations. Such decisions require support in the form of knowledge, tools, and calculative devices that incorporate multiple benefits of urban nature into financial risk assessments. Few financial professionals are trained in green finance or sustainability. It will therefore be crucial to work with financial actors to co-create such knowledge and tools, while opening the conversation up on what constitutes a 'good' return on investment in sustainability terms. The latter is particularly important because urban nature projects are likely to generate long-term benefits that cannot always be captured in monetary terms, or they reduce risks rather than generate profits.

Equally, working with nature will always generate public goods alongside private benefits, and new forms of co-finance that can sustain the mixed economy of returns on investment which urban nature generates are needed. This can provide the basis for diversifying the forms of finance and financial actors who engage with urban nature and open new collaborative approaches for sustaining urban nature over time.

Existing and ongoing investment into incumbent physical structures and building technology will affect the relative risk and return of 'grey' versus more innovative nature-type infrastructure as assets and will therefore also affect the decision-making about investing in urban nature. Important aspects to consider in this decision-making include the suitability of mainstream buildings to external greening (for example, their carrying capacity and slope of roofs); the depreciation rates of the existing urban infrastructure; the perceived risk and costs of implementing urban nature due to the need for its maintenance and 'withering away'; and the suitability of existing buildings and infrastructure to handle climate change (for example through the absorption of precipitation).

Another important challenge in large and fast-growing cities is the provision of affordable housing, which is often a key policy priority. Because this priority calls for the fastest and the cheapest ways to build, green urban spaces may become threatened as such development lowers available offsetting space for nature and undermines the need to implement strong green tender procedures. If the governments at various levels are passive in mainstreaming urban nature projects or even impede them, it will be particularly important to activate the civil society that can advocate for and realise these projects in a bottom-up fashion. The attention across public and private actors as well as in community-led initiatives for urban nature is growing.

Despite this growing recognition, however, the earlier-mentioned challenge of developing suitable and shared principles for calculating multiple benefits and risks of urban nature remains. In addition, the general for-profit paradigm by investors limits the competitive potential of urban nature projects against traditional investment assets. This leads to a conclusion that advancing urban nature in cities will require not only financial investment but also political and cultural commitments, which will then create grounds for viable business models. Before one could speak of financial investment, the first step is to generate political investment from across a wide range of actors who share a vision and commitment to the use of urban nature. Building trust and a sense of collective endeavour across multiple stakeholders is important, as it is them who will eventually bring finance to the table for urban nature to flourish.

KEY LEARNING EXERCISES

1. **Individual Reflection:** Think of three reasons why it may be important to invest in urban nature in your city or a city that is close to the place where you live. What kind of urban nature projects need investment? Who could provide such investment?
2. **Peer Discussion:** In a group of 2–4 peers, one person acts as an advocate for more investments in urban nature in a city and the other peers take on one of the roles of key financial players who may help secure such investments but are not yet persuaded that the investments are important: a local political leader, a commercial bank, an insurance company, and a nature conservation NGO (select one role per person). Based on the reasons in the first exercise, the 'advocate' develops arguments to persuade each of the stakeholders. Change roles so that each peer an act as 'an advocate' and put their arguments forward.
3. **Explore Examples:** What possible barriers to and opportunities for investing in urban nature projects can you identify from the debate exercise with your peers? Suggest an example (real or hypothetical) of how the barriers could be overcome and the decision about the investment in an urban nature project could be made.

FURTHER RESOURCES

Bockarjova, M., Botzen, W. J. W., Bulkeley, H. A. and Toxopeus, H. (2022) Estimating the social value of nature-based solutions in European cities. *Scientific Reports*, 12, 19833.

European Commission – Directorate-General for Research and Innovation. (2022) *The Vital Role of Nature-Based Solutions in a Nature Positive Economy*. Luxembourg: Publications Office of the European Union.

Toxopeus, H. and Polzin, F. (2021) Reviewing financing barriers and strategies for urban nature-based solutions. *Journal of Environmental Management*, 289, 112371.

7 Innovating

INTRODUCTION

Urban nature and nature-based solutions in many cases offer a more sustainable alternative to urban development approaches than their frequently prioritised counterparts, including technology-driven grey interventions. In reality, these multifunctional and solution-oriented nature-based alternatives occur in close interaction with networks of urban infrastructures (roads, railways, waterways, buildings, etc.) that are themselves influenced by associated practices, processes, and actors. As part of the urban system, working with urban nature therefore calls for rethinking the entire process of sustainable urban development and associated physical structures, urban practices, actor networks, and institutional arrangements. In this process, policies and standards, stakeholders' roles, and existing practices of planning, implementation, and maintenance are scrutinised in the search for an intertwined and balanced functioning of technology and ecology.

In the process of rethinking, various pathways of innovation are generated for each intervention starting from an initial idea and its demonstration to its broader uptake within policy, industry, and society. Along the way, the interventions are influenced by sociospatial and structural conditions alike. The combination of different conditions, such as local visions, governance networks, financial models, institutional settings, localised learning capacities, and place-specific natural endowments and resources, strongly influences the development of urban structures. Broader-scale priorities and practices embedded in international value chains and infrastructures, policy regimes, market structures, and knowledge paradigms further affect their mainstreaming. Together, these place-based and structural conditions across scales keep urban development locked in its current state ('path dependency'), often relying on existing institutions and favouring traditional infrastructures over nature-based alternatives.

In this chapter, we explain how innovation pathways are shaped with focus on urban nature and nature-based solutions (see Box 7.1). First, we provide

Box 7.1 Key terms and concepts used in this chapter

Innovations: Innovations can be defined and grouped depending on whether the innovation component rests in the final end *product* or in the development of new approaches (*process*); whether it has been built on existing products, practices, services, and ecologies (*incremental*); or if it is substantially different from what exists in a particular context (*radical*). We also distinguish between (1) physical, (2) social, and (3) system innovations, which can be broken down into further subcategories as shown in Chapter 4.

Nature-based innovation systems framework (NBIS): The NBIS framework has its origin in the technological innovation system (TIS) framework with the inclusion of the ecological component to sociotechnical systems, such as ecosystems, landscape structure, and environmental justice. According to this framework, the following structures and functions constitute and influence the performance of a nature-based innovation system: agency, discourse and vision, legislation and policies, governance structures, collaborative arrangements, learning, resources, and place-based factors (van der Jagt et al., 2020).

Systems: A system can be broadly defined as 'a set of elements or parts that is coherently organized and interconnected in a pattern or structure that produces a characteristic set of behaviours, often classified as its "function" or "purpose"' (Meadows, 2008, p. 188). In the light of sustainable urban development, working with the interconnectedness of social, ecological, and technological systems is gaining increasing attention.

Urban infrastructure regimes: This refers to 'the stable configurations of institutions, techniques and artefacts which determine "normal" sociotechnical developments in a city and thus shape general urban processes and the urban metabolism' (Monstadt, 2009, p. 1937). Urban development, policy-making, and finance are some of the key functions within a regime that, among others, can create path dependency.

a typology of innovations for nature-based solutions. Second, we unpack the underlying conditions enabling and constraining the mainstreaming of these innovations through the nature-based solutions innovation system framework. We also discuss localised innovation processes (see Box 7.2). Third, we provide potential explanations for path dependencies, through urban development regimes that enable or constrain these initiatives and systems. Through these three sets of dynamics, we aim to provide an understanding about what shapes the pathways through which urban nature and nature-based innovations emerge and open the gateway to potential intervention points towards sustainability. Fourth, we present recent innovation pathways for urban nature through case studies from Winnipeg (Canada) and Edinburgh (United Kingdom) to explore the interconnections between nature, innovation, and urban sustainability that indicate the emergence of a global agenda.

Box 7.2 Cultivating urban nature – key lessons

Value Experimentation: Seeing is believing – experiments allow actors to try things out without losing too much.

Nature-based solutions are being developed in cities globally as forms of experimentation – novel approaches or innovations that are being developed in response both to the challenges cities are facing and opportunities for doing things differently. Large-scale formal experiments include testbeds, living laboratories (or living labs), and large-scale urban developments framed as innovative approaches for managing multiple urban challenges, from climate change to well-being. More informal but equally significant approaches to experimentation involve temporary installations, driven by a range of actors, as well as interventions taking place in existing urban landscapes driven by one or two actors – for example, in community gardens or existing public parks. The experimental qualities of nature-based solutions allow novel coalitions to be formed and risks to be taken in doing things differently, lowering the stakes involved if any intervention were not to succeed and allowing diverse approaches to be tried on for size. Yet despite the recognised value in experimentation, it is often seen as just a phase which should be succeeded by more formalised, certain, and regulated means of implementation. Experimentation may, however, be worth holding on to. It enables the development of knowledge in situ, further enabling the translation of generic information into locally relevant knowledge that meets the needs of communities and stakeholders. It allows for continual exploration and new possibilities, while at the same time recognising that not all new interventions will be a success. Iterative experimentation, which builds on what is already known and understood but which fosters an emergent, open approach to the development of nature-based solutions, may prove productive for generating greater momentum for their uptake in diverse urban contexts.

Innovation and Nature-Based Solutions

What is an innovation and how can we understand different types of pathways for nature-based solutions? These are the questions we address in this chapter. We offer a definition of 'innovation' and sketch a typology of nature-based solutions, while also shedding light on the conditions that enable or constrain nature-based innovation pathways. Local factors such as resources, natural processes in the built environment, societal and cultural frames of reference, structural conditions, and the specific combination and intensity of their interconnectedness are some of the most significant drivers carving the path for nature-based innovations. Furthermore, agency, discourses and visions, policy and governance structures, and localised learning capacities are all considered to be relevant factors for a nature-based innovation to perform well. We will explore how some of the conditions that are more structural in nature can, by constituting urban infrastructure regimes, both present barriers to and pave the way for nature-based innovations. We will also demonstrate the potential innovation pathways of urban nature and nature-based solutions in three highly discussed areas – climate adaptation, urban forests, and water management.

Typology of Innovating with Nature-Based Solutions

How can we think about innovations? Are they original ideas, creative thoughts or imaginations, new methods, more effective devices, or better solutions that sneak or break into our society? Regardless of the development of products, designs, or ideas, what matters is their novelty. And what is new depends on the perspective taken; it can be new to a particular context; for example, new to the organisation, new to the region or city, or new to the world – something that doesn't exist in a similar form anywhere else. In terms of urban nature and nature-based solutions, we can differentiate between (1) physical innovations (including both ecological and technological innovations), (2) social innovations, and (3) system innovations.

(1) **Physical innovations** include physical changes in the urban system, which can be both *ecological* and *technological innovations*, although they are mostly intertwined in the case of nature-based solutions. *Ecological innovations* are mostly concerned with new approaches to (a) the creation of new green or blue natural spaces, (b) the management of existing spaces, and (c) the restoration of ecosystems and their functionality. The restoration of the River Isar in Munich (Germany) is a good example of ecological innovation, with technological elements. Re-engineering the riverbed has been an infrastructural process. However, through the removal of concrete along the river, the floodplain has been restored and new natural spaces have been created, which has increased accessibility and water-related recreational activities for different social groups as well as enhanced biodiversity along the river (see Box 7.3). *Technological innovations* include the introduction of new or significantly changed products, technical processes, and infrastructures. The BiodiverCity

project in Malmö (Sweden) is an example of this type of techno-ecological innovation. In this project, multi-disciplinary actor groups developed new soil structures (product generation) and new working practices (process generation), along with

Box 7.3 Innovation pathways for climate adaptation

Climate change and related impacts, including climate variability and extremes, are an increasing threat to urban development. In fact, impacts such as extreme precipitation, inland and coastal flooding, heat stress, drought, and water scarcity are increasing in both intensity and number. In this context, nature-based solutions offer an important prospect for climate change adaptation and advancing urban planning to address complex urban challenges simultaneously.

They can comprehensively address climate risk in cities by reducing hazard exposure (for instance, through the establishment of nature protection areas or parks designed to inhibit the development of housing in risk areas, or establishing wetlands for improving water management in the outskirts of cities), reducing climate vulnerability (for instance, through green roofs, which typically help reduce heat stresses by regulating rooftop surface temperature and ambient air temperatures and thereby preventing heat island effects), and increasing response and recovery preparedness (for instance, through mobile planting systems during heatwaves). However, the integration of such measures for sustainable climate change adaptation in urban governance and planning is challenging because it requires changes at multiple levels, including both organisational and institutional levels. While systematic approaches for climate policy integration exist, in practice there is still a long way to go. Barriers are manifold.

Techno-Ecological Innovation for Climate Adaptation: Urban River Restoration (Munich, Germany)

The River Isar is the most important green corridor in the city of Munich. Since the beginning of the nineteenth century, this pre-alpine river has been increasingly regulated, both to reduce the risk of flooding and for power generation. However, flood risk and legal requirements related to flood protection necessitated its fundamental redesign. Consequently, the Isar Plan project was implemented. The obvious solution was to continue to elevate the river's dams. Instead, an innovative approach was taken to improve flood control and, at the same time, to restore the river's ecological functions and improve recreational opportunities for the city's population. The riverbed was widened into surrounding flood plains, existing embankments were removed, and a naturalistic system of riverbed rock ramps was implemented that allowed fish to move upstream. At the local level, the restoration of natural riverbanks and the widening of its channel reduced exposure to flood risk. The expansion of flood plains within the city created buffer zones that reduced vulnerability. At the organisational level, an inter-departmental working group was responsible for coordinating the project; this group provided support and fostered a multi-benefit approach. At the inter-organisational level, the project was designed by an inter-disciplinary group of professionals, both internal and external to the city administration, and citizens were involved in different phases. Today, the river Isar and its surroundings have been successfully transformed into an appealing green space and provide support for comprehensive flood protection and management.

introducing new plant species to create a more biodiverse and more attractive low-maintenance intensive green roof as a more sustainable alternative to the mainstream moss roofs.

(2) Social innovations encompass changes in social relationships, for instance through (a) policy actions, (b) changes in governance structures, (c) knowledge development about urban nature in a way that changes how urban nature is viewed and nature-based projects are designed and implemented in the city, (d) new economic models, and/or (e) alterations in cultural frameworks such as new meanings or values attached to urban nature. A good example is the governance approach of the City of Melbourne (Australia) to urban nature. Through the Urban Forest Strategy and related policy actions, strategic prioritisation was given to urban nature, and more specifically, urban forests. The development of different urban policy instruments, such as the Urban Forest Visual (digital tree map), the Urban Forest Fund, and precinct plans, has brought about new forms of collaboration among a variety of actors. For instance, the digital tree map, partly building on data collected by citizens and thus providing new ways of engaging with nature, also serves as a monitoring system of the city's tree stock. The development process of the precinct plans, including the artistic and creative endeavours of locals, has reconnected nature to particular cultural histories or forms of heritage, which have been absent or forgotten in the past decades (see Box 7.4).

Box 7.4 Innovation pathways for urban forests

Although cities worldwide increasingly regard vegetation as critical infrastructure providing health and well-being benefits for communities and a connection to nature that is difficult to find in urban areas, challenges to implementation and upscaling remain. Urban forestry is an emerging concept that not only incorporates trees, but other vegetation in streets, parks, plazas, river embankments, wetlands, railway corridors, community gardens, and on buildings as well as the soil and water that support them. Urban forests have been around for generations, but only recently, considering population growth, densification, and climate extremes, have they become valued for more than aesthetics and recreation.

The nature-based solutions highlighted here show that the benefits of urban forests span environmental, economic, cultural, and political domains. These benefits are increasingly recognised as an argument to persuade and engage local actors to work with and expand urban vegetation. This innovation also shows that the legal status and ownership of green spaces define their future. Creating resilient and sustainable urban landscapes that provide healthy and enjoyable places for people to live and work requires rethinking the role of green infrastructure. Nature-based solutions must include strong visions and strategic target-oriented planning, coupled with new governing modes and partnerships, often reallocating and sharing responsibilities with private actors.

Box 7.4 (cont.)

Social Innovation for Urban Forests: Urban Forest Fund (Melbourne, Australia)
As part of a comprehensive and integrated climate governance approach and a supporting financial scheme of the overarching Urban Forest Strategy, the Urban Forest Fund is a key initiative to address sustainability challenges in the City of Melbourne through supporting the greening of privately owned land. The Urban Forest Fund is a timely response to the city's challenges: heavy rains, floods, heatwaves, droughts, and strong population growth. In the past decade, the City of Melbourne has worked with a variety of innovative policy initiatives to increase its residents' quality of life. Many of these initiatives address the greening of public spaces; however, very few focus on the private realm, which today comprises 75 per cent of the city's land area. The Urban Forest Fund (2017–2021), a public–private partnership, aims to increase vegetation cover on privately owned land by providing 50 per cent financial support to (a) new green spaces, (b) tree planting, (c) green roofs and walls, (d) water-sensitive urban design projects, and (e) below-ground soil condition improvements for healthy vegetation. The Fund currently holds AUS$1.2 million in seed funding; if this is matched with an equivalent amount in private donations, 6000 m^2 of green roofs, 4600 m^2 of green facades, 900 m^2 of green walls, and 4000 street trees (1000 more than are now planted annually) can be achieved.

(3) System innovations refer to far-reaching changes in social, technical, and ecological dimensions and, most importantly, in the relations between them. These are multifunctional interventions as part of a large-scale transformation of a neighbourhood, new master plans, integrated catchment plans, and urban redevelopment projects. System innovations tend to emerge in the context of urban sustainability transitions making a meaningful impact in the market or society. An example includes the development of a wetland park in a free-trade harbour zone in Tianjin (China). Driven by the strategic prioritisation of urban nature, the 'sponge city concept' along with central financial arrangements (social innovation) and restoration activities of a previously polluted area (ecological innovation) have been combined with the development of new forms of green and blue infrastructure (technological innovation) to transform a highly industrial port into an attractive, liveable green area – rich in biodiversity and recreational activities (see Box 7.5).

Enabling and Constraining Factors of Nature-Based Solutions

Nature-based innovations and sustainability transitions emerge in a system of interconnected actors, networks, institutions, and infrastructures facilitating or constraining their development and diffusion. In this section, we will unpack the driving forces and constraining factors behind these innovations. To do so we call on the *nature-based innovation system framework* (van der Jagt et al., 2020) for further assistance. According to this framework, innovation drivers can be grouped into eight dimensions. The combination and the intensity of these dimensions define the trajectories of

Box 7.5 Innovation pathways for water management

Water infrastructure is critical for cities to maintain a clean sustainable water supply and build resilience to floods and droughts. Nature-based solutions for water challenges are innovative approaches to tackle social and environmental challenges. Growing urban populations around the world are causing a rising demand for water. Concurrently, changing climate conditions are increasing extreme events in cities, from drought to floods, with severe social and economic consequences. One in four large cities already face water stress and demand for water is projected to increase by 55 per cent by 2050. This calls for extensive renewal and expansion of urban water infrastructure, changes that provide opportunities to redesign, retrofit, and better manage water resources to deliver multiple benefits for all.

The nature-based solutions described here demonstrate views and practices to work with nature and technology while recognising the complexity of urban water systems, their relationship with the built environment and green infrastructure, and interconnections with communities and stakeholders. Rethinking water in cities, new partnerships and funding arrangements, new ways of working, enhanced public participation, increased collaboration, and long-term city planning are key factors to achieve environmental, social, and economic benefits and create healthier, more resilient, and more prosperous cities.

System Innovation for Water Management: Ecological Wetland Park in a Free-Trade Harbour Zone (Tianjin, China)

Combining landscape use, water purification, and nature conservation in a highly industrialised port area that had minimal biodiversity and degraded saline–alkaline soil makes the wetland park one of China's most innovative nature-based solutions. Tianjin, a port city and free-trade zone in northern China, faces pressing challenges from air and water pollution, persistent droughts, and rapid urbanisation at the expense of agricultural land. As a response, the city has become involved in China's Sponge Cities Project, with several pilot sites that aim to capture, store, and utilise at least 75 per cent of the rainfall by transforming the built environment. With financing from the Asian Development Bank, between 2010 and 2013 the state-owned Tianjin Harbour Construction and Development Company and the local government created an artificial wetland park on an approximately 63 ha parcel in a high-tech coastal industrial zone. The wetland park has three distinct functions: (i) wastewater treatment on a 17 ha water surface to minimise pollutant discharge; (ii) ecological restoration to increase biodiversity by planting 29,000 trees and 155,000 shrubs of over 130 species, as well as establishing three protected islands as habitats for vulnerable coastal species; and (iii) recreational space creation with 11 thematic zones to increase liveability and attract a skilled workforce. The park is a popular site to visit, not least by other local governments which seek to replicate its success.

nature-based innovations. The eight key drivers are: (1) agency, (2) discourse and vision, (3) policy, (4) governance structures, (5) collaborative arrangements, (6) learning, (7) resources, and (8) place-based factors (see Figure 7.1). Let us now take a closer look at what these dimensions entail and how they play out in different contexts of nature-based innovations in the built environment.

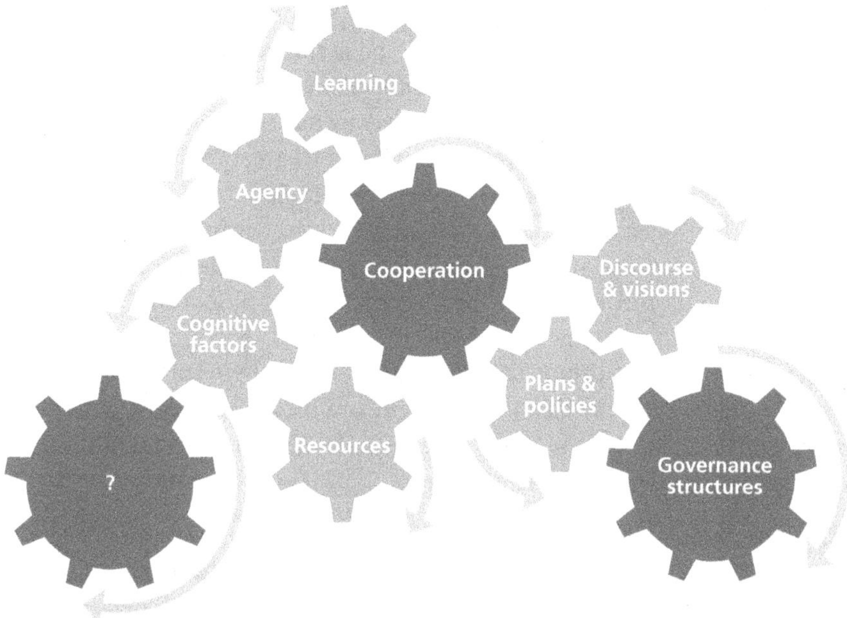

Figure 7.1 Nature-based innovation system framework

(1) The **agency**, the roles of and the capacity for actions of individuals and organisations, has a great influence on nature-based innovation pathways – by influencing other actors' actions, for instance through *leadership* and *power*, or forging them to engage in different partnerships and with diverse communities. Mayors have a powerful impact on creating a consistent political vision, along with planning practices, new forms of service provision, and the introduction of environmental strategies and regulations, which often translates into institutional *commitments* to sustainability.

Such high institutional commitment to sustainability can be seen, for instance, in the City of Melbourne (Australia), where a consistent political vision translated into the introduction of integrated policies along with intense citizen engagement. Or in Malmö (Sweden), where ecological innovations have been driven by a sustainability discourse originating from the United Nations Conference on Environment and Development in Rio de Janeiro (Brazil), which the mayor visited in 1992. His 'architect-vision' of a modern city based on sustainability principles intertwined with some individuals in the local administration and waterworks who were committed to experimenting with sustainable responses for local socioeconomic challenges both in the regeneration of declining neighbourhoods and new developments in brownfield areas. Individual and organisational commitments have translated into interdepartmental collaborations and multi-disciplinary working groups; and these practices have become institutionalised in the municipal administration in the past decades.

We can see similar commitments both at an individual and organisational level in other cities, too. In Munich (Germany), the mainstreaming of nature-based innovations relies on both individual and organisational commitments. The development of the city's Climate Adaptation Strategy was mostly driven by a newly employed and highly committed climate manager who had a great influence on the integration and implementation of blue and green climate adaptation measures in the city planning. The placement of a landscape architect in each development project team assures long-term organisational commitment to the integration of ecological knowledge and, through this, the mainstreaming of nature-based innovations. Other city administrations, for instance in Athens, Barcelona, and Leipzig, have committed to support urban gardening initiatives in the form of land or users' rights provision. However, the lack of long-term and balanced agency, including the lack of commitment, leadership, and power, can lead to project discontinuity and prevent nature-based innovations thriving.

(2) While agency plays a key role at individual and organisational levels, shared language and collective worldviews that incorporate the perspectives of diverse groups and organisations act at a broader societal level. **Discourses and visions** of urban sustainability, such as the 'eco city' or 'smart city', can translate into norms of action, eventually building up a momentum for change.

Augustenborg Ecocity in Malmö is a good example of how the sustainability messages of the Rio Summit (1992) have created a strong political vision in Sweden, which was put into action on the national policy agenda by creating the Local Investment Program for Sustainable Development to support a sustainable urban transition at a district level. The top-down vision, in this case, met the bottom-up needs expressed through strong agency and created a moment of change. As seen in this case, discourses and visions are closely linked to other innovation enablers, including agency, policy, learning, and place-based factors. In recent years, similar worldwide discourse – the 'sponge city' concept – has facilitated the mainstreaming of nature-based innovations in Tianjin, China.

Discourse can also create a status quo. While policies of the City of Melbourne mirror and benefit from the emerging concepts of 'resilient cities' and 'healthy cities', the public discourse around green roofs currently undermines their upscaling, as they are often perceived as costly and unsafe, requiring intense maintenance. Different visions of nature, such as community-based or unkempt nature, could also easily clash with the emerging multi-functional visions of nature-based solutions, whereby grey infrastructures may be seen to be more orderly, more controllable, and thus preferred.

(3) **Policies** are often sensitive to discourses and visions, especially when these shift their ways. National environmental policies, regional planning strategies, and urban plans can be used to directly and indirectly steer sustainable practices to align expectations, to enhance stewardship, to ensure financing, and to ensure public engagement in nature-based innovations. These policy processes can also be seen as collaboration platforms for sharing and aligning views, learning, and building

networks while engaging different actors. In this context, due to their place-based capacities, cities and municipalities can also be seen as arenas for negotiating place-based discourses and visions, partly because the envisioning takes place at the municipal level and partly because the actions can directly demonstrate feasibility, with the potential of city-to-city learning. According to a recent study, of 520 assessed nature-based solutions in Europe, most had been implemented in response to local policies (Dignum et al., 2020). Radical innovations, however, occur more often without a connection to existing policies, whereas systemic innovations are more common when urban plans include an explicit section on nature-based solutions or green infrastructure. Notably, however, the occurrence of both nature-based innovations and related local policies is dependent on the city's culture of openness towards newness and innovation.

Green infrastructure development, including urban gardens, is often prone to local regulations, property markets, and zoning. In Athens, Barcelona, and Leipzig, for instance, the municipality provided land-use rights to the respective communities, which allowed for urban nature to thrive, cultural frames to stretch, and communities to learn while being empowered. Urban nature experimentations and radical innovations are important components of policy learning, as they may prompt wider regulatory changes where existing land-use and other policies would otherwise prevent their implementation. Staying with the example of Augustenborg EcoCity in Malmö (Sweden), the municipal storm-water management policy, which was under development during the neighbourhood regeneration project, greatly benefitted from the practical experience gained from implementation of the nature-based drainage system as part of the ecocity's sustainability solutions.

(4) The involvement of a broad range of actors, the distribution of their decision-making power and responsibilities, as well as the different collaborative arrangements they are engaged in have a great influence on the development and diffusion of nature-based innovations. As discussed in detail in Chapter 5, these **governance structures** span horizontal and vertical scales and different sectors and disciplines. They are not only inherently influenced by policies at multiple levels, but for the successful development of nature-based innovations they also require a flexibility and a balance both in the variety of actors and in the distribution of power. In this colourful landscape of actors, local governments are often key actors and the initiators of nature-based innovations – especially those of incremental nature – while radical, social, and systemic nature-based innovations are typically supported by national- and EU-level structures (Dignum et al., 2020).

In the City of Melbourne, actor diversity, that is, bringing together researchers, policy-makers, businesses, and local communities to co-create urban nature-based innovations, was crucial for the development of the Urban Forest Strategy and the implementation of its related actions and demonstration projects. The multi-level governance structure and formal and informal social networks have greatly facilitated knowledge development, contributed to the mobilisation of agency and resources, and supported the further development and implementation of urban policies.

On the other hand, insufficient capacities to integrate diversity and bridge fragmentation lead to a lack of clarity in authorities, diffusion in responsibilities, and thereby uncoordinated actions or even non-actions, which often hampers innovation – for example in the form of project discontinuity often caused by insufficient attention given to issues of justice. Therefore, it is crucial to recognise and address the challenges of decentralised governance through, for instance, strong leadership, the clear allocation of responsibilities, and the transparent attribution of finances. At municipal level, for instance, assigning the responsibility for green space development to a specific entity may be more effective than trying to integrate it into common practice urban planning.

In practice, however, at an organisational level, this can be carried out in various ways. Linking back to a previous example, in Munich, one landscape architect (from the green space department) is assigned to each development project team (at the city planning department). This way, green space development is organisationally centralised but physically decentralised, which positively contributes to the mainstreaming of nature-based innovations. While these kinds of arrangements are crucial in overcoming challenges associated with fragmentation across scales and between sectors, they also require strategic thinking and a high level of collaboration.

(5) **Collaboration** is closely connected with governance structures; however, due to its fluid nature, the multiplicity of actors and practices potentially involved, and its centrality as a key element of system functions, it is highlighted here as a separate aspect. Collaboration around the development of nature-based innovations can take the form of professional networks and partnerships among different stakeholders, as well as the engagement of citizens. The conditions and quality of collaboration strongly determine the trajectory of an innovation, which in turn influences the potential benefits for the actors involved. Public–private partnerships, science–practice platforms, urban living labs, and transdisciplinary working groups are conducive to organisational commitment, knowledge development and exchange, learning, experimentation, visioning, resource pooling, and mobilisation, thereby contributing to reflexive policy-making.

Intermediaries and network activities that keep processes transparent and continuously align to the interests, concerns, and capacities of stakeholders enhance trust-building and relational capacities, these being key conditions for successful collaborations and for urban nature-based innovations to thrive. The positive role of city networks and regional partnerships is also notable in nature-based innovations, not least because such networks can facilitate inter-municipal or city-to-city learning. In networks, cities share best practices by observing nature-based projects elsewhere, learning about their pros and cons, and potentially adopting them.

Collaboration around nature-based innovations also requires processes to engage citizens in urban nature projects (also see Chapter 8). Citizens and community groups are not only the primary beneficiaries of many nature-based innovations, but their local knowledge and related place-based factors are also a valuable resource in the planning, development, and maintenance of urban nature. In many bottom-up initiatives, such as urban gardens or nature-based innovations addressing water scarcity, citizen engagement is key to initiating and/or bringing about sustainability transformations and improving public support for municipality-led interventions. In cities with high levels of private landownership, institutional private actors, such as housing associations, developers, landowners, and investors, are also important actors to build collaborations within urban nature-based innovations.

Working together with these actors can significantly improve the development, implementation, and upscaling of urban nature and nature-based solutions. A clear benefit of Melbourne's public participation model, among others in the Urban Forest Strategy and its related policies, is enhanced inclusivity in the planning and decision-making process. A deeper engagement with local knowledge and place-based conditions has, in turn, shown increased citizen understanding of the entire city as a socioecological system, which has resulted in better-informed and thus more relevant urban policies and action plans, consequently leading to higher-impact implementation. Urban gardens in Barcelona are also illustrative examples of how partnership working enables urban experimentations, also bringing about an increased consideration of justice issues.

(6) Different forms of **learning** are also key to support capacity building for nature-based urban development. Traditional *education and training* of different stakeholders not only raises awareness of the multiple benefits of nature-based solutions, but it can also increase confidence and capacity in their implementation, while creating a feeling of ownership of the project or the piece of nature itself in the neighbourhood. *Research, evaluation, and monitoring* can further refine and improve different aspects of nature-based innovations to ensure the sustained delivery of benefits. What is relevant to research, evaluate, and monitor, however, is greatly context-specific and can range from the assessment of ecosystem services to socioeconomic conditions and governance dynamics. The absence of evaluation strategies, for instance, is often an indicator for weak stakeholder commitment.

Despite the recognised support of evaluations in urban policy-making, many nature-based innovations, especially radical ones, are not monitored and very little data exist on how diverse local actors are involved in the evaluation process (Dignum et al., 2020). The disengagement of local communities – as the main beneficiaries of nature-based innovations – seems a particularly important missed opportunity here (Dignum et al., 2020). Their participation in evaluations could not only deepen commitment, but also allow for feedback on the suitability of the applied solution with the local needs (Heiskanen et al., 2015). *Experimentation*, both as practice-based learning-by-doing and as a means to govern transformation in cities, is an important approach to test local-level projects and processes as a response to different perceptions, current challenges, and future uncertainties. It is often called localised learning because it relies on the development of formal and informal local networks and institutions, and as such, focuses on place-bound needs, challenges, and possibilities as well as the desirability of innovation in these contexts.

While capacity building and the evaluation of urban nature projects can lead to stakeholders' increased understanding of, for instance, the multiple benefits of nature-based innovations, experimentation can bring about new approaches to the governance of urban nature, often intertwined with social learning. In this multi-actor environment, values and identities are often questioned and redefined, and new ideas and methods enter the discussion space, providing an opportunity for innovations to emerge, to be tested, or refined. These are especially crucial aspects when it comes to the governance of common resources. The Mexico City Water Fund (2015) has emerged in a partnership of non-governmental, governmental, and business actors to address a common need for water security by channelling investment from associated organisations towards projects that meet collectively agreed priorities. This has been the first water security project in Latin America that aimed at addressing environmental, economic, social, and political challenges at the same time. The Water Fund carries multiple aspects of learning.

On the one hand, the Water Fund plays an important intermediary role as a trusted, transparent, and well-defined entity providing a space for rethinking basic assumptions about water and for framing the problems and the solutions in new ways, in a public discourse where water has historically been priced low – with high subsidies – and considered as a public good that cannot be assigned a monetary value. On the other hand, the Water Fund provides a new mechanism, a business model that traces and calculates the full costs of different pathways for water provision, which helps decision-makers to find ways for more accurate water pricing. It also offers a new perspective to big water users (such as utility companies and industries) on their investments, and to water utilities on how to see their role not only as constructors of infrastructure but also providers and protectors of water sources. To be able to ensure an effective and just mechanism, novel modelling methodologies have been developed. To show that specific interventions are having impactful outcomes, the selected projects, and more specifically their ecological and economic qualities, are monitored.

(7) The presence and adequate use of different **resources** such as knowledge, human capital, financial factors, and technologies strongly shape innovation pathways. In the context of learning, we have already discussed the importance of *knowledge development* in different areas. For instance, not only technical, but also local ecological, climatological, and sociocultural knowledge – and often the interaction of these – is needed to develop, implement, and properly maintain different types of urban nature. Distributional and qualitative data on current blue and green structures and their forms of governance can further inform and enhance urban nature-based innovations. Beyond knowledge, human capital or so-called *soft skills* are equally important in the implementation of nature-based innovations, including networking, negotiation skills, conflict handling, and confidence building.

Access to *financing*, the diversity of sources, and sound financial planning are often perceived as key enablers of successful nature-based interventions. While how nature-based innovations are financed today is still dominated by institutionalised spending, grant programmes, and subsidies, there are some promising business models emerging on the horizon. These typically engage with multiple actors, most importantly including the business sector, with the intention to capture values that different stakeholders see in the proposed nature-based innovations. New governance structures, such as trusts and partnerships – or the water and forest funds discussed above – help to leverage funding from new sources which may include community and private resources, for instance through crowdfunding and donations. Notwithstanding this diversity of potential options, financing still originates from specific spatial scales. Nature-based innovations are mostly funded from local government budgets; this is especially the case in innovative city environments as opposed to less innovative environments, where there appear to be fewer nature-focused funding opportunities (Dignum et al., 2020).

Finally, the availability of *technologies* is another key condition for some types of nature-based innovations to emerge. For instance, in the case of green rooftops, high transaction costs (such as lack of knowledge and experience), high upfront costs, and non-available substrate technologies have limited the uptake and mainstreaming of green roofs in the City of Melbourne. On the other hand, the access to technologies can support different implementation processes, resource monitoring, or knowledge management. Such an example is the i-tree software, which supports multiple cities around the world to monitor and manage their tree stocks.

(8) Nature-based innovations tend to be specific to a place; and as urban and political geographers have shown, the different aspects of places have considerable effect on different urban processes. In this section, we discuss how various '**place-based factors**' can shape the pathways of nature-based innovations. These include but are not limited to the built environment, natural processes and resources, societal processes, and cultural frames of reference.

Urban nature and nature-based innovations are developed in close relation to the *built environment*. They are either attached to or situated between grey, green, and blue structures, which consequently affects their functionality. Returning to the example of green roofs, we have seen that their diffusion in the City of Melbourne has been partly hindered by social, financial, and technical factors, in addition to the built structure. Simply, cities with large areas of low-rise buildings are more suitable for extensive green roofs than high-rise neighbourhoods, which the City of Melbourne is characterised by. This is not only because of the harder rooftop accessibility but also because more space is occupied by building infrastructure in general.

Another good example of how built structures influence the emergence of nature-based innovations is the development of an open storm-water management system in Augustenborg ecocity (Malmö, Sweden). The proximity of the River Rise and the pre-existing 'park city' structures from the 1950s provided enough space for green space redevelopment integrating new multi-functional features complemented with blue structures, which were then connected back to the river. Furthermore, the availability of vacant spaces can also make alternative greening feasible, such as temporary and/or movable urban gardens.

Natural processes and resources also affect nature-based innovations. Local climatic conditions and soil characteristics, for instance, not only influence plant productivity, but also the urgency of human actions and response, for example in the case of heavy rainfall or extreme droughts. There is an ongoing interaction between natural processes and urban responses, as demonstrated by recently developed green plans and forest and tree strategies. Many of these explicitly build on the knowledge gathered on these natural processes; see, for example, the Urban Forest Strategy of the City of Melbourne.

Societal processes, such as urbanisation or tourism, similarly influence the availability and scope of nature in cities, while also giving rise to multiple contestations. It is important to note that these megatrends can trigger both negative and positive processes. The renaturalisation of the River Isar in Munich shows how the citizens' need for access to the river created more green space for recreational activities (positive environmental, social, and health outcomes), which in turn resulted in more littering and increased human presence, causing habitat disturbance (negative environmental outcomes). Increasing population growth and mobility may easily lead to environmental degradation, but we have to see that it could also prompt the demand for urban transformation, for example by stimulating the rethinking and revitalisation of certain neighbourhoods and providing job opportunities.

Finally, *local cultural frames of reference* can also influence nature-based innovations. These are often referred to as different norms, values, practices, or attitudes, such as consumption habits, entrepreneurial orientations, levels of trust, artistic activities, or aesthetic preferences shaped by historical and geographical processes. Local cultural frames of reference can also give rise to territorial differentiation and may create particular urban patterns in wider institutional transformations (Wolfram & Frantzeskaki, 2016).

Structural Conditions for Nature-Based Solutions

It is important to see that the conditions discussed in the previous section can both enable or constrain the mainstreaming and uptake of nature-based innovations. In this section, we focus on some of these conditions, so-called 'structural conditions', which can be conceptualised as embedded in urban infrastructural regimes (see Case Study Box 7.1 and Case Study Box 7.2). When structural conditions are static and mutually aligned, they can keep urban development locked in its current state, and thus facilitate path dependencies. In the case of nature-based innovations, this often means that pre-existing urban infrastructural regimes lead to favouring grey over green (and blue) infrastructure.

Established regimes have the tendency to hold existing sociotechnical systems in place, and as such they are typically barriers to innovative approaches, such as nature-based innovations. Conversely, unstable regimes can open a window of opportunity for innovations to emerge, which might lead to a 'regime shift'. To better understand how regimes and regime shifts shape urban nature-based innovations, and it is critical to take a deeper look into the structural conditions that constitute urban infrastructure regimes.

Physical infrastructures and technologies, the built environment, and structures supporting energy, transport, and water represent long life-span investments, and as such shape political choices and decision-making on urban development long after they have been established. These established structures are difficult to alter in favour of 'newer' or 'more sustainable' solutions. A typical example of this is how housing shortages and densification are crowding out urban nature in many European cities.

Urban infrastructure and the built environment are not only formed by physical structures, but also by the *physical geography*, the natural environment, and its ecological characteristics. Climatic conditions and natural resources, for instance, affect the growth of vegetation or water flows, which can thereby influence socio-technical developments, for example the space and extent of housing and water infrastructure and the extent and quality of urban nature being integrated into it.

The urban environment is shaped by a variety of actors; these actors are *embedded in different sectors, organisations, and networks*. The roles, responsibilities, and interactions among them, as well as the rules, routines, and power relations shaping these interactions, are key determinants of urban infrastructure regimes. Pre-existing actor networks, rules, routines, and power can create barriers to nature-based solution innovations that may require new types of collaborations, rules, routines, and power relationships. Moreover, the lack of agreed goals and alignment of time frames among different actors, as well as mistrust and contestations, can hinder the development of nature-based innovations. In city administrations, 'siloed' budgeting and fragmented responsibilities often constitute barriers to integrated decision-making about innovating with nature.

Case Study Box 7.1 River City (Winnipeg, Canada)

Winnipeg is a 'river city', yet public waterfront access and development have been limited by increasingly frequent and severe floods, erosion, loss of vegetation, and land-ownership patterns. However, over the last decade, interest in the city's riverfronts has grown significantly. The city is on a flat and very broad floodplain near the geographic centre of North America, halfway between the Atlantic and Pacific Oceans, at the confluence of the Assiniboine and Red rivers. Known as the 'Gateway to the West', Winnipeg is a transportation, logistics, and financial centre, as well as a thriving cultural, sports, and education hub of the Prairie provinces. Winnipeg is both the coldest provincial capital – the winter is 4–5 months long – and one of the sunniest cities in Canada.

Significant public and private investments were made along the confluence of the Assiniboine and Red rivers, known as 'The Forks'. Winter use of the riverfront has changed dramatically in recent years, as the frozen river was transformed into one of the world's most vibrant and innovative public spaces in winter. After decline and decades of abandonment, the revitalisation of the brownfield area was led by a development corporation, The Forks North Portage Partnership (FNPP), in the 1990s. The Forks is now regarded as the city's most vibrant zone, and one of the top public spaces in North America, welcoming more than four million visitors every year.

Case Study Box 7.1 (cont.)

To attract people and sustain commercial activities during the long winter period, FNPP began to maintain ice trails for skating and outdoor activities on the frozen river in the mid-2000s. The ice trails also provide exposure to rich urban wildlife during the winter season and connect otherwise distant neighbourhoods, thus functioning as a transportation and commuting route with a variety of access points, reducing the need for motorised traffic. The Forks is more vibrant and has more visitors during the winter than during any other season, allowing social innovators, artists, and businesses to flourish.

The Forks was essential to catalyse the innovative use of abandoned urban space and riverfronts in an entrepreneurial way, especially during the winter, thus demonstrating that even a harsh winter climate can be a success factor in a city. Due to the success of The Forks, Winnipeg started to turn its attention to the rest of the riverfront where other opportunities exist. With its innovative approach, The Forks opened up the conversation of what more could be done with the rivers, and greatly contributed to the change in quality of life during the long Winnipeg winters.

Figure 7.2 Winnipeg, Canada

Furthermore, the *cultural values* and *guiding principles* of these urban actors, such as their objectives, priorities, rationales, visions, values, and perceptions, also shape their strategies and actions in relation to sustainable city development. When these values and principles translate into norms of action, they can create a momentum for change, a sustainable transformation process, as we have seen in the case of Augustenborg ecocity in Malmö. However, they can also be barriers to sustainability, when, for example, economic efficiency or reconstruction regimes dominate urban decision-making.

Urban planning, through *policy* and *regulations*, subsidy and procurement programmes, voluntary agreements, and experimentations, aims to integrate different stakeholder interests while paving the path of urban development in the long term. However, these policies typically address existing problems engaging with currently existing technologies and approaches and therefore often reinforce the status quo, rather than support innovative approaches.

While *knowledge* and *expertise* are often linked with innovations, it is important to recognise that established knowledge bases and related technologies underpinning the functioning of regimes and decision-making might be challenging to change. In the context of nature-based innovations, a diversity of knowledge and continuous knowledge development, exchange, and dissemination are crucial conditions for breaking through dominant knowledge and technology frames.

Economic mechanisms and *user behaviour* also affect the direction of urban development. For example, recent urban sustainability discourses about economic growth and degrowth, and thereby the commodification of urban nature, have received some criticism. It will be interesting to see how this line of criticism is going to shape the uptake of nature-based innovations or the perceived demand of citizens for types of urban nature. It will also be interesting to see how the currently high public interest in sustainability issues will shape urban decision-making processes and whether it will increase the demand for more sustainable urban infrastructures, such as nature-based solutions.

Financial arrangements and the availability and types of resources are key structural conditions of urban infrastructure regimes; not only due to urban development costs, but also because financing urban structures and resources creates special bonds, so-called structural relations, among urban actors, which in turn can define the norms of their actions. In this context, austerity, subsidies, or the lack of a viable business case can determine actors' behaviour and thereby the likelihood of a regime shift. As the benefits of nature-based innovations are rarely integrated in currently used financial evaluation tools, they are often marginalised in urban development decisions.

Case Study Box 7.2 Little France Park (Edinburgh, UK)

The case of Little France Park shows how the interaction of different sociotechnical regime conditions can decelerate or deviate urban green space development. The Little France Park has been part of urban planning for over two decades and has gone through multiple challenges. One of the key barriers to development has been the conflicting visions over land use. As the city is growing, housing pressure has been making green spaces attractive sites for new developments. At the same time, green spaces act as excellent climate adaptation measures, as well as contributing to enhanced public health and increased biodiversity. The different stakeholder interests and disagreement between municipal departments in the initial phase resulted in a large amount of land having to be sold off to developers.

Case Study Box 7.2 (cont.)

Today, the area is halfway developed, but it is now re-envisioned by a public–private partnership between Edinburgh and Lothians Greenspace Trust as a pilot showcase, with the aim of delivering multiple benefits through nature, such as health and well-being, water storage, and biodiversity. Different features of the parkland, bioswales, green areas, and a green corridor have been developed with the aim to improve the health and well-being of the local community and enhance interactions between the local community and professionals working in this area. A hospital and a science park are being developed adjacent to the parkland, demonstrating a focus on green connectors which can act both as travel routes through the area and green belts connecting green spaces and habitats.

As we have seen, conflicting visions and interests over land use have been one of the critical hurdles to the parkland's development. This can partly be explained by conflicting regime values and guiding principles. According to the original development plans, the Little France Park project was to be an engineered river restoration for flood prevention, without considering the multiple benefits of nature-based innovations. This meant that green space development – along with its potential social benefits – was not the city's priority.

Stakeholder beliefs and promises about neighbourhood development further fuelled the conflict. For example, some residents believed that by expanding the neighbourhood, more schools and libraries would be developed and project developers also promised to construct new amenities. While some parts of the city administration regarded the site of Little France Park as attractive for housing development, this example shows how regime actors can influence development. Financial structures, municipal budget cuts and austerity, along with land-ownership issues further challenged the development of Little France Park.

Figure 7.3 Edinburgh, UK

OVERALL REFLECTIONS

In this chapter, we have focused on the underlying conditions and driving forces that support the development of urban nature and nature-based innovations. This is especially important as nature-based solutions are still marginalised, fragmented, and highly uneven within and between cities. By identifying conditions and socio-technical regimes that enable or hinder nature-based innovations, we can generate a better understanding of how to mainstream nature-based innovations in urban development.

As nature-based innovations are inherently place-based and ecologically and institutionally interdependent in the urban environment, it is important to look at this interconnectedness from a systems perspective. In this chapter, we have discussed an innovation system framework, defined and categorised innovations, and outlined eight factors that are relevant for understanding patterns of nature-based innovations. These include agency, discourses and visions, policy, governance structures, collaboration, learning, resources, and place-specific natural factors. The combination and intensity of these factors shape nature-based innovation pathways. Through the multiple case studies, we have also sought to demonstrate the importance of differences between urban environments and how different funding structures, policy, and public-sector institutions influence the emergence of nature-based innovations. Whereas policy visions and plans are key drivers for urban innovations, the influence of certain stakeholders, such as city networks and citizens, on innovations tends to be highly variable. Explicit mechanisms for localised learning from innovations and the involvement of citizens therein appear insufficiently developed.

Finally, to better understand nature-based innovation pathways we investigated urban infrastructure regimes that can pose potential challenges to the development, implementation, and mainstreaming of nature-based innovations, as well as generating opportunities for mainstreaming when windows of opportunities emerge. More specifically, we have discussed structural conditions constituting these urban regimes. We have illustrated how structural conditions and their interaction can influence nature-based innovation pathways. Notably, the change of course in urban development, regime shifts, or breakthroughs will require the consideration of change in the above structural conditions, with special focus on integrated governance approaches, novel financial arrangements, and the adaptation to local socioecological conditions.

KEY LEARNING EXERCISES

1. **Individual Reflection:** Choose a nature-based innovation in your neighbourhood and think about the factors that could have affected its development. In your opinion, what could have been the enabling and hindering factors of this development? Who could be the actors enabling and hindering this nature-based innovation?

2. **Peer Discussion:** Describe the potential development of the nature-based innovation in your neighbourhood to 2–4 peers and let them do the same. Collectively compare the emergence of these examples by identifying in what geographical, political, and sociotechnical contexts they have emerged and what types of sociotechnical regimes have affected (enabled or constrained) their emergence. Who were the regime actors? Which interests, visions, and resources did they hold? How did these actors influence the development of the nature-based innovations?
3. **Explore Examples:** You are a project leader at a municipal department responsible for the development of green areas in the city. You are planning for the creation of a small park with a playground and recreational activities for the residents in one of the growing city areas. The park will be created within 1–2 years. Prepare a scenario for the park development. Describe the factors that, in your view, would define the success of your scenario.

FURTHER RESOURCES

Dignum, M., Dorst, H., van Schie, M., Dassen, T. and Raven, R. (2020) Nurturing nature: exploring socio-spatial conditions for urban experimentation. *Environmental Innovation and Societal Transitions*, 34, 7–25.

Dorst, H., van der Jagt, A., Toxepeus, H., et al. (2022) What's behind the barriers? Uncovering structural conditions working against urban nature-based solutions. *Landscape and Urban Planning*, 220, 104335.

van der Jagt, A., Raven, R., Dorst, H. and Runhaar, H. (2020) Nature-based innovation systems. *Environmental Innovation and Societal Transitions*, 35, 202–216.

Part III

Navigating Pathways

To break the dominance of grey infrastructure, new approaches are needed for the development, implementation, and mainstreaming of urban nature and nature-based solutions (see Box P3.1). What are the key conditions and driving forces for urban nature and nature-based solutions to emerge as core elements in urban sustainability transitions?

Part III focuses on the politics and policy of urban nature and nature-based solutions by discussing contested issues and the role of engaging stakeholders and co-creating. It also discusses potential transformative pathways towards mainstreaming urban nature and nature-based solutions (see Box P3.2).

Politicising: This chapter introduces the politics and policy of urban nature and nature-based solutions, stemming from a diversity of flexible governance modes and novel financial arrangements with the strong involvement of local communities. It also examines how the politics and policy of urban nature and nature-based solutions are being played out in different parts of the world. This chapter aims to widen the scope and raise awareness of contested policy issues and how different communities can be excluded from decision-making and the benefits of nature in cities.

Key points:
- Highlighting some key contested issues for urban nature and nature-based solutions and the battlegrounds for urban sustainability at the intersection of nature and cities.
- Presenting innovative initiatives for nature-based solutions showcasing alternative governance and alternative finance.
- Case studies: Innovative Park Management Model (Newcastle, UK) and East-Boston rail-to-trail Greenway (Boston, USA).

Co-Creating: This chapter provides critical insights in the important role urban citizens play in urban nature and nature-based solutions. More specifically, it focuses on how citizens and communities interact with and value nature in cities, what resources they offer and need for this interaction, with what associated costs and revenues and under what conditions. This chapter presents and seeks to inspire different novel approaches of engagement and their associated benefits, which can range from local community empowerment, creation of greater senses of ownership, enhancement of urban citizenship and belonging, and decreasing social exclusion.

Key points:
- Exploring grassroots action on urban nature and nature-based solutions and when bottom-up actions meet top-down goals.
- Presenting the variety of engagement approaches related to nature in cities from design through implementation to maintenance.
- Case studies: Urban Gardens (Leipzig, Germany) and Roerplein Pocket Park (Utrecht, Netherlands).

Box P3.1 Spotlight on implementation – climate adaptation

Climate change and related impacts, including climate variability and extremes, are an increasing threat to urban development. In fact, impacts such as extreme precipitation, inland and coastal flooding, heat stress, drought, and water scarcity are increasing in both intensity and number. In this context, nature-based solutions offer an important prospect for climate change adaptation and advancing urban planning to address complex urban challenges simultaneously. They can comprehensively address climate risk in cities by: (i) reducing hazard exposure, for example through the establishment of nature protection areas or parks designed to inhibit the development of housing in risk areas, or by improving water management in the outskirts of urban areas by wetland maintenance; (ii) reducing vulnerability, for example through green roofs; and (iii) increasing response and recovery preparedness, for example through mobile planting systems during heatwaves. However, the integration of such measures for sustainable climate change adaptation in urban governance and planning is challenging as it requires changes at a local, institutional, and inter-institutional level. While systematic approaches for climate policy integration exist, in practice there is still a long way to go. Barriers are manifold. At the same time, there is an increasing number of projects to learn from.

Climate adaptation is a key driver for mainstreaming nature-based solutions in cities

Box P3.2 Exploring the pathways for nature in cities

Promising pathways for mainstreaming nature-based solutions in cities include climate change, biodiversity challenges, economic regeneration, social inclusion, and sustainable development. We find a variety of complementary pathways that can help to foster more sustainable cities for the future.

Biodiversity challenges: Nature-based solutions and urban nature can contribute to responding to biodiversity challenges through conserving nature, restoring nature, and mobilising people's ability to thrive with nature. In the meantime, urban policies and strategies that aim to address biodiversity loss also hold great potential to drive the wider application of nature-based solutions.

Climate change: Nature-based solutions and urban nature are increasingly integrated in urban development practices. They can help to effectively address the climate crisis. These natural climate solutions in cities can both reduce the impacts of climate change (adaptation) and reduce greenhouse gas emissions (mitigation).

Economic regeneration: Nature-based solutions and urban nature are able to encourage economic regeneration through improving economic vitality and providing attractive places to live and work.

Sustainable development: Nature-based solutions and urban nature can contribute to shifting direction towards sustainable development and reconnecting cities, people, and nature.

Social inclusion: Greater understanding of social inclusion is vital to decision-making about mainstreaming nature-based solutions. Social inclusion in this context means understanding how vulnerable, marginalised, and under-represented voices are included (rather than excluded) in processes and practices to expand nature-based solutions and urban nature.

Mainstreaming: Mainstreaming urban nature and nature-based solutions requires that we understand the key challenges and opportunities that are facing projects on the ground. This chapter revisits the main themes of the textbook, providing concise conclusions about the key points, arguments, and findings presented in the previous chapters and summarising the key implications for urban nature and nature-based solutions in the context of transformative pathways for sustainability. To break the dominance of grey infrastructure, new approaches are needed for the development, implementation, and mainstreaming of nature in cities.

Key points:

- Summarising and connecting the main messages of the textbook including the challenges and opportunities for urban nature and nature-based solutions from policy to practice.
- Presenting urban nature and nature-based solutions in the context of transformative pathways for sustainability.
- Case studies: Passeig de Sant Joan Green Corridor (Barcelona, Spain) and the City Forest (Sofia, Bulgaria).

8 Politicising

INTRODUCTION

In previous chapters we discussed how to enable urban nature through governance and financial arrangements, and by activating innovation pathways. In this and the following chapters we will focus on how to navigate the pathways and obstacles that may arise, by offering insights into the politics and policy of urban nature.

Nature, both as an idea and as something that we want to promote and embrace, has never been neutral. In the city, nature and nature-based initiatives aimed at sustainability bring to light a diversity of interests and conflicts around what we think urban nature should be and who should benefit from it. This also foregrounds nature's connection to other political struggles in a contemporary city, such as those

Box 8.1 Key terms and concepts used in this chapter

Ecogentrification or green gentrification: Gentrification is defined as a process of 'middle-class settlement in renovated or redeveloped properties in older, inner-city districts formerly occupied by a lower-income population' (Ley, 2009, p. 273). In this context, ecogentrification (also known as green gentrification) is an urban process through which the introduction of 'green' or sustainable features increases the attractiveness of an area along with property prices, leading to the exclusion of certain socioeconomic groups.

Greenwashing: This is the pretence of environmentally friendly behaviour of corporations or institutions, who artificially make themselves look ecologically friendly or committed; for example, by persuading the public through marketing and PR that their products, services, aims, and policies are environmentally friendly, but without any substantial change in their practices in this direction.

Multi-functionality: In contrast to mono-functional engineering solutions, multi-functionality in the context of nature-based solutions refers to the ability to simultaneously deliver more than one ecological, social, or economic function – while synergies are sought between these functions and trade-offs are intended be minimised.

Neoliberalism: An economic doctrine that prioritises self-regulating markets, broadly speaking free from political intervention, as a guiding principle for social and economic organisation.

Urban political ecology: A conceptual approach to urbanism concerned with uncovering the deeply politicised character of all socionatural processes. Urban political ecologists understand the 'metabolism' of cities as consisting of dynamic, interconnected, and co-produced. The concept of 'urban metabolism' (see Chapter 2), which underpins this approach, is described by Heynen (2014, p. 599) as 'a dynamic process by which new sociospatial formations, intertwinings of materials, and collaborative enmeshing of social nature emerge and present themselves and are explicitly created through human labor and non-human processes simultaneously'.

for greater social equality and different visions of economic development. This chapter delves into a range of contested issues and the emerging politics around nature-based solutions (see Box 8.1). It examines the battlegrounds for urban sustainability at the intersection of nature and cities, aiming to raise awareness of the contested side of urban nature.

We consider some of the negative consequences that can result from nature-based solutions and their embeddedness in the common structural inequalities of the city. Marginalised communities in particular may be excluded from the benefits of urban nature if inequalities are not sufficiently addressed in the design and implementation of nature-based solutions. Unveiling contested issues and the battlegrounds of urban sustainability points us to an open question that hinges upon the 'just right' conditions that are needed for nature-based solutions to thrive.

This chapter first opens with a discussion on the different visions of nature that are present in cities. This is followed by an examination of two particularly conflicting visions – which we discuss by pointing to the tensions between neoliberalism and the common good in 'green' urban development: the extent to which nature in the city is to be mobilised as a tool for public welfare versus as one for private profit. The second part of the chapter situates nature-based solutions in the context of three specific debates that illustrate their political and contested nature. The first of these is the extent to which the drive for multi-functionality in nature-based solutions can be a double-edged sword. The second looks at the tensions between green growth and gentrification, and the pitfalls of greening exclusionary urban change. And finally, the third considers the need to address issues of justice and equity within nature-based solutions. Through case studies, the chapter highlights enabling conditions that can drive the systemic, just, ecologically sustainable, and genuine integration of nature into urban life and policy (see Box 8.2).

Box 8.2 Cultivating urban nature – key lessons

Ensure Equity: Too often, the benefits that nature provides are unevenly distributed across urban communities.

The benefits that urban nature brings are too frequently concentrated in neighbourhoods and communities that are already thriving. Historical patterns of urban development have led those areas of cities that experience multiple forms of risk and deprivation to have limited access to nature and the benefits it provides, whereas multiple social and cultural barriers serve to exclude individuals from access to nature on the basis of their gender, age, or ethnicity. It is therefore vital that urban nature does not serve to reproduce inequalities in the city. By increasing the value of land, urban nature projects can lead to gentrification, further marginalising minority communities and creating forms of nature where access is either physically or culturally limited to those who can afford it or conform to social norms established by the majority groups. Even where urban nature projects do not exacerbate or replicate inequalities, they may do little to actively work against them – recognising past injustices and seeking purposively to intervene to readdress them will be necessary if we are to ensure equity in the city. Urban nature projects can start from a proactive engagement with equity concerns and account for their role in either addressing or embedding inequalities. Smaller, diverse forms of urban nature that are distributed across different neighbourhoods and communities can reduce the impacts of gentrification. Engaging with diverse communities in the design, implementation, and upkeep of urban nature can ensure that those forms of nature are provided in cities that are valued by the citizens who currently have limited access to urban nature. Opening up existing nature within the city to those who have historically been excluded and ensuring that majority groups give ground to others will all be needed if urban nature projects are to ensure equity over the long term.

Competing Visions of Nature-Based Solutions

What kinds of nature are to be sustained in cities, by whom, and for whose benefit? These questions are often at the heart of struggles for greater sustainability in cities. Furthermore, the very idea of urban nature or nature-based solutions can be understood in multiple and often contrasting ways. As argued by urban political ecologists Erik Swyngedouw and Nik Heynen (2003, p. 903), 'the material production of environments is necessarily impregnated by the mobilisation of particular discourses and understandings (if not ideologies) of and about nature and the environment'. These different discourses and understandings of nature lead to different priorities in, and modes of, governance of nature-based solutions, which can reinforce existing (and generate new) social and political inequalities in cities.

Nature-based solutions can create a space for different visions of the city and nature to emerge. Where they lead to contestation, new knowledge and paths towards urban living and urban governance may emerge (Sekulova et al., 2021). Urban political ecology scholars acknowledge this when they advocate for 'the recognition of radically different possible socio-environmental futures and the proliferation of new socio-environmental imaginaries' as a prerequisite to a more democratic politics of the environment in cities (Swyngedouw, 2007, p. 13).

At the heart of decision-making in the governance of nature-based solutions are questions about the needs that they serve, their costs, benefits, and effectiveness. While nature-based solutions can be argued to be valuable for the sake of nature itself (see Chapter 3), more often than not anthropocentric functions are prioritised and this has significant impacts on the kinds of nature that are permitted and promoted in cities. Thus, for example, aesthetic preferences for carefully managed green spaces that look 'neat and tidy' (for example on green roofs, in pocket parks, or in residential estates) tend to contrast with the types of nature that are required to promote biodiversity and look more 'messy and chaotic'. However, enhanced ecological knowledge and an increased awareness of threats to biodiversity can lead to changes in aesthetic preferences and political priorities. We see this in cities where communities or private developers are implementing landscaping schemes that address biodiversity needs while seeking to appeal to dominant perceptions of attractive design. Examples of this are, for instance, rewilded rivers with natural meanders or the integration of wildflower meadows with pollinator-attracting plants in urban parks, communal gardens, residential developments, or green corridors. Smaller-scale rewilding projects are also increasingly promoted by communities and activists using pocket spaces such as the perimeters of urban trees.

Inevitably, the full realisation of initiatives that in one way or another promote urban nature can further be impeded by competing land-use interests. Anthropocentric functions mostly dominate decisions over whether to implement nature-based solutions and, if so, which kind. The prioritisation of anthropocentric functions means that traditional grey solutions are often promoted or preferred over nature-based solutions due to perceptions of their greater functionality, lower costs, and/or likely economic benefits for society or private companies. Urban nature may further be moulded in specific ways to allow trade-offs between different functions, such as in the straightening of rivers or the inserting of concrete spaces into otherwise green–blue landscapes. Attempts to combine uses also often compromise the ability of nature-based solutions to deliver their full ecological potential. While potentially offering a compromise between economic and environmental aims, urban agriculture, for instance, further reduces the space available for the promotion of biodiversity.

Where nature-based solutions are seen as preferable and chosen for implementation, it is important to ask which functions, and *whose needs*, are prioritised. Defined as 'solutions', some types of nature may, for instance, be used as 'quick fixes' or to support and reinforce neoliberal growth agendas. As explained by Sekulova et al. (2021, p. 2), nature-based solutions may be 'deployed and instrumentalized to defend dominant economic representations, and especially so through the introduction of a "solutions"-oriented lens'. Decision-making around nature-based solutions frequently obscures the existence of multiple, competing, and contrasting views of nature – or socionatural representations – in the city.

At best, the unreflective implementation of nature-based solutions in the name of economic growth fails to address urban inequality and, at worst, deepens it. Sekulova et al. (2021, 2) argue 'the "natures" embedded in interventions are often redefined, reimagined, exported and rearticulated without addressing – or addressing enough – the increasingly uneven relations of power manifested in urban socio-ecological systems'. This means that they not only prioritise anthropocentric functions over the needs of 'nature', but they also risk reinforcing social injustice. In contrast, a 'just urban socio-environmental perspective', as discussed by Swyngedouw and Heynen (2003, p. 901), would require asking 'serious questions about the multiple power relations [...] through which deeply unjust socio-environmental conditions are produced and maintained'.

Context-related socioeconomic inequalities themselves also sometimes impede the implementation of nature-based solutions. Where entrenched structural problems persist and state or communal resources are limited, the needs of local residents for employment, housing, schools, social amenities, and mobility infrastructures, for instance, often clash with desires for more green space. Where publicly owned space is in short supply in cities, communal green spaces may be given up in exchange for schools and other social infrastructure, contributing in turn to the densification of cities. The deeper issues with structural inequalities and the ownership of urban space that this reflects cannot be tackled by nature-based solutions alone. Indeed, the latter may be seen as window dressing or a luxury compared with more urgent immediate needs.

Neoliberalism and the Common Good

One of the key political debates in the mobilisation of nature-based solutions is the extent to which these prioritise public profit versus public welfare. This debate is deeply shaped by two parallel trends of recent years. First, a trend within the late twentieth and early twenty-first century around the neoliberalisation of nature, whereby elements of the biophysical world are privatised, assigned prices, managed through market exchanges, and operationalised through 'light-touch' regulation with limited state intervention (Kotsila et al., 2020). Second, and more recently, a politics of austerity following economic crisis, which has been characterised by the restructuring of local states under conditions of severe budget cuts (Gray and Barford, 2018).

Further, in contexts such as formerly socialist states, economic crisis far preceded the 2008 financial crisis, leading in many cases to urban shrinkage and significant population decline (Haase et al., 2016). In many parts of the Global South, cities have meanwhile had to tackle economic instabilities related to long-term conditions of global inequality, colonialism, and dependency, reinforced by new social, environmental, political, and economic insecurities that often lead to urban population growth, which cities struggle to support economically. Conditions of precarity, economic decline, and austerity may, controversially, incentivise the use of nature-based solutions as a way of overcoming budgetary constraints in cities, enhancing the appearance of otherwise derelict spaces and/or supporting livelihoods (Estrada et al., 2020).

In order to finance and implement urban nature projects, cities have in recent years increasingly involved private stakeholders, both for-profit and non-profit, following a general trend in neoliberal urban governance to promote public–private partnerships and multi-actor coalitions (Jessop, 2002). While this has proved immensely beneficial for the realisation of many urban nature projects, the extent to which public interest is maintained in such cases, alongside a 'long-term equitable access to nature', has been called into question (Sekulova et al., 2021, p. 2). Toxopeus et al. (2020) thus argue that the involvement of private actors in 'hybrid governance' arrangements, which we discussed in Chapters 5 and 6, can help to unlock much-needed funding, enabling urban nature projects that are likely to enhance the quality of life for city residents.

Where private investors become involved or nature-based solutions are governed through public–private partnerships, accountability and transparency inevitably go through a transformation and therefore can become difficult issues. A model for accountability and transparency on nature-based solutions governed through public–private partnerships is evolving in Newcastle upon Tyne, in the UK, where a new parks management model was developed in 2016–2017 to relieve public coffers at a time of austerity (see Case Study Box 8.1). Park management tasks have since been taken over by a charity that operates via an executive team and a board of trustees, with representation of key organisations including the City Council as well as local health providers and universities. However, while the trust acts in the public interest, it is not democratically accountable in the same way that municipal officers, local government agencies, and politicians are.

The Hellenikon Metropolitan Park in Athens, a public park on the site of the former Hellenikon International Airport, likewise emerged in the context of economic crisis. To create it, the public property was privatised and sold at a low cost to

Case Study Box 8.1 Innovative Park Management Model (Newcastle, UK)

Beyond the ongoing processes of regeneration, flood risk due to changing climatic conditions, and ageing infrastructure, Newcastle is facing challenges related to governance capacity – both because of the need to join up capacities across different agencies and because of the current climate of austerity. In this context, public spending reductions and austerity have been key drivers for the development of new nature-based solutions and novel practices for maintaining the city's Victorian parks. To address austerity, Newcastle City Council (NCC) is developing a new business model to advance an old vision of urban parks as public green spaces which promote public health.

Between 2010 and 2017 the city's budget for parks was cut by 90 per cent. In 2017, the city ran a public consultation on the proposed transfer of operations, delivery, and maintenance of parks and allotments from the City Council to a new charitable trust. The proposed business plan stipulates that the land remains owned by the City Council, while the trust should generate new and diverse revenue streams through the sale of multi-functional services, commercial activities, and the engagement of citizens as volunteers for the maintenance of the green zones. In light of budget cuts, continuing to maintain parks as a public service was not considered an option within the proposed business plan. Enabling an interim measure while a longer-term solution was found, the Public Health Authority recognised the health benefits of parks and provided £1 million per annum (2015–2019).

In late 2017, Newcastle City Council decided to implement the Newcastle Parks Trust and transfer care of 33 city parks and over 50 hectares of allotments to a newly formed charity for this purpose. Important savings were expected from the agreed parks management plan. However, inequalities due to the limited ability of deprived neighbourhoods to mobilise volunteers and raise funding through commercial services in their parks were not taken into consideration. Similarly, citizens' and community groups' requests that parks were funded by the city as public goods were overlooked, despite concerns that the new business model could lead to a creeping privatisation and commercialisation of the parks. This is related to civil groups' concern that the charitable trust that is proposed to run the parks may not be democratically accountable.

Yet, for the local authority, the financial performance of the proposed business model was the primary criterion for evaluating success or failure. The emphasis on making parks a venue for quick returns has clearly compromised social and ecological benefits. In this sense, prioritising certain benefits and services these parks can offer is a function of whose visions, needs, and voices are included in the negotiations prior to and during the implementation of nature-based solutions. Although Newcastle's park management model is based on a charitable trust that seemingly functions as a social enterprise, it still acts outside democratic accountability. As with many other nature-based solutions across the world, public–private partnerships or hybrid governance models often compromise ecological or social goals over economic priorities.

Case Study Box 8.1 (cont.)

Figure 8.1 Newcastle, UK

international investors and developers. The benefits of this privatisation for the public are questionable (Kiss et al., 2019). A development such as this could be seen as a form of greenwashing: future housing developments connected to the park may seem sustainable although they may in fact lead to a loss of habitat and biodiversity. Greenwashing is a particularly pernicious problem for urban nature projects. Without the application of adequate monitoring and evaluation systems, it can lead to less credibility in the implementation of nature-based solutions.

Lack of credibility can also become an issue due to different cost/benefit calculations. To attract investments, nature-based solutions may be marketed as low risk/high profit. Where this clashes with how private investors estimate costs and potential profits, the uptake is likely to be limited. Costs of and responsibilities for maintenance are key to the long-term success of urban nature projects but may be underestimated or overlooked at the planning stage. In as far as private developers and land managers consider these long-term costs and see them as a significant risk to the development, it erodes their willingness to invest. This was observed in the case of Melbourne's Urban Forest Strategy, where divergent cost estimates for installation and maintenance limited the uptake by developers and land managers, who were hesitant to risk cost overruns. In Malmö's BiodiverCity project, similar concerns about the cost of nature-based solutions arose due to uncertainties over the responsibility or budgets assigned to any party for maintenance.

It is further questionable whether privately funded, owned, or co-sponsored nature-based solutions can serve social and environmental justice interests. Lack of affordability and a design that appears exclusionary can mean that the amenities and benefits of such urban nature projects do not reach people with lower incomes, and profit-oriented investors may be averse to, for instance, mixed developments that include social housing for fear of reduced market returns. If social housing is included, inequalities may still arise due to locational differences and profit calculations.

Multi-Functionality and Nature-Based Solutions

Multi-functionality is one of the key features of nature-based solutions, but it is also the root cause of many of their contradictions. When looking at the conceptualisation and implementation, the planning and performance, or the expectations and outcomes of nature-based solutions, inconsistencies tend to arise. How can a single project fulfil multiple promises and deliver ecological, social, and economic benefits at the same time? In fact, it often cannot; and the result is compromised functions, negotiated benefits, and spatial and temporal trade-offs.

Urban planning is a highly politicised process, and thus the means through which different performance criteria for nature-based solutions are prioritised, trade-offs in benefits negotiated, and where nature-based solutions get located are affected by many political factors. Political priorities, city budgets, the costs and financial management of nature-based solutions, and the potential consideration of community interests are just a few of these. And even if nature-based solutions seek to be promoted on the basis of multi-functionality or co-benefits, they are often implemented opportunistically, based on one preferred criterion. In the City of New York, for instance, siting decisions for green infrastructure are primarily driven by either stormwater management or green space accessibility (Meerow, 2020). Depending on planning decisions, one is planned at the cost of the other, implying that related co-benefits might also be compromised.

In the entrenchment of grey infrastructure, it is also questionable whether urban nature can provide 'enough' ecosystem services (air quality, noise reduction, temperature regulation, carbon storage). It is uncertain whether nature-based solutions can be regarded as the most sustainable solution to address certain urban challenges, if current urban lifestyles, along with consumption and production patterns (that is, car usage, industrial pollution) remain the same. Many European city governments face the politics of struggle between different needs and demands that can compromise short-term and long-term sustainability. They need to compromise between density and greening – providing housing to a growing urban population today versus creating green space-based recreational opportunities for long-term well-being.

How should more green infrastructure be introduced into a city that is planned around car-dominated infrastructure and trees – which are typically regarded as obstacles rather than part of a solution – to tackle environmental and social challenges? Are green-field developments necessary and on what compromises? New eco-districts, for instance, tend to exhibit promising sustainability and climate change adaptation outcomes, but their promoters 'forget' to account for the biodiverse ecosystems that are to be replaced. The list goes on. Without integrated approaches in urban planning and governance that are built upon sustainability principles that have been inclusive and negotiated, individual efforts of nature-based solutions might remain marginal.

The viability of multi-functionality pledges from nature-based solutions requires a more transparent decision-making process supported by public scrutiny and evidence-based evaluations, especially of the short- and long-term impacts across social, environmental, and economic aspects. Considering social impacts in urban policy-making, for instance, could prevent gentrification processes and the potential displacement of socially vulnerable communities when new green infrastructure developments are planned. It is therefore important to remain critical of how to capture the full benefits and potential of nature-based solutions.

Green Growth and Gentrification

Recent research in European and North American cities has identified that 'green' cities tend to have higher costs of living than their 'non-green' counterparts. This trend, for example, finds a tangible expression through positive associations between green rhetoric and lower affordability (Garcia-Lamarca et al., 2021). As put by Sekulova and colleagues, 'the caveat of nature-centered projects is that the associated economic benefits seem to mostly accrue to a few more privileged classes and groups, or those able to capture new green rents from both the greening of their neighbourhood and new land redevelopment projects' (Sekulova et al., 2021, p. 3; Shokry et al., 2020).

Residents and social movements are often worried about the negative consequences of nature-based solutions. As suggested, nature-based solutions offer a multiplicity of social and environmental benefits, but they can also cause or accelerate gentrification – for example, by bringing tourism and real estate speculation, as in cities such as Barcelona, Boston (see Case Study Box 8.2), and Dublin (Kiss et al., 2019). In the long term, the benefits of green improvements could be counteracted by the negative long-term effects of gentrification, including a loss of longstanding social networks and an erosion in the sense of belonging experienced by long-standing residents.

Nature-based solutions have the potential to transform economic and real estate dynamics of cities in a multiplicity of ways, many of which are still unknown. Research has pointed to the extent to which nature-based solutions can often be enrolled within narratives and practices of 'exclusivity', whereby the full benefits of nature-based solutions are not equally shared by all. In Montpellier's Parc Marianne eco-district, for example, where the 30 per cent of social housing has been located outside the district itself, proximity to urban nature is directly related to income levels.

Case Study Box 8.2 East-Boston Rail-to-Trail Greenway (Boston, USA)

Boston is undergoing rapid population growth and economic transformation, while struggling to address water pollution and climate change. The newly adopted climate plan addresses these two key sustainability challenges. Bottom-up initiatives, such as the East-Boston Greenway, intend to tackle deeper societal challenges such as social inequalities through green space provision and accessibility. Boston is one of the oldest cities in the United States, located on the northern Atlantic coast. While constituting a significant intellectual, economic, and political role in the region, the city is deeply segregated by income and race, and is also grappling with growing economic and racial inequality.

More than half of East Boston's residents have a Hispanic background and racial wealth disparities are high, although the neighbourhood is experiencing acute gentrification and displacement. Converting the long-abandoned Consolidated Rail Corporation (Conrail) track into a linear park and multi-use pathway has been a promising initiative to tackle some of the social challenges the city is facing. Historically, East Boston has less parkland per resident than elsewhere in the city, and its parks are mostly on the periphery of the neighbourhood, where the waterfront is located.

After Conrail abandoned the tracks in the 1950s, they became a dumping ground for old cars and other trash, threatening public health in the area. In the 1980s, a discussion organically emerged to convert this 'eyesore' into something that would add to the community in terms of beauty and recreation. In 2007, these ideas turned into action, with the aim to create a 5.3 km pathway through different areas of East Boston along with

Figure 8.2 Boston, USA

Case Study Box 8.2 (cont.)

more than 4.8 hectares of green open space. Thanks to community activists this greenway intends to connect local residents of a historically segregated, working-class, multi-racial area to transportation, to the waterfront, and to other neighbourhoods, while offering a safe backyard for young children to ride their bikes and play.

The Greenway is also integrated into a larger plan for green climate resilience infrastructure in Boston. While both bottom-up and top-down efforts have been made to address sustainability issues in the area, the equitability and viability of greening, however, is questionable. Newer developments actually block access to green space without new access points being created. It brings up the issue of how nature-based solutions that are funded, owned, or partly supported by private institutions can serve the public interest and social welfare, and thus how to avoid eco-gentrification and social and racial injustice.

In Tianjin's Ecocity there are concerns about an increase in house prices and an associated reduction of affordable housing. The extent to which nature-based solutions are tied to practices of urban exclusivity can be seen in their deployment in real estate packages (for example green roofs in expensive residential or commercial urban developments) or through an economic 'free ride' where high-end housing or hotel developments benefit from adjacent natural assets – a move that is increasingly being challenged by residents and environmental justice groups (Sekulova et al., 2021).

Understanding how different urban nature projects interact with the more traditional funding schemes and economic flows of cities might shed light on both their viability and the extent to which particular nature-based solutions might lead to exclusionary forms of urban growth. For example, take large-scale rewilding and naturalisation activities at urban district scale versus green features at building scale commonly included as part of real estate packages. The latter are often an important marketing tool within urban development strategies acting as primary motors for economic growth. In contrast, the former have been identified as potentially leading to economic slowdown, with little quantitative evidence for these types of nature-based solutions directly contributing to job creation, business start-ups, and growth in general. '. . . financial markets are unable to provide a return on large-scale investment in urban greening without tying it to a form of real estate development or commercial retail industry . . . it is easier to make profit on grey developments with green aesthetics than on mass rewilding across all poor suburbs' (Sekulova et al., 2021, p. 3).

Greening, Equity, and Justice

An emerging agenda around urban nature 'has sought to ask whether and how the "greening" of cities may actually reinforce inequalities or lead to new forms of social exclusion' (Tozer et al., 2020, p. 1). It is increasingly clear that the social and environmental benefits of nature-based solutions are easily eroded if issues of social polarisation and socioeconomic inequality are not tackled (Sekulova et al., 2021). This points to the relevance of addressing issues of social equity and justice in the design and implementation of nature-based solutions, via, for example, inclusivity mechanisms ingrained in their governance. Studies suggest that the use of participatory methods alongside a purposeful effort to direct urban nature projects towards green-deprived neighbourhoods, or socioeconomically vulnerable groups through the deployment of participatory methods, can be an effective way to address issues of urban environmental justice.

Social justice is a particularly relevant topic in gentrification-prone areas such as waterfronts where, given the high demand for waterfront locations, redevelopment processes are associated with commercial and business space as well as high-end residential developments. In Boston, for instance, regulations on social housing and rents have resulted in a waterfront that reflects social and racial inequalities. The population in the Seaport District is only 3 per cent black and 89 per cent white, with a median household income of nearly $133,000, the highest in Boston. A contrasting example is presented by the Isar Plan in Munich, a multi-stakeholder river restoration plan financed by the Munich municipality and the region of Bavaria, and executed between 2000 and 2012. Here, following the values of biodiversity and civic engagement, the resulting waterfront delivered an accessible amenity for many residents. But even here the price of nearby housing is increasing.

In the case of nature-based solutions, successful inclusivity means addressing other aspects as well as the visual and often evident issues of social exclusion associated with green urban spaces, for example the lack of or differential accessibility to nature (as discussed in the previous subsection). When planning for urban nature, justice is to be thought 'in deeper and broader ways', considering also 'the deeply-nested structural divisions that create or lead to particular exclusionary practices and the production of uneven social landscapes in the first place' (Sekulova et al., 2021, p. 3). In Sofia and Cape Town, for example, Tozer and colleagues have examined to what extent nature-based solutions have managed, in the respective contexts of post-socialist and post-apartheid transitions, to address deeply seated environmental, social, and racial privileges (Tozer et al., 2020). Their research shows that justice issues around urban nature are not limited to access and distribution (of, for example, green spaces). It requires looking at the range of social, relations involved, such as potential inequalities in how people connect to and value nature, as well as differences in the needs and sociocultural preferences in relation to nature.

Therefore, 'inclusive nature-based solution governance in transition cities needs to ensure that governance processes support more equitable distribution as more diverse perspectives on which kinds of socio-nature are seen to have value and for whom, in diverse urban contexts' (Tozer et al., 2020, p. 9). Similarly, Kotsila et al. (2021) evaluate the justice potentials of urban gardens, focusing on the extent to which practices of social care and support are key determinants for the transformative possibilities of urban nature. Care work, as an undervalued form of reproductive labour that is based on nurturing and emotional support, stands in tension with the valued productive work typical for the capitalist mode of production – a tension that finds an expression in a differential allocation of time commitments towards production and reproduction. In a study of eight municipally supported community gardens across Athens, Dublin, Leipzig, and Barcelona, Kotsila et al. (2021) found that care and support, albeit threatened by the fast temporalities of easily quantifiable benefits such as garden productivity, are key mechanisms behind the sustenance and just distribution of urban nature benefits.

OVERALL REFLECTIONS

In this chapter we argue that the ways in which the benefits of urban nature are distributed depends strongly on how competing visions of nature are reconciled in the governance and finance of nature-based solutions. A single project on nature-based solutions often cannot fulfil the multiple promises of increased urban nature in cities. Instead, multiple projects and initiatives are needed to deliver ecological, social, and economic benefits at the same time, and this involves negotiated benefits as well as spatial and temporal trade-offs.

Anthropocentric functions tend to be prioritised in urban planning. As a consequence, grey solutions may be given preference over nature-based solutions, or the latter are constructed in the ways that compromise their ecological and/or social value. Therefore, social engagement and considering social impacts in urban policy are crucial to prevent displacement, exclusivity, and gentrification in the planning process of new green infrastructure developments.

Neoliberal governance regimes increasingly involve private investors in the development and funding of urban nature projects. The expertise and resources that these actors bring to the table are often welcome but divergent priorities and cost/risk calculations can lead to reduced public benefits, communal resources becoming private property, a deepening of social inequalities, and a loss of democratic accountability and transparency.

When poorly planned, nature-based solutions might reinforce inequalities or generate forms of social exclusion. Advancing nature-based solutions that work socially requires prioritising issues of socioeconomic inequality. This can be achieved via explicit commitments towards social values and a reduction in social polarisation, alongside extensive participatory mechanisms for the planning and implementation of nature-based solutions in cities.

KEY LEARNING EXERCISES

1. **Individual Reflection:** Select and visit a nature-based solution in a city that is familiar to you. Draw a transect – that is, a map that shows which functions different spaces in and around this nature-based solution serve. For example, mark residential and commercial areas, spaces for leisure activities, storm-water management systems, and any other elements that you consider deliver

a particular function. Supplement the transect with annotations by adding your observations to the map in comment boxes. Note down any potential clashes in interests or questions that may arise concerning competing visions of urban space and urban nature that may be influencing the development of the nature-based solution.

2. **Peer Discussion:** In a group of 2–3 search for local media reports and any other relevant sources of information to find answers to your questions about competing visions and interests, and how/whether these have been reconciled in the project in question. Who benefits the most? Which interests are marginalised and why? How have these questions been addressed in the governance of this project?
3. **Explore Examples:** Search for 2–3 other examples of urban nature developments in any other city where the interests of local residents and representatives of the different interest groups (for example local government, commercial, or non-governmental actors) have clashed. What are their perspectives, interests, and needs? What would you propose to improve the dialogue and reach a consensus?

FURTHER RESOURCES

Haase, D., Kabisch, S., Haase, A., et al. (2017) Greening cities – to be socially inclusive? About the alleged paradox of society and ecology in cities. *Habitat International*, 64, 41–48.

Sekulova, F., Anguelovski, I., Kiss, B., et al. (2021) The governance of nature-based solutions in the city at the intersection of justice and equity. *Cities*, 112.

Toxopeus, H, Kotsila, P., Conde, M., et al. (2020) How 'just' is hybrid governance of urban nature-based solutions? *Cities*, 105.

9 Co-Creating

INTRODUCTION

Cities are characterised by a paradox: as compact spaces that bring high numbers of diverse people together, they are also often marked by deep inequalities and social divisions. As discussed in the previous chapter, this results in contestations and includes highly uneven access to urban nature as well as unequally distributed environmental risks. However, as we will show in this chapter, urban nature can also be co-created by and with city residents, thus becoming a rich source for engaging with and shaping our cities in more inclusive ways.

Co-creation extends beyond formal governance. It includes hands-on engagement in bottom-up initiatives such as community gardens, tree planting/maintenance schemes, stewardship for communal green spaces, and/or small-scale greening projects (for example, tactical urbanism). It also includes political activism through raising awareness, lobbying and/or protesting for greater environmental justice, socioecological equality, and (urban) sustainability. As such, co-creating cities and urban nature can be considered from both instrumental as well as normative perspectives. This chapter focuses on co-creating cities and urban nature with citizens as a key condition for achieving greater social justice, reflecting diverse needs and interests, and achieving stronger accountability.

Municipalities, environmental NGOs, and urban developers increasingly recognise the benefits of citizen participation in the co-creation of cities and urban nature. They have, in many global contexts, developed governance processes that aim at greater collaboration with, and more active participation of, citizens in urban planning and development. Citizens are increasingly considered as experts in their own right and as stakeholders who have a right to be consulted on issues that concern them and who can make valuable contributions to addressing these issues. A raft of new governance methods has been developed to improve opportunities for citizen participation in planning processes, including those involving urban nature.

How and why citizens become involved in the co-creation of cities and urban nature has much to do with questions of justice (see Box 9.1). This chapter therefore starts with a discussion of the three key forms of justice (*procedural*, *recognitional*, and *distributional*) that are addressed by and constitute reasons for enhanced citizen participation. Building on this discussion of justice, this chapter then outlines different forms of participation that have been applied in the design and implementation of nature-based solutions (see Box 9.2). Challenges and obstacles are discussed before concluding with suggestions for how to tackle them.

Box 9.1 Key terms and concepts used in this chapter

Citizen participation: Is a process through which individuals actively take part in the making of decisions about issues that affect them. Included in the definition of 'a citizen' are not only those with formally recognised citizen statuses, but often also those who, independent of their formal status, have a stake in the decisions taken, for instance by virtue of their current residence.

Co-creation: The shared generation of ideas, visions, and innovations. It requires the involvement of actors who bring different interests, perspectives, and expertise to the table. These actors usually represent different stakeholder or status groups.

Distributional justice: Addresses the question of how access to (green, nature-based) amenities is distributed in society (assessing availability, accessibility, attractiveness,

Box 9.1 (cont.)

and other aspects), but also how the costs and benefits accruing from these amenities are distributed among the population.

Justice: Is a normative concept that is closely tied to moral understandings of what is fair and 'deserved'. It describes both a process and an outcome. Scholars in the field of environmental justice mostly use the concept to describe actions and processes that are aimed at alleviating inequalities in the distribution of environmental harms, risks, benefits, and provisions. Concerning co-creation and citizen participation, three aspects of justice are relevant: distributional, procedural, and recognition.

Procedural justice: Concerns the level and form of civil participation in decision-making around urban nature interventions. Interrogating procedural justice in nature-based solutions involves asking questions about the extent to which the planning, design, implementation, and evaluation of urban nature projects is open to input by citizens, who is represented (or not) in these participatory processes, and how much these processes influence decision-making.

Recognitional justice: In urban nature governance, this refers to the recognition of different needs, values, and preferences that depend on people's (intersectional) identities and characteristics, such as gender, race, age, and ethnicity.

Box 9.2 Cultivating urban nature – key lessons

Embrace Diversity: There is no one-size-fits-all nature-based solution – beauty is in the eye of the beholder.

Diversity is what allows nature to thrive. Urban nature initiatives that embrace diverse knowledge, values, beliefs, and contributions are able to foster both ecological and social diversity. Embracing diversity means allowing different voices and views to be heard, and this may involve creating room for challenging accepted ways of knowing nature and established practices. Learning from diverse experiences across multiple communities and different places can provide a powerful means for recognising the value that nature can bring to the city. Rather than seeking consensus, it may be more fruitful to allow diverse and competing ideas about what nature should be and who should decide to co-exist in the urban landscape. Rather than allowing the domination of one form of nature over others, cities can provide fertile grounds for contested and conflicting forms of what kinds of nature are considered valuable, beautiful, or necessary. Establishing this diversity will mean empowering those whose voices are not often heard. While creating space for voluntarism and stewardship can be a way to give expression to diverse views, these approaches can often remain confined to those who can afford to provide their time and expertise without compensation. Embracing diversity requires recognising that communities and individuals who are not able to participate in this way still have legitimate concerns and desires for nature and that they need to be empowered and resourced to enable their voices, experience, and values to be engaged.

Co-Creating Just Cities through Citizen Participation

Justice concerns are central to co-creation and citizen participation in urban greening (cf. Agyeman et al., 2003; Angelouvski et al., 2020; Kabisch et al., 2016; Toxopeus et al., 2020). In this section, we show how they relate to questions of inclusion and accountability in governance, to the problematics of representing different interests and needs, and to concerns with the uneven distribution of resources. To address these interrelated questions and concerns, it is helpful to distinguish between the three different aspects of justice, namely *procedural, recognitional*, and *distributional* justice.

Citizen participation in the co-creation of cities and urban nature holds numerous benefits for enhanced procedural, recognitional, and distributional justice. Where citizens have opportunities to become engaged in the design, implementation, and maintenance of shared urban green spaces and/or of other forms of urban nature, such as green facades and roofs, they exert a direct influence over how their city looks and feels. Becoming engaged in concrete aspects of spatial design and in the (mostly communal) effort to maintain and improve urban green spaces also means forging a hands-on experience of co-owning urban space through co-creating it. In addition to numerous other social and cultural benefits, urban nature thus holds a rich and significant potential for enhanced citizenship and urban democracy, thus contributing to *recognitional justice*.

In terms of *distributional justice*, participation in planning processes and/or concrete bottom-up projects for urban nature has been shown to support senses of inclusion and belonging in communities. Collaborative governance here allows people to experience themselves as part of something bigger: supporting others and contributing to communal life can be fulfilling for participants and enable them to form or join new social networks. For urban residents without formal citizen status and/or those marginalised through social inequalities and cultural exclusions, urban nature projects can further open a route to exercising core social, economic, and political citizenship rights as members of urban communities (Isin, 2000; Staeheli et al., 2002).

Participation in planning processes also enables social learning (Kenter et al., 2015; Raymond et al., 2014) and the acquisition of new, hands-on skills and expertise. Urban nature also often acts as a vehicle for greater inclusion in itself, as it offers opportunities otherwise foreclosed to urban residents from poorer backgrounds due to the lack of access to private green space and recreational facilities, thus contributing to *distributional justice*. Practical engagement in urban greening projects such as community gardening or park stewardship programmes has thus been shown to support participants' health and well-being, while at the same time contributing to environmental education (Schram-Bijkerk et al., 2018; Soga et al., 2017).

On a political level, the benefits of citizen co-creation extend to *procedural justice* in as much as they enhance the effectiveness and legitimacy of governance (cf. Cárdenas et al., 2021; Fisher et al., 2015; Kabisch et al., 2016). Citizen participation allows for original, context-specific ideas from community members to find their way into planning, thus enriching urban life and city landscapes. Participatory governance can be more responsive to diverse values and needs. Decisions can be better justified and communicated to the wider urban community. Becoming part of democratic decision-making is, ideally, an empowering experience that makes inclusion a lived reality and instils a sense of ownership that enables long-term stewardship and engagement. Urban nature projects in turn benefit greatly from citizen participation in their visioning, development, and maintenance. Where citizens have been involved from the start in the design and implementation of urban nature projects, greater senses of stewardship through care and long-term responsibility may emerge that make them more sustainable.

This final issue also concerns the place of nature in co-creation processes. Ecological concerns frequently motivate citizens to become involved in co-creation processes. Where this is the case, they act as advocates for urban nature. Because nature itself is not a governance 'actor' with a voice of its own in governance processes, this advocacy can be seen as one way to extend *recognitional justice* to the interests and needs of non-human cohabitants of cities. Urban nature in turn, however, also supports many justice goals, such as better access to shared resources like public green spaces, protection against environmental risks, or improved health (*distributional justice*).

Shared public green spaces such as parks, alleys, botanical gardens, tree-lined streets, green school grounds and playgrounds, community gardens, allotments, riverbank greens, or urban waterscapes provide much-needed space for social interaction and encounter, which is crucial for generating senses of community and urban citizenship. They also provide opportunities for interacting with and learning about more-than-human natures, thus potentially igniting and/or furnishing a sustained interest in ecology and nature preservation. Urban nature is not only an 'object' of citizen participation here, but also an important medium for it. In this respect, it can thus be considered as a co-creator of more inclusive, just, and cohesive cities, alongside citizens and other actors in urban governance processes.

Forms of Citizen Participation for Nature-Based Solutions

We can broadly distinguish between six forms of citizen participation, based on who the initiator is and who are the supporters or collaborators. Citizen participation can be: municipality-initiated; citizen-initiated and implemented with municipality support; NGO-initiated; citizen-initiated and implemented with NGO support; citizen-initiated and implemented with a broad coalition of collaborating partners; and citizen-initiated and maintained through collaboration between community participants.

Municipalities often include citizens in decision-making by statute and as a requirement of funding schemes (see Box 9.3). Some have dedicated departments or staff organising public information, consultation, and participation processes, which may follow legal requirements. Local NGOs and/or international and national NGOs with local agencies form part of civil society and are thus themselves

Box 9.3 Applying participatory methods in urban planning and environmental assessment

Planning departments increasingly involve diverse stakeholders in the design and evaluation of new plans, scenarios for changes in land use, and/or the development of specific projects. Such 'participatory integrated assessment' (PIA) tends to make use of selected public participation methods like focus groups, or simulation and gaming techniques to include local knowledge and additional information in the assessment processes (cf. Ridder & Pahl-Wostl, 2005; Salter et al., 2010). It seeks to bridge the gap between the requirements for expert knowledge on specialist issues on the one hand and the diversity of legitimate stakeholder interests on the other.

PIA aims to include community representatives in the selection of impact indicators, in data collection and analysis, in the communication of findings, and in the development of concrete interventions. Just like in other participatory processes, such comprehensive involvement in PIA is argued to improve the quality of decision-making by enabling tailored, context-specific assessments that are adapted to stakeholder needs, enable social learning, and enhance the legitimacy of decisions, while reflecting diverse values and allowing the examination of different possible responses to uncertainties and changes over time (Fontaine et al., 2014; Salter et al., 2010; Stern & Dietz, 2008).

However, recent reviews have pointed to several difficulties, including problems with reconciling expert assessments with stakeholder priorities and values, relaying scientific findings without compromising on reliability, weighing the needs of decision-makers for user-friendly assessment against the complexity of scientific findings, and the complicated process of combining qualitative evaluations and deliberation processes with quantitative indicator-based assessments. Raymond et al. (2014) criticise that stakeholders are often only involved in instrumental ways, that is, through the ranking of pre-given indicators, rather than fully included in the processes of co-producing knowledge and deliberation, whereas others highlight issues with democratic deficits (cf. Stern & Dietz, 2008). Entrenched interests and hierarchies can be reinforced by uneven processes that privilege experts and those seen as key stakeholders while marginalising non-experts and interest groups that face social, cultural, and economic barriers to inclusion.

The exclusive or complementary use of qualitative creative and discourse-based methods in PIA, such as focus groups, storytelling, participatory diagramming, and workbook methods, is one way in which these issues can be tackled. Such methods can be used as part of so-called Delphi and charrette processes of deliberation, which enable participants to develop an understanding of alternative views and scenarios through a step-by-step consultation process and feedback loops. A broader range of stakeholders can thus be included and wider sets of values and priorities assessed, while discursive processes also enable social learning, consensus building, and the extrapolation of non-consensual issues and views.

Participatory modelling and the application of 'reduced-form', interface-driven computer models can allow mediation between a participant and scientific knowledge. Stakeholders can be involved in the development of models or use of computer-based models and simulations in deliberation processes. Ideally, the latter are developed in response to stakeholder proposals and expert opinions, thus allowing both the opportunity of reflection of different values and scientifically informed decision-making.

Box 9.3 (cont.)

While specific applications of PIA vary in terms of the methods they use and how much interaction and co-development they allow, the following key stages are usually applied: problem definition; design of research strategy, identification of appropriate assessment tools, and/or co-development of tools and indicators; identification of required data, data availability, and data gaps; data collection/input; data analysis, modelling, visualisation, scenario development; deliberation of findings and decision-making; and decision-making and implementation.

Following Arnstein's (1969) widely adopted 'ladder of citizen participation', stakeholders representing a wide range of interest groups should ideally be involved at all stages. In practice, however, such comprehensive involvement is rarely possible and also not necessarily suitable. Therefore, for decision-makers to address potential democratic deficits, it is often best not to consider assessment tools as stand-alone mechanisms for participation but to ensure that they are fully embedded in wider deliberation processes and designed in formats that allow access to different user groups. Expert facilitators or knowledge brokers can also be employed to lower participation thresholds.

often organisational structures that have emerged from citizen activism. They may collaborate with municipalities to promote and/or implement participatory schemes, or they may act as advocates for specific interests including, for instance, citizen inclusion in decision-making. As part of this, NGOs often play a key role in public education, training, and empowerment.

Practitioners and researchers have developed a raft of methods for participation that seek to ensure the inclusion of diverse community members, the counterbalancing of hierarchies and power structures, and the implementation of deliberation processes that enable consensus building or, at minimum, compromise. Some of them are summarised in Table 9.1. A specific example is the Liberties Greening Strategy in Dublin, Ireland. To design and construct new green amenities in the city centre, the city council implemented an innovative and socially inclusive management style, comprising a variety of workshops. Organised by urban landscaping and design companies, the workshops concentrated on gathering and defining different ideas, needs, and demands from local citizen groups and residents. The communal meetings were promoted through leaflets and posters. They were held in local venues at times convenient to citizens (that is, evening hours). However, while open access to the workshops promoted inclusivity, it also caused minor tensions due to the wide-ranging expectations of diverse participants.

Another example is the Spence Neighbourhood Association in Winnipeg, Canada. This initiative was aimed at tackling systemic poverty, violence, and unhealthy lifestyles through the development of vacant green spaces for the benefit of inner-city communities. One of the more ambitious aspirations of the initiative was the creation of a socially innovative and sustainable Healing Village, planned and governed by indigenous people. The process involved community organising through neighbourhood associations, as well as the promotion of individual and

Table 9.1 Citizen participation tools and methods

Approach	Description
Future Workshop	A Future Workshop is a useful tool for tackling complex problems where many, often contradicting, views need to be reconciled. The idea is to bring together people from various backgrounds who share interest in a common issue.
Round Table	A Round Table is a meeting of formal decision-makers and other societal actors. It is a useful tool to understand the expectations, perceptions, and needs of participants and to include their knowledge in the decision-making. It can be a part of Participatory Scenario Planning.
Participatory Planning Workshop	The idea of a Participatory Planning Workshop is to bring together the expertise of citizens and planners. It is a good tool to reach the goals of a concrete, predefined question.
Citizen Panel	A Citizen Panel is a large, demographically representative group of citizens meeting regularly. It is a suitable tool to identify local priorities and assess public preferences and opinions. It is typically used by statutory agencies, particularly local authorities and their partners.
District Forum	District Forums are organisational structures. They are a suitable tool to improve the situation in a certain area of the city in the long term. They consist of citizens from parts of the city not necessarily designated by planners, but rather from the areas identified by inhabitants.
Appreciative Inquiry	Appreciative Inquiry (AI) is a useful tool to identify valuable aspects of a topic, to assess which resources a community has access to, and to see how positive aspects can be multiplied. It can be conducted through a range of methods, including one-to-one interviews and group discussions.
Public Spirit Workshop	Public Spirit Workshops can build meaningfully on an initial process of appreciative inquiry. They are a suitable tool to connect citizens based on intrinsic motivations to find solutions for complex challenges. It is a project approach that needs a longer period, from six months to up to two or three years.
District-Based Community Work	The aim of District-Based Community Work is to improve the living conditions in disadvantaged residential areas with the help of the local population. It is the working principle of professional social work and includes alliance building with a broad range of key community actors, including residents' organisations, local employers, and training agencies. Community work in the district functions as an intermediary between life in the district and public institutions.
Environmental Education	Environmental Education teaches how natural environments function and how humans can manage behaviour and ecosystems sustainably. It is a good tool to equip citizens with the knowledge needed for them to be able to act and participate in the society as agents of change. It integrates disciplines such as biology, chemistry, geography, or physics.
Advocacy Planning	Advocacy Planning is a suitable tool for long-term planning. Citizens' advocates (specialists experienced in the planning process) advise and assist them in representing their interests in committees.
Community Organising	Community Organising is a useful tool for citizens to constructively shape their own city. It is a method to build citizen organisations, for example in disadvantaged neighbourhoods. They are brought together and supported to stand up for their own interests.

collective responsibility for the developed green spaces, which included community gardens and edible parks. Close cooperation between municipality, community groups, and indigenous leaders was seen as the key factor in the successful implementation of the method and the initiative as a whole.

Nature-Based Solutions, Activism, and Participation

While so far we have focused on municipality-and/or NGO-initiated citizen participation, below we discuss bottom-up initiatives and direct actions by citizens who claim their rights to cities and to urban nature through the appropriation of urban spaces and/or through the protest actions. From smaller-scale guerrilla gardening, communal gardening, and tactical urbanism projects to larger civil society movements and/or taking one's concerns to the streets, there are numerous actions taken by citizens as members of civil society that address pressing concerns and inequalities from the bottom up, independent of municipal or NGO facilitation.

These happen in response to societal crises, which create food shortages, negative impacts on livelihoods and well-being because of environmental degradation, or social unrest. These also occur with an aim to address long-standing societal needs and structures of inequality. Frequently, such hands-on activism involves the use of marginal lands with low investment values, for example derelict brownfield sites or vacant plots. It may also involve demands for the maintenance and/or creation of communal spaces in (parts of) cities that exhibit high levels of investment and privatisation (cf. Kotsila et al., 2020; Tozer et al., 2020).

Where communities begin to cultivate marginal lands and produce food locally, improve environmental quality, and/or aesthetically enhance the area, they often invest limited private financial resources for the greater good as well as less tangible resources such as their knowledge, skills, time, and voluntary labour. This can lead to experiences of solidarity and non-marketised social relations as well as bottom-up democracy, in addition to direct benefits from the land cultivation. However, it can also have unintended negative consequences, the most severe of which include exploitation and gentrification (cf. Estrada et al., 2020; Kotsila et al., 2020; Pudup, 2008; Rosol, 2010; Staeheli et al., 2002).

Community gardening can therefore significantly enhance the attractiveness of a neighbourhood, leading to an appreciation of property values and potentially rising rents that push out less well-off residents. Activist schemes may also be exploited when neoliberal urban governments see them as an opportunity to save on public investment by substituting communal responsibilities with (under-sourced) private actions. Those who invest their time and effort voluntarily to derive benefits for their communities risk becoming exploited and/or further marginalised.

Similarly problematic, although increasingly used to bolster public coffers, are crowdfunding and municipal sponsorship schemes to invest in urban nature and other urban development programmes (cf. Topoxeus & Maas, 2018; Tozer et al., 2020). While such forms of finance allow citizens to contribute directly and immediately where political processes and changes appear too cumbersome and slow, it clearly privileges those who can pay, giving them an opportunity to shape their city without the need to negotiate and compromise with the interests of other actors. Co-creation is not always a smooth process, and there are a number of obstacles to it, which we discuss in the following section.

Obstacles to Co-Creation and Participation

Ensuring public participation in urban nature governance is not without challenges. These challenges frequently relate to the three forms of justice outlined above. Thus, citizen participation may be obstructed by hierarchical structures and unsuitable processes (*procedural justice*). It may neglect and reinforce resource issues that stem from social inequalities (*distributional justice*). Further, the diversity of interests between different citizens and community groups can be hard to reconcile (*recognitional justice*).

Ideally, participatory schemes and processes enable citizens from all social groups to contribute and different communities to be represented. Indeed, the whole point of citizen participation is to bring a greater diversity of views to the table. This inevitably means that it is necessary for public engagement to be organised in such a manner that different interests can be articulated, negotiated, and reconciled.

Risks such as exploitation, tokenism, and manipulation further need to be considered and tackled. It is widely recognised that to empower citizens, they need to see the effects of their contributions, experience the process as respectful and sincere, be sufficiently resourced and supported, and ideally be involved at all stages of a project or planning cycle. Arnstein referred to these concerns in 1969, with the 'Ladder of Participation' (see Figure 9.1), which visualises differences in the degree, depth, and effectiveness of citizen

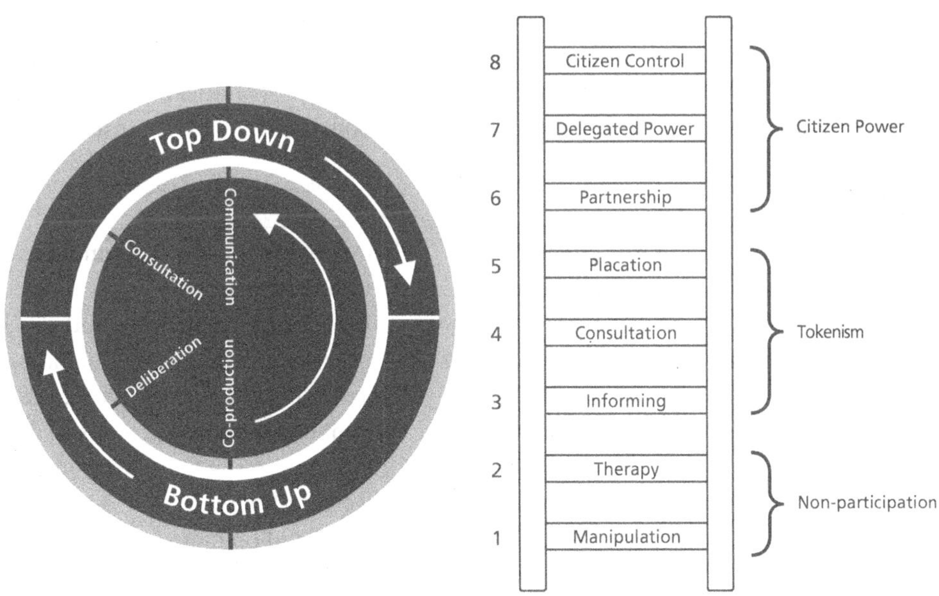

Figure 9.1 Ladder and wheel of participation

participation, moving from manipulative and tokenistic non-participation to increasingly more active forms of participation. The 'Ladder of Participation' implies a rather linear, one-directional orientation towards the highest levels of empowerment. However, what is most appropriate can differ between contexts and issues, depending for instance on project stage, goals, scope, and types and number of participants.

Authors such as Reed et al. (2018) and Davidson (1998) therefore propose the alternative metaphor of a 'wheel' of participation and empowerment, which 'promotes the appropriate level of community involvement to achieve clear objectives, without suggesting that the aim is always to climb to the top of the ladder' (Davidson 1998, p. 14). As Table 9.2 illustrates, the challenges that participatory projects and processes face include four key factors: political and legal; economic and financial; social and cognitive; and technical and procedural.

Ways of Tackling Obstacles to Participation

To reap the full benefits of citizen participation, processes and methods of engagement need to be both enabling and tailored to specific contexts and challenges. While participatory governance is a key route towards tackling the social sustainability challenges of 'inclusive and effective governance' and 'social justice, inequality and social cohesion', these goals can only be achieved if urban inequalities and the diversity of values and interests are addressed.

Table 9.2 Four challenges for participatory projects and processes

Political and legal factors	Economic and financial factors	Social and cognitive factors	Technical and procedural factors
Hierarchies between citizens, experts, and actors with powerful interests that create uneven playing fields.	Lack of funding for citizens' work and for bottom-up initiatives.	Insufficient valuation of, and support for, volunteer contributions by citizens.	Lack of expertise with citizen participation. Insufficient time given to consultation processes.
Missing or weak legal basis for including the outcomes of participatory processes in decision-making.	Lack of other resources or obstacles for accessing them, such as limited public or communal space, insufficient access to information. Dependence on predetermined funding requirements.	Unrealistic expectations of citizens' time, budgets, and other resources. Unrealistic participant expectations, e.g. concerning the weight of partial views and opinions or the timescales involved before results can be seen.	Complex bureaucratic processes and regulations, including inaccessible regulatory language. Mismatched timescales and time pressures that are tied to unrealistic expectations.

Urban nature projects can often be used to tackle such inequalities, for instance by providing public green spaces in deprived neighbourhoods or improving air quality and other environmental conditions in the worst-affected urban quarters. Without sensitivity to economic and political power differentials, however, they can just as likely become the preserve of those who are able to pay and who have the resources to make their voices heard. Unless counteracted, implementation of urban nature projects can lead to gentrification and worsening inequalities. If we aim to create 'cities for the many, not the few' (Amin et al., 2000), it is important to attend carefully to exclusions in participatory governance and to use the latter to address such exclusions and inequalities.

Below we focus on what *municipalities* and *civil society organisations* can do to advance democratic processes for the co-creation of urban nature. Municipalities are particularly important players in this arena because they often have the agency, power, and resources to make decisions about urban nature projects as well as who, when, and how people should be involved. On the other hand, civil society organisations are important in building the links between the citizens and the municipality and act as catalysers of inclusive and efficient public participation processes.

Municipalities can promote effective and democratic citizen participation in the face of the above-mentioned obstacles via two major routes: to provide tangible (for example, finance) and intangible (for example, knowledge) resources for the citizens to set up and maintain their own bottom-up initiatives; and to develop and implement participatory governance processes across the different levels of urban administration and decision-making. Governance processes and practices that are particularly suited to enhancing inclusion in and through urban nature projects are presented in Table 9.3.

Table 9.3 Municipal governance processes and practices to enhance inclusion in nature-based solutions

Processes and Practices	Measures and Activities
Providing expertise and advice, incl. on funding	Urban quarter management Citizen advice bureaus Environmental educators
Organising public consultations	Participatory scenario planning Online and postal surveys Citizen assemblies Planning forums Round tables Planning cells Visioning workshops Written commenting options (e.g. on plans, strategic visions, and proposals) Municipal offices to facilitate consultation

Table 9.3 (cont.)

Processes and Practices	Measures and Activities
Organising and contributing to communal events	Festivals Seasonal fairs/plant-sharing Information evenings Public education events Walking/cycling tours Mobile labs
Providing and (co-)funding to communal spaces and publicly owned or leased land	Community centres Urban parks and gardens with meeting spaces People's colleges Environmental education centres
Long-term engagement	Visionary long-term municipal strategies Permanent budget allocation Longitudinal evaluation processes
Providing funding	Community budgets Pump-priming funds Regular budgetary contributions Inclusion of community schemes in master plans and in larger funding applications Competitions and awards Salaries to enable community groups and associations to employ staff Financial compensation for volunteers
Providing and supporting educational resources	Training/education centres Environmental education through eco-walks and meetups Educational school packs Organising hands-on volunteering opportunities and environmental education activities

Civil society organisations are often crucial for providing the 'missing links' between municipal governments and their citizens. This is particularly important when participatory processes are not yet well-established or represent a common practice. Co-creation with the support of civil society organisations also enables a greater diversity of interests to be brought to the table and therefore, for many commentators, represent a sign of a healthy democracy. The roles of civil society organisations can range from being a 'thorn in the side' of urban administrators and policy-makers to specialist consultants, project collaborators, subcontractors, educators, facilitators, advocates, lobbyists, and more. From this wide range of possible roles, it is apparent that no recommended practices and support structures will suit all societies, purposes, and contexts. In Table 9.4, we highlight several key

Table 9.4 Mechanisms by civil society organisations to advance the co-creation of nature-based solutions

Type	Description
Advocating	Advocating for citizen groups and issues that might otherwise be excluded or marginalised due to unequal access to expertise, capital, or other resources – these groups and interests may include children, residents without formal citizenship, and other disadvantaged groups.
Lobbying	Lobbying for change on behalf of specific groups or of otherwise voiceless interests, including urban nature and biodiversity.
Mediating	Mediating between different interest groups, especially in decision-making processes.
Facilitating	Facilitating collaborations, alliance building, and setting up new networks.
Consulting	Consulting community groups and providing access to knowledge, expertise, and resources, e.g. through environmental and policy education.
Supporting	Supporting community groups with planning applications, petitions, and participation in planning consultations.
Consulting	Consulting municipalities and (co-)implementing projects.
Supporting	Supporting citizen groups with funding applications and the acquisition of financial resources, for example through crowdfunding and fund-raising events.
Recruiting	Recruiting diverse citizens for new urban nature projects and campaigns.
Representing	Representing projects in the media, at exhibitions, and through other forms of public engagement.
Demonstrating	Demonstrating the benefits of inclusion to key actors in urban nature governance

mechanisms by which NGOs and other civil society organisations can support more participatory governance for urban sustainability through urban nature.

In addition to these more formal routes to tackling some of the main challenges of citizen participation, municipalities and NGOs can do more to promote the flourishing of bottom-up initiatives through the provision of resources such as access to communal space, publicly owned land, networking opportunities, libraries, public education, and information technology. However, this requires an underlying approach to governance that is aimed at sharing the risks and unequal burdens that result from uneven socioecological and economic development more equally and redistributing resources for the common good (see Case Study Box 9.1 and Case Study Box 9.2).

OVERALL REFLECTIONS

Citizen participation is a key instrument for achieving greater environmental justice in the co-creation of urban nature. At the same time, urban nature offers opportunities to ensure greater equity and social justice. This chapter suggests that it is helpful to distinguish between the three different aspects of justice, including procedural,

Case Study Box 9.1 Urban Gardens (Leipzig, Germany)

Leipzig has recently re-established itself as a major economic and cultural centre in the eastern part of Germany. A key aspect of change has been its landscape transformation building on its semi-natural assets, such as urban woodlands, alluvial forests, municipal parks, and garden colonies, as well as a varied system of rivers, brooks, and recently reopened canals. However, some of the environmental gains made as a result of tackling industrial pollution, renaturing post-industrial landscapes, and regenerating urban green spaces are placed at risk today by increasing pressures on land and related sustainability challenges. Many of these link back to its changing socioeconomic and political fortunes over the last few decades, such as environmental legacies of industrialisation, consequences of economic recovery and population growth after decline, rising inequalities, traffic-related air pollution, predicted extreme heat, loss of natural habitats, and decreased biodiversity.

Citizen-led green space initiatives have played a key role in the city's transformation process, while shaping various municipal schemes to revitalise Leipzig's East Quarter, which is one of the city's most structurally disadvantaged yet most culturally vibrant areas. Some of these revitalisation measures include the use of vacant plots as communal gardens, such as Queerbeet and Bunte Gärten, along with a larger-scale project to build a green mobility corridor: Parkbogen Ost. These initiatives have been facilitated by municipal measures, by public investments, and by collaborations between the city, NGOs, citizen groups, local businesses, and landowners. By providing space for social interaction, these initiatives aim to stimulate social integration by offering opportunities for urban gardening, as well as supporting informal environmental learning.

The Querbeet garden in Leipzig was initiated by a small group of gardening enthusiasts in 2012 who negotiated temporary use of a vacant plot. The garden is managed through cooperation, co-creation, and democratic self-governance. Besides temporary use rights that were provided by the city, the initiative received reconstruction funding from federal, national, and EU sources (for example, Urban Reconstruction East, Social City, National Projects for Urban Construction, Improvements in Regional Economic Structures, ESF, and EFRE). The members of the garden seek an active engagement with community politics, local and global food provisioning, and environmental education and protection. The group collaborates with a local club of young people and a refugee home, providing space for garden-based interaction between local and immigrant residents.

As this example shows, urban gardens are spaces for co-creation and interaction with nature while also contributing to environmental justice. This is not only because green-deprived neighbourhoods or socioeconomically vulnerable groups participate in governing urban nature and amenities are distributed better in the city, but also because the very process of consultation can bring out new and valuable voices, views, and values. Despite the increasing social and healing role of urban gardens, they are still considered to be less prestigious and thus less durable in comparison with other types of nature in cities and, as such, often face reallocation, having an uncertain economic future, or running low on volunteer time.

Case Study Box 9.1 (cont.)

Figure 9.2 Leipzig, Germany

Case Study Box 9.2 Roerplein Pocket Park (Utrecht, Netherlands)

Population growth combined with climate change impacts are the main sustainability challenges for Utrecht. The city is rapidly growing with around 340,000 citizens, which puts pressure on urban green spaces. The city expects to grow to 400,000 inhabitants by 2030, which will mainly be achieved by infill development. Utrecht is taking a systems perspective to address the objective of creating a healthy and climate-resilient city and actively seeks integrated approaches involving civil society.

The Roerplein pocket park is created in line with this perspective in a highly paved neighbourhood with little green space. It is an example of a Neighbourhood Green Plan project, initiated by Utrecht Municipality to support local multi-functional urban nature interventions – through public funds and managed by local citizens. In this co-creation process, citizens can propose a variety of quite small-scale plans that enhance the neighbourhood and the municipality funds ideas meeting their criteria, which are mostly related to accessibility and policy congruence.

In the case of Roerplein, the municipality funded an idea by a group of local citizens to turn a paved public square of a residential area into a green square.

Case Study Box 9.2 (cont.)

Community interest in the garden grew through the involvement of a social entrepreneur who facilitated the design of a green square, using a range of communication strategies and techniques including interaction with local school children. The pocket garden has been designed and implemented through back-and-forth exchanges between citizens and the municipality with the social entrepreneur acting as a mediator.

This mediation triggered the emergence of a self-organised team of local citizens supervising and maintaining the plot, which in turn helped other goals to surface, such as improving social cohesion, attractiveness and safety of the neighbourhood, promoting biodiversity, and supporting recreation. The pocket park was implemented in 2015 and is currently maintained by citizens. Given the relatively negative attitude towards green spaces within the neighbourhood, one of the main success factors was that it was organised by the community and residents.

Figure 9.3 Utrecht, Netherlands

recognitional, and distributional justice. Furthermore, participation in planning processes also enables social learning and the acquisition of new, hands-on skills and expertise as well as creating the foundations for the implementation of nature-based solutions.

The specific forms of citizen involvement and degrees of empowerment differ between contexts and issues. They depend, for instance, on project stage, goals, scope, and types and number of participants. We can broadly distinguish between six forms of citizen participation, including municipality-initiated; citizen-initiated and implemented with municipality support; NGO-initiated; citizen-initiated and implemented with NGO support; citizen-initiated and implemented with a broad coalition of collaborating partners; and citizen-initiated and maintained through collaboration between community participants.

Public participation in urban nature governance is not without challenges. Obstacles such as political and legal factors, economic and financial factors, social and cognitive factors, technical and procedural factors, and environmental factors can significantly hamper participation and undermine justice aims. It is therefore of paramount importance that processes and methods of engagement are designed to be both enabling and tailored to specific contexts and challenges. Municipalities and civil society organisations can often take a lead to advance democratic processes for the co-creation of urban nature.

Effective and democratic citizen participation can be promoted by municipalities by providing tangible and intangible resources and through developing and implementing participatory governance processes across the different levels of urban administration and decision-making. Civil society organisations can support such governance processes by acting as a missing link between municipalities and citizens. Overall, co-creation extends beyond formal governance. It includes hands-on engagement in bottom-up initiatives and political activism too.

KEY LEARNING EXERCISES

1. **Individual Reflection:** Identify 2–3 urban nature initiatives active in your nearest city. Think and explain with examples what distributional, procedural, and recognition justice would mean in each of the initiatives that you have selected. What, in your view, could be done to make these initiatives more socially just?
2. **Peer Discussion:** In groups of 2–4 identify which mechanisms and practices municipalities and civil society organisations can adopt to support more co-creative governance processes. What are their advantages and disadvantages?
3. **Explore Examples:** Read the quotes and interview excerpt on citizen participation in urban nature projects (see Box 9.4) and answer the following questions: What are the key challenges identified by the interviewees? What could municipalities do to address these challenges?

Box 9.4 Insights from participation in nature-based solutions

'Participatory approaches are not without challenges, in tempering the input of powerful voices and interests, and in managing stakeholder expectations by clearly defining the boundaries within which input and participation is sought.' – from Melbourne.

'It is difficult to have a result in only 4 years, when the vision is to green the entire city. Building a vision and changing what is going on in people's head, how they think about greening takes time. It is successful, but a long-term project, you cannot measure the direct success of the project after so short time ... In long-term it will be a success, but now in short term, you cannot see so much impact of this project in Munich.' – from Munich.

'[Municipal] investments for the long term, no, that does not exist. They call it the project-carrousel – you always have to come up with something new to get funding. Projects that are already up and running and have proven their importance, you won't get funding for them. So we just keep on inventing events, projects, you name it.' – from Utrecht.

'It is very hard to coordinate people and make them work together [...]. The social worker chooses the participants, but she doesn't know of the everyday processes in the garden. She wouldn't know, for example, that some people cause problems or never show up. This type of project needs time to develop and social contact is very important. This is when success is starting to show, because something bigger starts to be created, beyond the physical aspect of it.' – from Athens.

'The general approach is that every once in a while, the city can initiate, can build something, can implement measures, get something off the ground, but then, the decisive issue is always whether there is local engagement, local groups, engaged citizens, who become active or stay active.' – from Leipzig.

FURTHER RESOURCES

Anguelovski, I., Brand, A. L., Connolly, J. J., et al. (2020) Expanding the boundaries of justice in urban greening scholarship: toward an emancipatory, antisubordination, intersectional, and relational approach. *Annals of the American Association of Geographers*, 110, 1743–1769.

Bulkeley, H., Edwards, G. A., and Fuller, S. (2014) Contesting climate justice in the city: examining politics and practice in urban climate change experiments. *Global Environmental Change*, 25, 31–40.

Tozer, L., Hörschelmann, K., Anguelovski, I., Bulkeley, H. and Lazova, Y. (2020) Whose city? Whose nature? Towards inclusive nature-based solution governance. *Cities*, 107.

10 Mainstreaming

INTRODUCTION

Throughout the different chapters of this textbook, we have discussed how urban nature and nature-based solutions can provide a range of ecological, social, and economic benefits. They are therefore increasingly positioned as solutions to address urban sustainability challenges. We have also shown that despite promises, mainstreaming nature in cities has been limited to date. In the previous chapters, we examined the state-of-art, the conditions, barriers, and opportunities from theory to practice, as well as governance, financing, and innovation in the context of nature-based solutions. This in turn underpins how to understand and support the work with nature in cities from different perspectives, which can lead to the mainstreaming of urban nature and nature-based solutions.

Mainstreaming urban nature relates to strategic intervention in the governance, financial, and urban development domains to enable the functioning of nature-based solutions over the long term and support their potential to deliver ecological, economic, and social benefits (see Box 10.1). To identify the pathways to mainstream urban nature, it is key to understand how urban nature and nature-based solutions can be governed (Chapter 5), how current investment and finance regimes are shaping decision-making practices in urban environments (Chapter 6), and what innovation pathways for urban nature exist (Chapter 7). To go further, we examined the politics around nature-based solutions (Chapter 8) as well as the role of community engagement and co-creation in urban nature projects (Chapter 9). Behind all of this knowledge and understanding sits conceptualising (Chapter 2), valuing (Chapter 3), and developing nature-based solutions (Chapter 4).

Mainstreaming urban nature and nature-based solutions is widely advocated; however, due to a multitude of reasons discussed in the previous chapters of this textbook, it has not been systematically implemented. Many urban stakeholders are still unsure about the actions needed to change this situation. To address this, this chapter provides a strategic approach and identifies key factors that may enable mainstreaming of urban nature and nature-based solutions. The approach builds on the frameworks developed for mainstreaming environmental policy, climate adaptation, disaster risk reduction, and other cross-cutting domains, as well as on empirical evidence.

In this chapter, we identify and discuss strategic actions on different levels that are essential for mainstreaming nature-based solutions. We also discuss enabling factors, which hold the potential to work across different domains and to address hurdles or to tap into opportunities for implementing and maintaining nature-based

Box 10.1 Key terms and concepts used in this chapter

Intermediaries: These are individuals or organisations that can move back and forth in the 'middle area' between different sectors or contexts and act as a 'go-between'. In terms of nature-based solutions, intermediaries can map the landscape of actors involved and broker relationships among actors, foster collaborations and build trust, and they can translate knowledge from diverse sources.

Mainstreaming: Strategic intervention in the governance, financial, and urban development domains to enable the functioning of urban nature innovations over the long term and support their potential to deliver ecological, economic, and social benefits.

Urban infrastructure regime: This refers to 'the stable configurations of institutions, techniques and artefacts which determine "normal" socio-technical developments in a city and thus shape general urban processes and the urban metabolism' and which operate over multiple scales (Monstadt, 2009, p. 1937).

Box 10.2 Cultivating urban nature – key lessons

Nurture Intermediaries: New relationships and trust are needed to expand urban nature.

Intermediaries, key individuals or organisations, form a valuable but often overlooked role in providing the glue that holds coalitions of actors together to realise urban nature-based solutions. Intermediaries help map the landscape of actors involved and broker relationships among actors, foster collaborations, and build trust. They can translate knowledge from diverse sources and make it relevant for locally specific conditions, in turn building capacity on the ground for the uptake of tools and knowledge generated elsewhere. Yet the presence of intermediaries is often more a matter of good fortune than intentional design of urban nature forms. More explicitly recognising the need for intermediaries and including them from the outset in the design and implementation of specific urban nature-based solutions can be one way of ensuring that the capacities needed for the success of such projects are established. Another means is through fostering new institutional arrangements or co-governance initiatives that develop and hone intermediary functions and provide a means through which to deliberate on how the costs and benefits of such projects can be shared over time. Developing and supporting intermediaries should be an urgent priority in cases in which urban nature forms are being implemented in the context of previous histories of conflicts over land use or where there has been a contestation over policy priorities among stakeholders. Intermediaries are not only able to foster trust and consensus, but they also create spaces where dissent and contestation can take place and the desired outcomes for urban nature projects can be deliberated among diverse groups.

solutions (see Box 10.2). The focus is on enabling factors along with key challenges, and opportunities related to each factor, illustrated with examples and case studies. We also touch upon how the combination of coordinated actions and conditions can lead to different mainstreaming pathways – depending on the sustainability challenges and goals in focus.

Mainstreaming Nature-Based Solutions

Mainstreaming nature-based solutions relates to strategic intervention on different levels and in different but interconnected domains of governance and policy, finance, and urban development to enable the functioning of urban nature over the long term and support their potential to deliver ecological, economic, and social benefits. In this chapter, we explore the key factors and strategic actions that can unlock the potential for mainstreaming nature-based solutions. By exploring these factors, we seek to offer pathways to overcome the barriers to mainstreaming nature-based solutions.

As we have discussed in this textbook, for urban nature to thrive and for nature-based solutions to become mainstream, they need to become a common practice and a regular element in the urban infrastructure regime (see Figure 10.1). As such

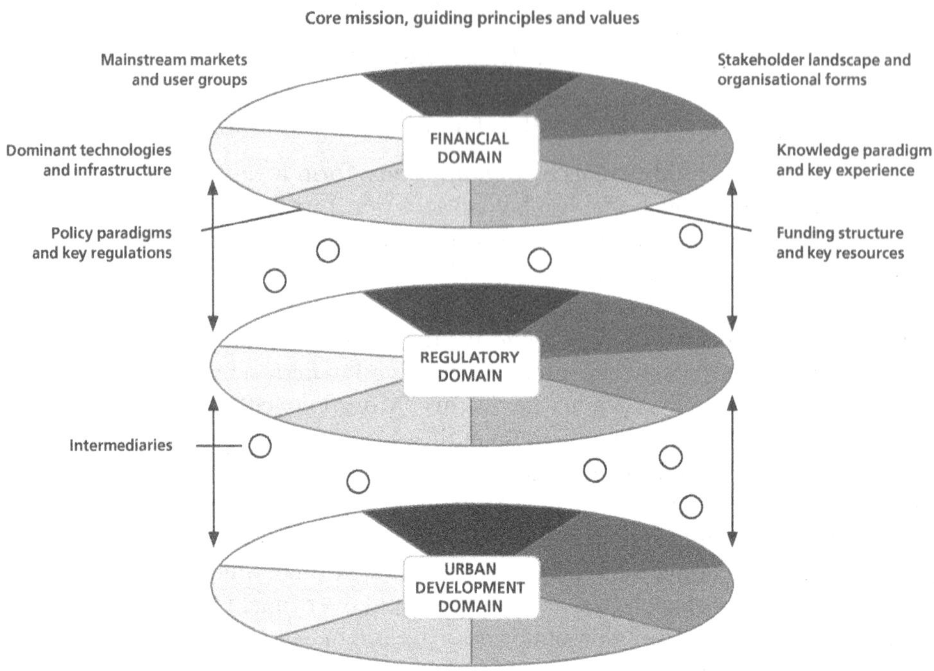

Figure 10.1 A conceptualisation of the urban infrastructure regime

regimes are also evolving and are being shaped by different domains, that is, regulations, financing, and urban development, and by how actors work with urban sustainability challenges (Dorst et al., 2021), it is especially important that the actions for nature-based solutions become coordinated across domains. This is a key to catalyse the mainstreaming of nature-based solutions.

Strategic and coordinated actions supported by enabling factors can facilitate the uptake of alternative practices and realise their potential. This may be possible, for example, by creating new actor constellations, nurturing joint capacities, uncovering and mobilising new forms of resources, transforming the perceptions of urban problems and finding innovative solutions to them. Individually, the actions on each level and each factor can generate incremental change towards the uptake of nature-based solutions. However, by aligning them with one another their impact can be larger. The actions and the enabling factors can be combined in a variety of ways which will determine the pathways for mainstreaming of nature-based solutions.

For example, to mainstream nature-based solutions for climate change mitigation and adaptation, it may be relevant to engage insurance companies and promote investments in risk reduction. At the same time, enabling factors in the form of regulations and certification schemes that promote offsetting are critical for mainstreaming nature-based solutions for biodiversity. In other words, the effectiveness of the mainstreaming pathways will depend on the types and focus of nature-based solutions, their context, and urban problems that are desired to be addressed.

Aligning strategic actions and enabling factors that seek to address only one sustainability goal can result in mainstreaming forms of urban nature that deprioritise or undermine achieving other important goals. That is why mainstreaming urban nature and nature-based solutions that can contribute to achieving several sustainability goals requires actions that mobilise multiple enabling factors. At the same time, it is important that we focus on certain sustainability challenges, such as climate change and biodiversity, so that we are explicit about the problems in focus and the suggested solutions.

Strategic Actions and Mainstreaming on Different Levels

Mainstreaming nature-based solutions needs to take place through strategic interventions at all levels from the local and operational scale to the institutional and inter-institutional levels. Only through uniting top-down and bottom-up efforts can we create a holistic and distributed governance system for achieving sustainable change. However, in practice, considerable efforts are still needed to mainstream nature-based solutions in cities. Many current approaches remain characterised by individual actions and the implementation of separate structures and mechanisms. Based on Wamsler and Pauleit (2016) and Wamsler et al. (2017), we identify six key types of strategic actions for contributing to mainstreaming nature-based solutions.

(1) Add-on mainstreaming: Implementing initiatives that are not part of the core work by the implementing actor but that can directly engage with measures related to urban nature or nature-based solutions. Pilot or demonstration projects on nature-based solutions can create shared learning and knowledge as well as show how nature-based solutions work in practice.
(2) Programmatic mainstreaming: Changing the core work of the implementing actor by including design and implementation aspects of urban nature or nature-based solutions into on-the-ground operations, projects, or programmes.
(3) Managerial mainstreaming: Changing formal and informal corporate structures, for example organisation of working units, personnel, and finance, presentation of job descriptions, to institutionalise the design and implementation of urban nature projects and nature-based solutions.
(4) Intra- and inter-organisational mainstreaming: Expanding the collaboration with other sectors, units, and actors (that is, other governmental organisations, non-governmental bodies, knowledge institutes, community actors, and individuals) to develop knowledge and understanding, build capacities, and advance collective action when working with urban nature and nature-based solutions.
(5) Regulatory mainstreaming: Changing regulations, policies, strategies, and other governance tools to support the integration of urban nature and nature-based solutions.

(6) Directed mainstreaming: Supporting mainstreaming of urban nature and nature-based solutions at a higher level, for example, by financing specific projects or promoting them in other ways, educating staff, or assigning specific roles and responsibilities to personnel working with such projects.

Enabling Factors and Mainstreaming across Different Domains

We have outlined strategic actions at different levels. Next, we will explore mainstreaming across the dominant domains of policy, governance, finance, and urban development. In practice these are very much interlinked, and we are also linking mainstreaming on different levels with the underlying and enabling factors (see Table 10.1). These enabling factors include public policy, strategic priorities, and certification schemes; partnerships, networks, and collaboration; finance, incentives, and insurance; markets, land value, and contractual agreements; and demonstration projects and data monitoring.

Table 10.1 Enabling factors for nature-based solutions

Key Factors	Key Messages
Public policy, strategic priorities, and certification schemes	Provide a public mandate Regulate for zero net loss Align with strategic priorities Promote certification schemes
Partnerships, networks, and collaboration	Create intermediaries Generate partnerships Facilitate community-based action Include in contractual agreements
Finance, economic incentives, and insurance	Provide economic incentives Engage insurance sector Stimulate institutional investment for risk reduction Incorporate in green investment products
Markets, land value, and contractual agreements	Develop markets Build co-financing arrangements Work with investment cycles Target areas of low land value
Demonstration projects, data monitoring, and valuation models	Establish demonstration projects Grow practitioner expertise Improve data and monitoring Advance valuation models

Public Policy, Strategic Priorities, and Certification Schemes

There is a need for a clear mandate at multiple levels and sectors that is also aligned across levels and sectors. Mandatory greening policies and related funding schemes are still scarce in policy agendas. There are, however, several cases showing that when policy-makers give a clear direction for the inclusion of green or nature-based features in urban development guidelines, investors and developers are more likely to opt for nature-based solutions in their projects. Greening mandates can be advocated through a variety of policy instruments and at multiple policy levels, from local and regional to national and European. That is, for instance, by setting clear requirements or detailed specifications in tenders and procurement policies or, whenever possible, designing mandatory regulations. Furthermore, integrating urban nature-based solutions criteria into existing urban development tools, such as green certification schemes for buildings and infrastructure, can also open new pathways for mainstreaming.

The Biodiversity Net Gain regulation in England, the Public Procurement Law in Spain, and the Federal Building Code in Germany present good examples of how different types of compulsory national policy instruments can stipulate the mainstreaming of urban nature. In England, it is through incentivising developers to mitigate and offset their development projects' negative environmental impact through implementing onsite or offsite biodiversity measures. In Spain, supported by the procurement law, municipalities must integrate additional sustainability criteria into their procurement processes, which in turn facilitates longer-term engagement with and higher investments from the private sector. In Germany, stipulated by the Federal Building Codes, municipal and district-level land-use plans (for example, Landscape (Master) Plan, Preparatory Land Use Plan, and Binding Land Use Plan) are powerful instruments to promote green roofs in new developments.

Hamburg, for instance, also tapped into the opportunity of other urban priorities and developed an ambitious green roof strategy as part of the climate adaptation plan – mainstreaming green roofs (a specific type of urban nature) under a different policy objective. Local governmental policies, with or without a top-down mandate, can effectively integrate nature-based solutions in urban development. The Green Space Factor, for instance, has stipulated the integration of nature into new development projects across a multitude of European cities. Swedish municipalities have used it as a planning tool to set clear and detailed requirements (that is, thresholds) for the environmental and social quality of urban greenery for developers when developing on municipally owned land.

Voluntary certification schemes, due to their sustainability focus and target-oriented nature, can provide knowledge on the value obtained from these nature-based solutions through clear indicators and monitoring tools. This in turn can encourage developers and engineers to increase the sustainability quality of constructions. It can also attract investments into these solutions, and in the long term it can provide a good base for introducing non-voluntary standards. In the

Netherlands, the UK, and Sweden, for instance, sustainability certification schemes are increasingly considered in portfolios of real estate investment.

While nature-based policy agendas are indeed favourable for delivering multiple sustainability benefits, aligning urban nature narratives with and integrating the multiple benefits of nature-based solutions into other policy goals can present an equally good opportunity for mainstreaming. By aligning the narratives and benefits of urban nature and nature-based solutions with existing priorities, such as urban and energy transition, climate change adaptation and mitigation, water supply management, circular economy, and healthy urban living, their relevance and community of practice can be widened (see Case Study Box 10.1).

Case Study Box 10.1 Passeig de Sant Joan Green Corridor (Barcelona, Spain)

Barcelona faces sustainability challenges – air pollution, noise, and heat island effect – due to intensive car traffic and limited green space in the city. In addition, biodiversity is threatened because of urbanisation, industrial development, and accelerated economic growth. As a response, in 2012, Barcelona City Council introduced the '(re)naturalisation' concept, aiming to enhance the built environment with elements that introduce, restore, or reinforce green space. The goal is to increase green space per inhabitant by one square metre by 2030.

Among key measures for urban greening, Barcelona has a policy to promote green corridors including urban gardens, green roofs, and green inner-yards in residential buildings. One of the first green corridors, which seeks to strengthen ecological and social connectivity, boost the local economy, and improve functionality and use of public spaces, is a 1.2-km-long boulevard, 'Passeig de Sant Joan'. The greening of the boulevard was performed by the Ecology, Urban Planning and Mobility Area. The project was finalised in 2015.

Passeig de Sant Joan boasts rich vegetation, broadened pavements with semi-permeable surface, and areas for children and recreation. Not least due to the dedication of the city council and targeted funding, the project has delivered multiple co-benefits for the citizens and urban biodiversity. These include noise abatement and pacification, local heat reduction due to increased shading, and an increase in biodiversity. Several sustainability solutions like vegetation with structural complexity and species that preserve and enhance biodiversity have been intentionally incorporated in the planning of Passeig de Sant Joan.

However, the project faced two sets of challenges. First, while the first part of the corridor had a variety of species, the second part did not. This was due to specific aspects of planning, implementation, and maintenance. Second, the implementation process has hardly accounted for public opinion. District authorities of Eixample coordinated the public participation process, which nevertheless resulted in a 'boulevard' design. Such design is criticised for benefiting commercial interests (that is, ground-floor businesses) instead of intensifying the use of green areas by the public to promote social interaction.

Case Study Box 10.1 (cont.)

Figure 10.2 Barcelona, Spain

In Cape Town, the Atlantis Aquifer Clearing Project by the Nature Conservancy aims to increase the water supply in the city by removing invasive plant species – which are thought to use millions of litres of water per year, much more than indigenous species – from the city's largest aquifer. While this initiative is part of the city's water supply strategy and a response to the severe drought Cape Town experienced from 2015 to 2018, it also creates jobs and acts as a training programme by employing plant-clearing teams from nearby disadvantaged communities. In addition, this pilot is part of the Water Fund for Cape Town, a public–private partnership which intends to convene various levels of government, industry representatives, and other stakeholders to find new ways to fund and coordinate wider efforts to clear invasive plant species as a water supply strategy.

While public policy agendas hold multiple opportunities for mainstreaming, they also carry some challenges. It is important to note that whereas mandatory requirements can result in positive policy outcomes, without clarity in instructions and detailed requirements they could also undermine the multi-functionality of urban nature, and can result in low-quality green spaces, for example with low biodiversity value or unsatisfactory climate adaptation or health benefits. Another key observation is that single-focus policies (for example, biodiversity) usually cannot incentivise multi-faceted actions, that is, address multiple sustainability challenges at once. In addition, without clarity and details on how to achieve high-quality accessible urban nature, such policies even risk exacerbating other sustainability issues in cities.

It is also challenging to integrate nature into the core requirements of voluntary certification schemes, which focus on circularity, energy issues, and material use. At the same time, these schemes carry considerable institutional support and extensive industry expertise, which can be critical for the mainstreaming of nature-based solutions. One of the challenges in cities is limited space, which often results in conflicting policy goals and undesired results. For example, placing carbon offsetting initiatives in urbanised areas with no or little green space may not only delay natural offsetting but also attract development of grey infrastructure, thereby exacerbating the risk of biodiversity loss. The multitude (or the lack) of specifications in building regulations poses further challenges for integrating urban nature into new developments.

As shown in our examples, the mainstreaming of nature-based solutions calls for the development of evidence (for instance, the biodiversity benefits of nature-based solutions) and synchronising policy agendas followed by strategic actions. The latter should be achieved – first, by coordinating strategic priorities in policy-making at multiple levels, and second, through intra- and inter-institutional changes, that is, by working across silos within or between government departments, and public and private sectors.

Partnerships, Networks, and Collaboration

Creating intermediary units and stipulating partnerships – both within and across public- and private-sector organisations – hold a strong potential to bridge fragmented institutional structures and create a platform for nature-based solutions – from co-design to development and maintenance. Partnerships are also critical for the support of mandatory urban greening policies and for the actions on the ground, including community-based support of local urban nature-based solutions. Intermediaries – key individuals, professional groups, or organisations – play a key role by bridging actors, departments, organisations, sectors, and disciplines and thereby facilitating their communication, collaboration, and coordination.

For example, to navigate the challenges of the fragmented building sector in the Netherlands, central contact points were created under the Building Agenda policy programme. They act as intermediaries among project developers, energy supply companies, and funders to catalyse the implementation of the projects on climate neutrality, circularity, and sustainable energy transformations, which require complex solutions and expertise from multiple domains and disciplines. Municipality-driven initiatives have also applied similar approaches to promote nature-based solutions in urban development projects. They have employed managers and established teams responsible for the integration of green infrastructure and nature-based solutions in development projects.

One such example is from Utrecht, where a project office was established inside the municipal structure to implement a sustainable closed-circuit water system. This office has its own director and councillor, who are relatively independent in their decision-making power. Intermediaries not only ease communication, facilitate collaboration, and represent the stakes of urban nature along the entire development process, but can also provide expertise while mitigating the risk of mal-implementation. Intermediaries, institutionalised roles, clarity about responsibilities, and/or formalised procedures can be effective ways of mainstreaming nature-based solutions into urban development projects. As such, installing a green roof on the top of an office building becomes less risky once the installation and maintenance are managed by one responsible actor.

Partnerships and collaboration can remedy multiple obstacles for urban sustainability, including siloed policy- and decision-making in governmental organisations, knowledge gaps in designing and implementing nature features in cities, as well as support governance and funding mechanisms. For example, the City of Melbourne (see Case Study Box 2.1) and the BiodiverCity project in Malmö (see Case Study Box 4.1) brought together representatives of academia, government, private sector, and local community to co-design nature-based solutions in experimental projects. The co-creation processes supported knowledge exchange, capacity building, and resource mobilisation, while contributing to urban policy development.

Establishing co-funding and co-governance mechanisms for working with nature in cities forms a basis for long-term partnerships while enabling mutual learning and hands-on experience. There are multiple ways to make the partnerships work. In Barcelona, for instance, the Urban Ecology Directorate is responsible for municipal sustainability policies through bridging the gap between the departments working with mobility, environment, and planning to deliver the municipal climate plan, which includes experimenting with urban greening. One of such experiments is the 'superblocks', where parts of roads and their crossings are turned into pedestrian sites with green areas, recreation spaces, bike lanes, and public transport infrastructure.

Multi-stakeholder dialogues called 'City Deals', which are sponsored by the government, have emerged both in the United Kingdom and the Netherlands as one experiment to bring together urban actors to align policy and practice – not least by identifying and reconsidering the policy barriers preventing urban nature from thriving. In the Netherlands, one such experiment is the National Roof Plan (previously Green Deal 'Green Roofs'), which is the government-funded public–private partnership to create new business models for green roofs. The partnership includes key actors including municipalities, water utility companies, firms delivering roofs, and residents. It enables mainstreaming of green roofs in the Netherlands, for example by negotiating sewage tax reduction for owners of buildings with green roofs. Apart from financial support for the green roofs, the partnership advances multi-functional green roof development based on co-created visions and collective expertise by collaborating actors. The multiple benefits delivered by these green roofs include enhanced biodiversity, cooling, water retention, and improved aesthetics.

External funding schemes, for instance through the EU funding programmes, also incentivise collaboration. As such, the EU Green Capital award supported the uptake of the green infrastructure concept in Hungary, resulting in increased collaboration among various municipal units in Budapest. Another example of a partnership that helps mainstream nature-based solutions in cities is Network of Local Governments + Biodiversity in Spain, which includes more than 300 municipalities. The platform supports the Spanish National Strategy on Green Infrastructure by contributing to knowledge and policy development on biodiversity and nature-based solutions. The network partnered with the national federation of municipalities and provinces and associations of green infrastructure companies and parks to develop the best practice guide on green infrastructure for cities.

Partnerships and collaborations extend to urban residents and communities. The engagement of locals in nature-related activities not only increases the understanding of urban nature, but can also create a sense of ownership, belonging, and empowerment. This in turn can be a firm foundation for various community-based initiatives which further support mainstreaming of nature-based solutions in cities. There are several ways to facilitate and support active citizenship and community-based actions, including co-governance and co-funding mechanisms, and enhancing environmental education. In Madrid, for instance, the Policy for Promoting Urban Gardens (2015) encourages residents to apply to develop so-called 'green zones' in public urban gardens, in this way preventing their commercialisation.

This policy and the rise of urban agriculture has become an important element of active citizenship and the social justice movement. In Utrecht, through the Neighbourhood Green Plan project, the municipality not only provides funding for bottom-up greening of neighbourhoods, but also recognises the importance of intermediaries and regular citizen involvement to successfully navigate these kinds of community initiatives. When public funding is lacking, however, locally organised funding platforms (crowdfunding, trusts, foundations, etc.) become particularly relevant. Raising awareness and providing easily accessible knowledge about the value of nature in cities can enhance community engagement in urban greening, which in turn contributes to its mainstreaming.

While intermediaries, partnerships, and community actions hold multiple opportunities for mainstreaming, they also come with challenges. On the one hand, the intermediary units have proven to be successful in taking joint action and coordinating responsibilities across siloed government departments (energy, mobility, housing, health). On the other hand, the dispersed authority that governs urban land and infrastructure and the benefits that are delivered to multiple stakeholders pose challenges to maintain urban nature in cities. In this context, generating new organisational forms and partnerships, improving citizen awareness, and supporting active citizenship are important for not only initiating and implementing nature-based solutions, but also maintaining them after their implementation. These

Box 10.3 Community actions in governance, funding, and education

Heeley Development Trust: Various ownership and management models are being implemented for green spaces, providing diverse sources for financing of nature-based solutions. These models often involve different kinds of engagement from the community. In Sheffield, UK, the Heeley Development Trust is the charity that came out of the community's work to transform the derelict space that was left after road plans had been shelved in 1996. In 1997, after it had raised the funding, the Trust took ownership of the 3.5 hectares of land through a 125-year lease from Sheffield City Council. In the past, the Trust depended on grants for its capital projects and maintenance. Recently, it has asked for voluntary subscriptions from nearby households to cover the costs. The new funding idea aims to save the derelict heritage buildings in its community. The rental fees contribute to the restoration and maintenance of heritage buildings and the remaining funding goes directly back into maintaining the Heeley People's Park. In the meantime, the Trust also provides adult education in the community and runs projects like Recycle Bikes and hosts the Heeley Festival and The Big Boulder in the park; most recently, the Trust has played a key role in keeping Meersbrook Hall in community hands.

Sea Heroes Community Garden: The Sea Heroes Community Garden was initiated by the citizens in a disadvantaged neighbourhood with no green spaces. While planning guidance – the Development Plan of Sea Heroes Quarter – identified the lack of green space in the neighbourhood, there were no plans to create new green spaces. To rectify this, the citizens collected 2500 signatures from the neighbourhood, convincing the municipality of The Hague that more green spaces were needed and to support the development of the community garden. The key goal was to create a garden in which children can play, organic fruits and vegetables can be grown, and people can enjoy recreation. Local citizens formed a board to oversee the project and coordinate their activities. The garden was designed by DGJ architects and volunteer students from the Technical University of Delft, based on ideas by the citizens and drawings from the school children. The project was financed by Stichting De Versterking, a foundation that bought the land from the housing corporation HaagWonen, various private funds (Fonds 1818, Jantje Beton, and Oranjefonds), a bank (Rabobank), the municipality of The Hague, a healthcare facility (Zorg Hotel Residence Haganum), and citizens themselves. The neighbourhood residents and volunteers of the organisation De Groene Eland maintain the garden. The creation of such green spaces supports activities and recreation, and promotes the health and well-being of citizens, which is particularly important for the elderly.

processes are not easy and require learning among key actors: from understanding and working through existing power relationships to reaching out to the most affected ones.

Finance, Economic Incentives, and Insurance

Public–private partnerships that build on co-financing arrangements, engage the insurance sector, stimulate investments, and provide economic incentives aligned with strategic interests hold a strong potential to bridge the knowledge gap on the benefits of nature-based solutions, mobilise finance for their implementation, and catalyse communication and understanding among urban actors.

In terms of risk reduction, it is important to involve insurance companies in the mainstreaming of nature-based solutions in cities based on from their risk reduction potential and avoidance of damage costs. For example, ClimateWise is a voluntary initiative in the UK with a global membership across the insurance industry, which is involved in a Resilient Cities project focused on how insurance companies can use investments to strengthen urban resilience. The members of ClimateWise identify climate risks and opportunities using a reporting framework.

Investments in urban nature-based projects depend on their climate risk reduction potential (both for climate adaptation and mitigation), and to realise this potential specific data need to be collected and models created. For example, climate change mitigation has been a rising priority in Sweden due to recent heavy rainfalls and heatwaves, and this has increased the focus on climate change adaptation. In Sweden, both municipalities and funding agencies are becoming increasingly concerned about climate change risks. Such awareness also changes their priorities, redirects funding, and stimulates alterations in urban planning practices to better adapt to extreme weather conditions. As a result, nature-based solutions become increasingly valued for their climate adaptation potential in Swedish cities, for example Malmö.

In relation to co-financing, it is imperative to develop public–private co-governance arrangements to facilitate co-funding of design, development, and maintenance of nature-based solutions in cities. For example, in Melbourne, Australia, the Urban Forest Fund was launched in 2017 to provide financial support to new greening projects on private land and buildings. The Urban Forest Fund specifically targets business, property owners, and developers to undertake greening measures, such as green roofs, walls, tree planting, and rainwater collection on private grounds. Under this public–private partnership scheme, the aim is to increase the amount of nature-based solutions across the city area by fund-matching projects dollar for dollar.

Providing economic incentives to support the development and uptake of nature-based solutions is an effective mechanism. Economic incentives can significantly help create market conditions to encourage the establishment of nature-based solutions. Currently, a prominent barrier for mainstreaming nature-based solutions is often the high financial cost connected with urban greening measures. Meanwhile, investments in nature-based solutions are constrained by uncertainties about the return on investment. One example of economic incentives comes from Hamburg, Germany, where the municipality has developed the first comprehensive Green

Roof Strategy. Its goal is to plant 100 hectares of green roof surface in the metropolitan area in the next decade. To support this process, the Hamburg Ministry for Environment and Energy provides financial support for green roofs so that building owners can receive subsidies to cover up to 60 per cent of installation costs.

Integrating urban nature-based solutions into infrastructure projects and renovation cycles increases their (multi-)functionality and it can save costs by reducing the need for additional costs and drawing on existing budgets. For example, in the UK, nature-based solutions are often linked to flooding and water treatment. Sustainable Urban Drainage Systems (SuDS) are considered by environmental regulators and local authorities as additional to the traditional systems approach. Some water utilities are increasingly interested in SuDS where they had previously focused on pipes and sewers. Thames Water, for instance, aims for SuDS implementation to expand in the coming decade, recognising that nature-based solutions can address water management as well as provide additional benefits for climate change risk mitigation.

Markets, Land Value, and Contractual Agreements

Aligned with the strategic interest, creating markets for nature-based solutions – for instance, by including them in contractual agreements or developing them in target paces with lower land value – might provide a more cost-effective means of urban greening (for example, street greens, pocket parks, and building-integrated greens). Positioning nature-based solutions as a solution offering wide societal, sustainability, and reputational benefits can support the development of demand for nature-based solutions, which in turn can stimulate supply. For example, the home insurance firm Interpolis in the Netherlands stimulated the green roof market by running a national marketing campaign featuring media celebrities who demonstrated green roof installations. The campaign explained how homeowners can prevent environmental damage by converting their roofs 'from grey to green', while contributing to biodiversity and sustainability. To make green roofs attractive, Interpolis offered a free roof inspection and a standard price through a collaboration with a green roof installation firm.

Alternative land use with a higher return on investment can create competition for urban nature-based solutions. Therefore, sometimes developing urban nature projects on land with a lower value can offer a more cost-effective urban greening solution. Furthermore, marginalised groups in cities are often likely to live in disadvantaged areas with limited access to parks and green space. Thus, developing nature-based solutions in such areas can produce significant social benefits and contribute to social inclusion. For example, a project by the Scottish Government Green Infrastructure Fund upgraded a former primary school plot with nature-based solutions. The site was transformed into a community green space with plantings, allotments, recreational spaces for children, outdoor exercise equipment, and educational areas.

Utility companies (water, waste, energy) and providers of network services (waterways, road and rail authorities) can be important actors for mainstreaming of nature-based solutions in cities. These organisations are either publicly owned or deliver their services based on long-term contracts, which means they need to comply with a set of regulations. Therefore, specific requirements on the increased use of nature-based solutions can be included in the delivery of core functions by them (for example, waste water treatment) or for land management (for example, railway sidings, roadside verges). Building on biodiversity offsetting regulation that has been mandatory in Germany since the 1970s, the City of Hamburg developed the NATURCENT regulation. Essentially an accounting system for urban nature, it incentivises real estate developers to minimise the loss of natural habitat in developments, and in cases where this cannot be avoided they can allocate funds or space, or both, to create or enhance natural areas in other parts of the city. The NATURCENT programme specifically focuses on the quality (rather than the quantity) of nature in the city, for example by investing in maintenance of parks.

Demonstration Projects, Data Monitoring, and Valuation Models

Demonstration or pilot projects of nature-based solutions can create shared learning and knowledge development as well as provide tangible examples of how nature-based solutions can work in practice. This can in turn create confidence among partners about their potentials and benefits (see Case Study Box 10.2). For example, the Porous Alley Demonstration Project in Boston involves nature-based solutions and roads, mostly involving the installation of porous asphalt to increase the permeability of pavement. It is a testing ground for new green technology. Porous asphalt has been applied in the streets and alleyways to recharge groundwater levels, in turn reinforcing the structural integrity of buildings while cleaning and filtering the runoff to prevent pollution of the river in Boston. The project provided the city and relevant stakeholders with the opportunity to learn by doing and build collaborations.

Case Study Box 10.2 City Forest (Sofia, Bulgaria)

Sofia is the largest, most dynamic, continuously growing city in Bulgaria, and the capital city. It is also Bulgaria's economic, cultural, and educational centre. The city has significant natural resource potential including hot thermal springs, long sunny days, rich biodiversity, and fertile lands. At the same time, this potential has not been realised, partially due to the lack of knowledge about ecosystem services, their benefits, and their importance. Sofia faces sustainability challenges stemming from its industrialisation during the Soviet era with hardly any attention given to environmental issues as well as the modern need to align urban economic growth with environmentally and socially sustainable development of the city. This also impedes the mainstreaming of nature-based solutions.

At the same time, in this environment, the City Forest initiative is one inspiring example of civic engagement. The idea unfolded after NGOs had started the initiative 'Sofia – Green Capital', resulting in Sofia taking part in the contest for the European

Case Study Box 10.2 (cont.)

Green Capital Award. Funded and realised by the active citizens of Sofia and an NGO Grupa Grad in collaboration with Sofia municipality, the initiative seeks not only to deliver ecosystem services, for instance climate regulation or air pollution abatement, but also to develop a community feeling and a sense of belonging by becoming a landmark in Sofia's green heritage.

'Sofia – Green Capital' envisions the planting of trees on neglected or marginalised urban land and the restoration of a green corridor allowing the fresh mountain air to penetrate the city. It thus seeks to reduce air pollution, capture and sequester CO_2, offer recreation and leisure opportunities, and contribute to the green footprint of the city. While there has been a significant involvement of citizens, not least thanks to the lead coordinator NGO, for example through voluntary tree planting, tree buying or donations, and crowd funding, the municipal support has declined over time.

Still, overall there is a struggle to align the strategic interest of local economic growth, expansion of the tourism sector, and land use for residential development with conservation activities. In general, there is often a risk associated with relying solely on citizens' voluntary engagement and donations in terms of emergence and implementation of such intervention, as it can lead to selective, small-scale, scattered activities on the one hand and municipal commitment on the other. At this stage, the municipality has yet to widen its scope of investment to other areas besides the reconstruction of parks and the NGO is still negotiating with the department of green systems that manages parks and green areas in the city to align the interests and assure land and resources amidst slow procedures and the unsatisfactory policy framework.

Figure 10.3 Sofia, Bulgaria

Mainstreaming nature-based solutions requires the development of evidence on performance through the use of 'big data' and new assessment tools that can support effective monitoring, evidence-building, and assessments of effectiveness in addressing key urban goals. For example, an EU Life project called 'My Building Is Green' aims to increase the resilience of social buildings and educational centres by implementing nature-based solutions. Three pilot schools in Spain and Portugal are participating in the project to develop evidence through the monitoring of how building-integrated greening for schools can respond to the heat island effect.

Encouraging investment decisions among public and private actors, and in this way catalysing the mainstreaming of nature-based solutions in cities, calls for evidence-based valuation models that specify, monetise, and clearly communicate the benefits and costs of urban nature projects to the key actors. For example, Natural Capital Accounting is an established valuation model in the UK. The Natural Capital Committee is an independent government advisory committee that consults the national government on the value of natural assets to the economy and provides policy input. The Natural Capital Committee also tests the guidance on valuing natural capital in specific places by partnering with pioneer projects throughout the UK.

OVERALL REFLECTIONS

Mainstreaming nature-based solutions requires strategic interventions on different levels and in key domains to enable the functioning of urban nature over the long term and support its potential to deliver ecological, economic, and social benefits. Strategic and coordinated actions along with enabling factors can open possibilities for nature-based solutions by bringing new agents of change together, generating new capacities, forms of resource, or thinking about urban problems and their solutions. Ultimately, mainstreaming nature-based solutions that can contribute to multiple sustainability goals requires efforts on a mix of factors that can work for all of these goals.

As suggested, actions are needed across the dominant domains: policy, governance, finance, and urban development. This requires strategic interventions from the local context to the institutional and inter-institutional levels. Overall, this demands connecting top-down and bottom-up efforts to establish a governance system for achieving sustainable and effective change. Based on Wamsler and Pauleit (2016), we identify six types of strategic actions for mainstreaming nature-based solutions, including add-on, programmatic, managerial, intra- and inter-organisational, regulatory, and directed actions.

Turning to domains, we can see that working across the urban infrastructure regime is key – in terms of the dominant domains of policy, governance, finance, and urban development. In practice these are interlinked. In order to influence the urban infrastructure regime, shaping and shifting enabling factors is crucial through a mix of actions. The enabling factors include public policy, strategic priorities, and certification schemes; partnerships, networks, and collaboration; finance, incentives, and insurance; markets, land value, and contractual agreements; and demonstration projects and data monitoring.

Nature-based solutions and urban nature hold great potential for addressing socioeconomic and environmental challenges in our cities. However, there are still challenges to tackle and opportunities to grasp when it comes to nature-based solutions. To unlock their potential requires creating enabling factors across the regulatory, financial, and urban development domains of the urban infrastructure regime that shapes approaches to urban sustainability challenges. Aligning actions, measures, and initiatives can activate synergies and create effective pathways for promoting the mainstreaming of urban nature-based solutions.

KEY LEARNING EXERCISES

1. **Individual Reflection:** Revisit the definition of the urban infrastructure regime provided in the chapter. Imagine that you need to explain this concept to someone who has not read this book. Use simple words and examples. To support your reflection, write down several examples of what constitutes regulatory, financial, and urban development domains in the urban infrastructure regime.
2. **Peer Discussion:** In groups of 2–3 each peer selects two of the six key types of strategic action that contribute to the mainstreaming of nature-based solutions. Discuss in your group and argue why and when your selected types of actions may be important and what challenges they may encounter when seeking to mainstream nature-based solutions in cities. Collectively think of situations when certain types of actions may be more effective than others.
3. **Explore Examples:** Choose one group of enabling factors for the mainstreaming of urban nature-based solutions, which are summarised in Table 10.1. Use examples (from this chapter or your own) to explain how and why your chosen group of enabling factors is important to mainstreaming nature-based solutions in cities. Think of situations when these enabling factors may create undesired or negative outcomes. What actions would you propose to avoid such outcomes?

FURTHER RESOURCES

United Nations Development Programme (UNDP) (2019) *Accelerating Climate Ambition and Impact: Toolkit for Mainstreaming Nature-Based Solutions into Nationally Determined Contributions*. New York, USA: UNDP.

van der Jagt, A., Tozer, L., Toxopeus, H. and Runhaar, H. (2023) Policy mixes for mainstreaming urban nature-based solutions: an analysis of six European countries and the European Union. *Environmental Science and Policy*, 139, 51–61.

Xie, L., Bulkeley, H. and Tozer, L. (2022) Mainstreaming sustainable innovation: unlocking the potential of nature-based solutions for climate change and biodiversity. *Environmental Science and Policy*, 132, 119–130.

References

Aalto, H. and Ernstson, H. (2017) Of plants, high lines and horses: civics and designers in the relational articulation of values of urban natures. *Landscape and Urban Planning*, 157, 309–321.

Agyeman, J., Bullard, R. D. and Evans, B. (2003) *Just Sustainabilities: Development in an Unequal World*. Cambridge, MA: MIT Press.

Amin, A., Massey, D. and Thrift, J. (2000) *Cities for the Many Not the Few*. Bristol: Policy Press.

Angelo, H. (2021) *How Green Became Good: Urbanized Nature and the Making of Cities and Citizens*. Chicago, IL: University of Chicago Press.

Angelo, H. and Wachsmuth, D. (2015) Urbanizing urban political ecology: a critique of methodological cityism. *International Journal of Urban and Regional Research*, 39(1), 16–27.

Anguelovski, A., Connolly, J. and Brand, A. (2018) From landscapes of utopia to the margins of the green urban life. *City*, 22(3), 417–436. https://doi.org/10.1080/13604813.2018.1473126

Anguelovski, I., Connolly, J. J. T., Masip, L. and Pearsall, H. (2018) Assessing green gentrification in historically disenfranchised neighborhoods: a longitudinal and spatial analysis of Barcelona. *Urban Geography*, 39(3), 458–491. https://doi.org/10.1080/02723638.2017.1349987

Anguelovski, I., Brand, A. L., Connolly, J. J., et al. (2020) Expanding the boundaries of justice in urban greening scholarship: toward an emancipatory, antisubordination, intersectional, and relational approach. *Annals of the American Association of Geographers*, 110(6), 1743–1769.

Arnstein, S. R. (1969) A ladder of citizen participation. *Journal of the American Planning Association*, 35(4), 216–224.

Baker, L. E. (2004) Tending cultural landscapes and food citizenship in Toronto's community gardens. *The Geographical Review*, 94(3), 305–325.

BCNUEJ. (2021) Policy and planning tools for urban green justice. Fighting displacement and gentrification and improving accessibility and inclusiveness to green amenities. GreenLuLus project report. BCNUEJ. www.bcnuej.org/wp-content/uploads/2021/04/Toolkit-Urban-Green-Justice.pdf

Bockarjova, M., Botzen, W. J. W., van Schie, M. H. and Koetse M. J. (2020) Property price effects of green interventions in cities: a meta-analysis and implications for gentrification. *Environmental Science and Policy*, 112(2020), 293–304. https://doi.org/10.1016/j.envsci.2020.06.024.

Brink, E., Aalders, T., Ádám, D., et al. (2016) Cascades of green: a review of ecosystem-based adaptation in urban areas. *Global Environmental Change*, 36, 111–123. https://doi.org/10.1016/j.gloenvcha.2015.11.003.

Brundtland Commission. (1987) *Our Common Future*. Oxford: Oxford University Press.

Bulkeley, H. (2019) Taking action for urban nature: growing effective governance solutions. NATURVATION Guide. https://naturvation.eu/result/taking-action-urban-nature-governance-solutions.html

Bulkeley, H. (2021) Climate changed urban futures: environmental politics in the anthropocene city. *Environmental Politics*, 30(2), 266–284

Bulkeley, H., Schroeder, H., Janda, K., et al. (2009) Cities and climate change: the role of institutions, governance and urban planning. *Change*, 28–30.

Bulkeley, H., Edwards, G. A. and Fuller, S. (2014) Contesting climate justice in the city: examining politics and practice in urban climate change experiments. *Global Environmental Change*, 25, 31–40.

Cabral, I., Costa, S., Weiland, U. and Bonn, A. (2017) Urban gardens as multifunctional nature-based solutions for societal goals in a changing climate. In Kabisch, N., Korn, H., Stadler, J. and Bonn, A. (Eds), *Nature-Based Solutions to Climate Change Adaptation in Urban Areas* (pp. 237–253). Cham: Springer.

Cárdenas, M. L., Wilde, V., Hagen-Zanker, A., et al. (2021) The circular benefits of participation in nature-based solutions. *Sustainability*, 13(8), 4344.

Castán Broto, V., Allen, A. and Rapoport, E. (2012) Interdisciplinary perspectives on urban metabolism. *Journal of Industrial Ecology*, 16(6), 851–861.

Castree, N. (2008) Neoliberalising nature: The logics of deregulation and reregulation. *Environment and Planning A: Economy and Space*, 40(1).

Castree, N. (2014) *Making Sense of Nature.* London: Routledge.

Chan, K. M. A., Balvanera, P., Benessaiah, K., et al. (2016) Why protect nature? Rethinking values and the environment. *Proceedings of the National Academy of Sciences*, 113(6), 1462–1465.

Clancy, C. and Ward, K. (2020) Auto-rewilding in post-industrial cities: the case of inland cormorants in urban Britain. *Conservation and Society*, 18(2), 126–136.

Cohen-Shacham, E., Walters, G., Janzen, C. and Maginnis, S. (eds.) (2016). *Nature-based Solutions to Address Global Societal Challenges*. Gland: IUCN.

Cronon, W. (1991) *Nature's Metropolis: Chicago and the Great West*. New York, NY: W.W. Norton and Company.

Davidson, S. (1998) Spinning the wheel of empowerment. *Planning*, 3, 14–15.

Davis, M., Abhold, K., Mederake, L. and Knoblauch, D. (2018) Nature-based solutions in European and national policy frameworks: Deliverable 1.5. NATURVATION. Horizon 2020 Grant Agreement No. 730243, European Commission, 50 pp.

Derickson, K. D. (2018) Urban geography III: Anthropocene urbanism. *Progress in Human Geography*, 42(3), 425–435.

Dignum, M., Dorst, H., van Schie, M., Dassen, T. and Raven, R. (2020) Nurturing nature: exploring socio-spatial conditions for urban experimentation. *Environmental Innovation and Societal Transitions*, 34, 7–25. http://doi.org10.1016/j.eist.2019.11.010

Dorst, H., van der Jagt, A. P. N., Runhaar, H. and Raven, R. (2021) Structural conditions for the wider uptake of urban nature-based solutions – a conceptual framework. *Cities* 116. https://doi.org/10.1016/j.cities.2021.103283.

EFTEC. (2013) Green Infrastructure's contribution to economic growth: a review. Final report for DEFRA and Natural England. Sheffield Hallam University/DEFRA. http://shura.shu.ac.uk/22114/1/11406_GI_Economic_Catalyst_Final_Report_July2013.pdf

Erixon Aalto, H. and Ernstson, H. (2017) Of plants, high lines and horses: civics and designers in the relational articulation of values of urban natures. *Landscape and Urban Planning*, 157, 309–321. http://dx.doi.org/10.1016/j.landurbplan.2016.05.018

Estrada, M., Kotsila, P., Hörschelmann, K., Lazova, Y. and Werner, A. (2020) Ensuring citizenship rights: cooperation and tensions in the governance of urban community gardens. *IOP Conference Series: Earth and Environmental Science*, 588, 1.15–1.19.

European Commission, Directorate-General for Research and Innovation. (2015) Towards an EU research and innovation policy agenda for nature-based solutions and re-naturing cities – Final report of the Horizon 2020 expert group on

'Nature-based solutions and re-naturing cities' (full version). Publications Office.

Fisher, D., Svendsen, E. and Connolly, J. (2015) *Urban Environmental Stewardship and Civic Engagement: How Planting Trees Strengthens the roots of Democracy*. Abingdon: Routledge.

Follmann, A. and Viehoff, V. (2015) A green garden on red clay: creating a new urban common as a form of political gardening in Cologne, Germany. *Local Environment*, 20, 1148–1174. https://doi.org/10.1080/13549839.2014.894966

Fontaine, C. M., Dendoncker, N., De Vreese, R., et al. (2014) Towards participatory integrated valuation and modelling of ecosystem services under land-use change. *Journal of Land Use Science*, 9(3), 278–303. https://doi.org/10.1080/1747423X.2013.786150

Gandy, M. (2003) *Concrete and Clay: Reworking Nature in New York City*. Cambridge, MA: MIT Press.

Gandy, M. (2004) Rethinking urban metabolism: water, space and the modern city. *City*, 8(3), 363–379.

Gandy, M. (2005) Cyborg urbanization: complexity and monstrosity in the contemporary city. *International Journal of urban and Regional Research*, 29(1), 26–49.

Garcia-Lamarca, M., Anguelovski, I., Cole, H., et al. (2021) Urban green boosterism and city affordability: for whom is the 'branded' green city? *Urban Studies*, 58(1), 90–112. http://doi.org/10.1177/0042098019885330

Ghose, R. and Pettygrove, M. (2014) Actors and networks in urban community garden development. *Geoforum*, 53, 93–103.

Girardet, H. (2004) *Cities, People, Planet: Liviable Cities for a Sustainable World*. London: John Wiley and Sons.

Gowdy, J. (2004) The revolution in welfare economics and its implications for environmental valuation and policy. *Land Economics*, 80(2), 239–257.

Gray, M. and Barford, A. (2018) The depths of the cuts: the uneven geography of local government austerity. *Cambridge Journal of Regions: Economy and Society*, 11(3), 541–563. https://doi-org.ezphost.dur.ac.uk/10.1093/cjres/rsy019

Grove, J. M., Cadenasso, M. L. and Pickett, S. T. (2015) *The Baltimore School of Urban Ecology: Space, Scale, and Time for the Study of Cities*. New Haven, CT: Yale University Press.

Guerry, A. D., Polasky, S., Lubchenko, J., et al. (2015) Natural capital and ecosystem services informing decisions: from promise to practice. *Proceedings of the National Academy of Sciences*, 112(24), 7348–7355.

Haase, A. (2017) The contribution of nature-based solutions to socially inclusive urban development – some reflections from a social–environmental perspective. In Kabisch, N., Korn, H., Stadler, J. and Bonn, A. (Eds), *Nature-Based Solutions to Climate Change Adaptation in Urban Areas* (pp. 221–236). Cham: Springer.

Haase, A., Rink, D. and Grossmann, K. (2016) Shrinking cities in post-socialist Europe: what can we learn from their analysis for theory building today? *Geografiska Annaler: Series B, Human Geography*, 98(4), 305–319.

Haase, D., Kabisch, S. and Haase, A. (2017) Greening cities – to be socially inclusive? About the alleged paradox of society and ecology in cities. *Habitat International*, 64, 41–48.

Heiskanen, E., Jalas, M., Rinkinen, J. and Tainio, P. (2015) The local community as a 'low-carbon lab': promises and perils. *Environmental Innovation and Societal Transitions*, 14, 149–164. http://doi.org/10.1016/j.eist.2014.08.001

Henrique, K. and Tschakert, P. (2019) Contested grounds: adaptation to flooding and the politics of (in)visibility in São Paulo's eastern periphery. *Geoforum*, 104, 181–192.

Henrique, K. P. and Tschakert, P. (2021) Pathways to urban transformation: from dispossession to climate justice. *Progress in Human Geography*, 45(5), 1169–1191. https://doi.org/10.1177/0309132520962856

Heritage Fund. (2017, November 2) Newcastle explores transfer of parks to trust. Heritage Fund. www.heritagefund.org.uk/news/newcastle-explores-transfer-parks-trust.

Heynen, N. (2006) Green urban political ecologies: toward a better understanding of inner-city environmental change. *Environment and Planning A*, 38(3), 499–516.

Heynen, N. (2014) Urban political ecology I: the urban century. *Progress in Human Geography*, 38(4), 598–604.

Heynen, N., Kaika, M. and Swyngedouw, E. (2006) *In the Nature of Cities: Urban Political Ecology and the Politics of Urban Metabolism*. Abingdon: Routledge.

Hodson, M. and Marvin, S. (2010) Can cities shape socio-technical transitions and how would we know if they were? *Research Policy, Special Section on Innovation and Sustainability Transitions*, 39, 477–485. https://doi.org/10.1016/j.respol.2010.01.020

Hörschelmann, K., Werner, A., Bogacki, M. and Lazova, Y. (2019) Taking action for urban nature: citizen engagement handbook. NATURVATION Guide. https://naturvation.eu/sites/default/files/result/files/citizen_engagement_handbook.pdf

Immergluck, D. and Balan, T. (2018) Sustainable for whom? Green urban development, environmental gentrification, and the Atlanta Beltline. *Urban Geography*, 39(4), 546–562. https://doi.org/10.1080/02723638.2017.1360041.

IPBES (2019) *Global Assessment Report on biodiversity and Ecosystem Services of the Intergovernmental Science–Policy Platform on Biodiversity and Ecosystem Services*, edited by E. S. Brondizio, J. Settele, S. Díaz and H. T. Ngo. Bonn: IPBES secretariat.

Irazábal, C. and Punja, A. (2009) Cultivating just planning and legal institutions: a critical assessment of the south central farm struggle in Los Angeles. *Journal of Urban Affairs*, 31(1), 1–23.

Isin, E. F. (Ed.). (2000) Introduction: democracy, citizenship and the city. In: *Democracy, Citizenship and the Global City* (pp. 1–21). New York, NY: Routledge.

Ives, C., Lentini, P., Threlfall, C., et al. (2016) Cities are hotspots for threatened species. *Global Ecology and Biogeography*, 25(1), 117–126.

Jessop, B. (2002) Liberalism, neoliberalism, and urban governance: a state–theoretical perspective. *Antipode*, 34(3), 452–472.

Kabisch, N., Frantzeskaki, N., Pauleit, S., et al. (2016) Nature-based solutions to climate change mitigation and adaptation in urban areas: perspectives on indicators, knowledge gaps, barriers, and opportunities for action. *Ecology and Society*, 21(2).

Kaika, M. (2005) *City of Flows: Modernity, Nature, and the City*. Abingdon: Routledge.

Kaika, M. and Swyngedouw, E. (2011) The urbanization of nature: Great promises, impasse, and new beginnings. In: Bridge, G. and Watson, S. (Eds), *The New Blackwell Companion to the City* (pp. 96–107). Hoboken, NJ: Wiley-Blackwell.

Kenter, J. O., O'Brien, L., Hockley, N., et al. (2015) What are shared and social values of ecosystems? *Ecological Economics*, 111, 86–99.

Kiss, B., Sekulova, F. and Kotsila, P. (2019) International comparison of nature-based solutions. Naturvation Project Report. https://naturvation.eu/sites/default/files/result/files/international_comparison_of_nbs.pdf

Kotsila, P., Hörschelmann, K., Anguelovski, I., Sekulova, F. and Lazova, Y. (2020) Clashing temporalities of care and support as key determinants of transformatory and justice potentials in urban gardens. *Cities*, 106, 102865. https://doi.org/10.1016/j.cities.2020.102865.

Kotsila, P., Anguelovski, I., Baró, F., et al. (2021) Nature-based solutions as discursive tools and contested practices in urban nature's neoliberalisation processes. *Environment and Planning E: Nature and Space*, 4(2), 252–274.

Lawson, L. (2005) *City Bountiful: A Century of Community Gardening in America*. Los Angeles: University of California Press.

Ley, D. (2009) Gentrification. In: Gregory, D., Johnston, R., Pratt, G., Watts, M. and Whatmore, S. (Eds), *The Dictionary of Human Geography* (5th ed.). London: Blackwell Publishers.

Light, J. S. (2009) *The Nature of Cities: Ecological Visions and the American Urban Professions, 1920–1960*. Baltimore, MD: Johns Hopkins University Press.

Maller, C. (2020) *Healthy Urban Environments: More-than-Human Theories*. London: Routledge.

Meadows, D. H. (2008). *Thinking in Systems*. White River Junction, VT: Chelsea Green Publishing.

Maestre-Andrés, S., Drews, S. and Savin, I. (2021) Carbon tax acceptability with information provision and mixed revenue uses. *Nature Communications*, 12(7017). https://doi.org/10.1038/s41467-021-27380-8 X

Meerow, S. (2020) The politics of multifunctional green infrastructure planning in New York City. *Cities*, 100, 102621. https://doi.org/10.1016/j.cities.2020.102621.

Monstadt, J. (2009) Conceptualizing the political ecology of urban infrastructures: insights from technology and urban studies, *Environment and Planning A*, 41(8), 1924–1942.

Ott, U., Pascual, T., Satterfield, M., et al. (2016) Opinion: why protect nature? Rethinking values and the environment. *Proceedings of the National Academy of Sciences of the United States of America*, 113(6), 1462–1465.

Parks, S. and Gowdy, J. (2013) What have economists learned about valuing nature? A review essay. *Ecosystem Services*, 3, 1–10.

Pascual, U., Balvanera, P., Díaz, S., et al. (2017) Valuing nature's contributions to people: the IPBES approach. *Current Opinion in Environmental Sustainability*, 26–27, 7–27.

Pauleit, S., Zölch, T., Hansen, R., Randrup, T. B. and van den Bosch, C. K. (2017) *Nature-Based Solutions and Climate Change – Four Shades of Green*. Cham: Springer.

Pickett, S. T., Burch, W. R. and Dalton, S. E. (1997) A conceptual framework for the study of human ecosystems in urban areas. *Urban Ecosystems*, 1(4), 185–199.

Pickett, S. T., Cadenasso, M. L. and Grove, J. M. (2008) Beyond urban legends: an emerging framework of urban ecology as illustrated by the Baltimore Ecosystem Study. *BioScience*, 58(2): 139–150.

Pickett, S. T., Cadenasso, M. L. and Childers, D. L. (2016) Evolution and future of urban ecological science: ecology in, of, and for the city. *Ecosystem health and Sustainability*, 2(7).

Pincetl, S. (2017) Cities in the age of the Anthropocene: climate change agents and the potential for mitigation. *Anthropocene*, 20, 74–82.

Polzin, F., Toxopeus, H. and Stam, E. (2018) The wisdom of the crowd in funding: information heterogeneity and social networks of crowdfunders. *Small Business Economics*, 50(2), 251–273.

Pudup, M. B. (2008) It takes a garden: cultivating citizen-subjects in organized garden projects. *Geoforum*, 39, 1228–40.

Raymond, C. M., Kenter, J. O., Plieninger, T., Turner, N. J. and Alexander, K. A. (2014) Comparing instrumental and deliberative paradigms underpinning the assessment of social values for cultural ecosystem services. *Ecological Economics*, 107, 145–156.

Reed, M. S., Vella, S., Challies, E., et al. (2018) A theory of participation: what makes stakeholder and public engagement in environmental management work?. *Restoration Ecology*, 26, 7–17.

Ridder, D. and Pahl-Wostl, C. (2005) Participatory Integrated Assessment in local level planning. *Regional Environmental Change*, 5(4), 188–196.

Rosol, M. (2010) Public participation in post-Fordist urban green space governance: the case of community gardens in Berlin. *International Journal of Urban and Regional Research*, 34(3), 548–563.

Rosol, M. (2012) Community volunteering as a neoliberal strategy? Green space production in Berlin. *Antipode*, 44(1), 239–257.

Rosol, M., Béal, V. and Mössner, S. (2017) Greenest cities? The (post-)politics of new urban environmental regimes. *Environment and Planning A: Economy and Space*, 49(8), 1710–1718. http://doi.org/10.1177/0308518X17714843

Salter, J., Robinson, J. and Wiek, A. (2010) Participatory methods of integrated assessment – a review. *Climate Change*, 1(5), 697–717. https://doi.org/10.1002/wcc.73

Schmelzkopf, K. (1995) Urban community gardens as contested space. *Geography Review*, 85(3), 364.

Schmelzkopf, K. (2002) Incommensurability, land use, and the right to space: community gardens in New York City. *Urban Geography*, 23(4), 323–343.

Schram-Bijkerk, D., Otte, P., Liesbet, D. and Breure, A. M. (2018) Indicators to support healthy urban gardening in urban management. *Science of the Total Environment*, 621, 863–871.

Schuetze, T. and Chelleri, L. (2015) Urban sustainability versus green-washing – fallacy and reality of urban regeneration in downtown Seoul. *Sustainability*, 8(33). https://doi.org/10.3390/su8010033.

Secretariat of the Convention on Biological Diversity. (2009) Connecting biodiversity and climate change mitigation and adaptation: report of the Second Ad Hoc Technical Expert Group on Biodiversity and Climate Change. Montreal, Canada: Technical Series No. 41.

Sekulova, F. and Anguelovski, I. (2017) The governance and politics of nature-based solutions. European Commission: NATURVATION.

Sekulova, F., Anguelovski, I., Kiss, B., et al. (2021) The governance of nature-based solutions in the city at the intersection of justice and equity. *Cities*, 112. https://doi.org/10.1016/j.cities.2021.103136.

Shokry, G., Connolly, J. and Anguelovski, I. (2020) Understanding climate gentrification and shifting landscapes of protection and vulnerability in green resilient Philadelphia. *Urban Climate*, 31, 100539. https://doi.org/10.1016/j.uclim.2019.100539.

Soga, M., Cox, D. T., Yamaura, Y., et al. (2017) Health benefits of urban allotment gardening: Improved physical and psychological well-being and social integration. *International Journal of Environmental Research and Public Health*, 14(1), 71.

Staeheli, L. A., Mitchell, D. and Gibson, K. (2002) Conflicting rights to the city in New York's community gardens. *GeoJournal*, 58(3), 197–205.

Stern, P. C. and Dietz, T. (2008) *Public Participation in Environmental Assessment and Decision Making*. Washington, DC: National Academies Press.

Swilling, M. (2015) Towards sustainable urban infrastructures for the urban Anthropocene. In: Allen, A., Lampis, A. and Swilling, M. (Eds), *Untamed Urbanisms* (pp. 19–32) London: Routledge.

Swyngedouw, E. (1996) The city as a hybrid: on nature, society and cyborg urbanization. *Capitalism Nature Socialism*, 7(2), 65–80.

Swyngedouw, E. (2006) Circulations and metabolisms: (hybrid) natures and (cyborg) cities. *Science as Culture*, 15(2), 105–121.

Swyngedouw, E. (2007) Impossible sustainability and the postpolitical condition. In: Krueger, R. and Gibbs, D. C. (Eds), *The Sustainable Development Paradox: Urban Political Economy in the United States and Europe* (pp.13–40). New York: Guilford Press.

Swyngedouw, E. and Heynen, N. C. (2003) Urban political ecology, justice and the politics of scale. *Antipode*, 35(5), 898–918.

Thomson, G. and Newman, P. (2020) Cities and the Anthropocene: urban governance for the new era of regenerative cities. *Urban Studies*, 57(7), 1502–1519.

Tizot, J. Y. (2018) Ebenezer Howard's garden city idea and the ideology of industrialism.

Open Edition Journals. http://doi.org/10.4000/cve.3605.

Toxopeus, H. and Maas, K. (2018) Crowdfunding sustainable enterprise as a form of collective action. In: Walker, T., Kibsey, S. D. and Crichton, R. (Eds), *Designing a Sustainable Financial System*. Cham: Palgrave Macmillan.

Toxopeus, H., Kotsila, P., Conde, M., et al. (2020) How 'just' is hybrid governance of urban nature-based solutions? *Cities*, 105. https://doi.org/10.1016/j.cities.2020.102839.

Tozer, L., Hörschelmann, K., Anguelovski, I., Bulkeley, H. and Lazova, Y. (2020) Whose city? Whose nature? Towards inclusive nature-based solution governance. *Cities*, 107, 102892.

United Nations, Department of Economic and Social Affairs, Population Division. (2018) World Urbanization Prospects: The 2018 Revision, Online Edition.

Van der Jagt, A. P. N., Raven, R., Dorst, H. and Runhaar, H. (2020) Nature-based innovation systems. *Environment Innovation Society Transitions*, 35, 202–216. http://doi/org/10.1016/j.eist.2019.09.005

Wakefield, S. and Braun, B. (2014) Governing the resilient city. *Environment and Planning D: Society and Space*, 32(1), 4–11.

Walker, T., Kibsey, S. D. and Crichton, R. (Eds). (2018) *Designing a Sustainable Financial System: Development goals and Socio-Ecological Responsibility* (pp. 263–288). Cham: Palgrave Macmillan.

Wamsler, C. and Pauleit, S. (2016) Making headway in climate policy mainstreaming and ecosystem-based adaptation: two pioneering countries, different pathways, one goal. *Climatic Change*, 137, 71–87. https://doi.org/10.1007/s10584-016-1660-y

Wamsler, C., Pauleit, S., Zölch, T., Schetke, S. and Mascarenhas, A. (2017) Mainstreaming nature-based solutions for climate change adaptation in urban governance and planning. In: Kabisch, N., Korn, H., Stadler, J. and Bonn, A. (eds) *Nature-Based Solutions to Climate Change Adaptation in Urban Areas. Theory and Practice of Urban Sustainability Transitions*. Cham: Springer. https://doi.org/10.1007/978-3-319-56091-5_15

Whatmore, S. (2002) *Hybrid Geographies: Natures Cultures Spaces*. London: Sage Publications.

While, A., Jonas, A. and Gibbs, D. (2004) The environment and the entrepreneurial city: searching for the urban 'sustainability fix' in Manchester and Leeds. *International Journal of Urban and Regional Research*, 28(3), 549–569.

Wolfram, M. and Frantzeskaki, N. (2016) Cities and systemic change for sustainability: prevailing epistemologies and an emerging research agenda. *Sustainability*, 8, 144.

Young, R. F. and McPherson, E. G. (2013) Governing metropolitan green infrastructure in the United States. *Landscape and Urban Planning Special Issue: Urban Ecosystem Services*, 109, 67–75. https://doi.org/10.1016/j.landurbplan.2012.09.004

Index

Page numbers in *italics* refer to Figures and Tables and those in **bold** refer to Boxes and Case Studies.

Printed by Integrated Books International,
United States of America